Beginning the Quest

The Eric Voegelin Series in Political Philosophy

How World Politics Is Made: François Mitterand and the Reunification of Germany, by Tilo Schabert

Worldview and Mind: Religious Thought and Psychological Development, by Eugene Webb

Rethinking Rights: Historical, Political, and Philosophical Perspectives, edited by Bruce P. Frohnen and Kenneth L. Grasso

The Philosopher and the Storyteller: Eric Voegelin and Twentieth-Century Literature, by Charles R. Embry

The Constitutionalism of American States, edited by George E. Connor and Christopher W. Hammons

Voegelin Recollected: Conversations on a Life, edited by Barry Cooper and Jodi Bruhn

The American Way of Peace: An Interpretation, by Jan Prybyla

Faith and Political Philosophy: The Correspondence between Leo Strauss and Eric Voegelin, 1934–1964, edited by Peter Emberley and Barry Cooper

New Political Religions, or an Analysis of Modern Terrorism, by Barry Cooper

Art and Intellect in the Philosophy of Étienne Gilson, by Francesca Aran Murphy

Robert B. Heilman and Eric Voegelin: A Friendship in Letters, 1944–1984, edited by Charles R. Embry

Voegelin, Schelling, and the Philosophy of Historical Existence, by Jerry Day

Transcendence and History: The Search for Ultimacy from Ancient Societies to Postmodernity, by Glenn Hughes

Eros, Wisdom, and Silence: Plato's Erotic Dialogues, by James M. Rhodes

The Narrow Path of Freedom and Other Essays,
by Eugene Davidson

Hans Jonas: The Integrity of Thinking,
by David J. Levy

A Government of Laws: Political Theory, Religion, and the American Founding, by Ellis Sandoz

Augustine and Politics as Longing in the World,
by John von Heyking

Lonergan and the Philosophy of Historical Existence,
by Thomas J. McPartland

Books in the Eric Voegelin Institute Series in Political Philosophy: Studies in Religion and Politics

Etty Hillesum and the Flow of Presence: A Voegelinian Analysis, by Meins G. S. Coetsier

Christian Metaphysics and Neoplatonism, by Albert Camus; translated with an introduction by Ronald D. Srigley

Voegelin and the Problem of Christian Political Order, by Jeffrey C. Herndon

Republicanism, Religion, and the Soul of America, by Ellis Sandoz

Michael Oakeshott on Religion, Aesthetics, and Politics,
by Elizabeth Campbell Corey

Jesus and the Gospel Movement: Not Afraid to Be Partners, by William Thompson-Uberuaga

The Religious Foundations of Francis Bacon's Thought, by Stephen A. McKnight

Beginning the Quest

LAW AND POLITICS IN THE EARLY WORK OF ERIC VOEGELIN

Barry Cooper

UNIVERSITY OF MISSOURI PRESS
COLUMBIA AND LONDON

University of Missouri Press
Columbia and London

University of Missouri Press, Columbia, Missouri 65201
Printed and bound in the United States of America

5 4 3 2 1   13 12 11 10 09

Library of Congress Cataloging-in-Publication Data

Cooper, Barry, 1943–
Beginning the quest : law and politics in the early work of Eric Voegelin / Barry Cooper.
p. cm.
Includes bibliographical references and index.
Summary: "Examines an analysis of the legal and political writing of Eric Voegelin during the 1920s and the 1930s. Cooper discusses Voegelin's first systematic effort to bring together the principles of philosophical anthropology with his understanding of comparative social science and examines Voegelin's The Authoritarian State and The New Science of Politics"—Provided by publisher.
ISBN 978-0-8262-1854-4 (alk. paper)
1. Voegelin, Eric, 1901–1985 2. Political science—History—20th century. I. Title.
JC263.V632C648 2009
320.092—dc22

2009008544

♾™ This paper meets the requirements of the American National Standard for Permanence of Paper for Printed Library Materials, Z39.48, 1984.

Designer and typesetter: Kristie Lee
Printer and binder: Integrated Book Technologies, Inc.
Typefaces: Minion

Publication of this book has been assisted by a contribution from the Eric Voegelin Institute, which gratefully acknowledges the generous support provided for the series by the Earhart Foundation and the Sidney Richards Moore Memorial Fund.

To Jim Doak, flying buttress

Interpretation is not the reproduction of an original but
merely a more or less weak means of making
abstruse material more accessible.

—ERIC VOEGELIN,
On the Form of the American Mind (1928)

Contents

Preface

"Inside baseball" has become a metaphor to describe sports reporters who rely on locker-room gossip rather than what happens on the playing field. There is an equivalent temptation for those who report on the playing fields of academe. In literary criticism, for example, one often finds arguments developed at great length and with a highly refined technical vocabulary that refer not to literature but to other critics. Likewise in political science one can find plenty of examples of articles, books, and papers that do little more than situate themselves in relation to other arguments rather than to political reality. This is true with respect to studies devoted to the exegesis of the writings of political scientists such as Eric Voegelin as well. If to some extent "inside baseball" is inevitable, that does not mean it must be the focus.

This book deals with a specific period of Voegelin's work. If it holds the interest of a reader, that reader is likely already to be familiar with Voegelin's best-known writings, all of which were written at a later date than were most of the materials covered here. In an earlier book, *Eric Voegelin and the Foundations of Modern Political Science,* I tried to make the case, as have many others, that Voegelin was a major thinker of the twentieth century. I do not make that case again here, which may mean for some readers that it is *such* inside baseball that it carries no interest at all for them. Even people familiar with Voegelin's later writing—in *The History of Political Ideas, The New Science of Politics, Order and History,* or his meditative interpretations of consciousness—might wonder whether an exegesis of positions and arguments that Voegelin discarded is worth the trouble either of reading or of writing. In any event, that an author such as Voegelin once considered a book worth writing is not necessarily persuasive to readers.

There is, however, continuity in Voegelin's work. This is not to say that he did not change his mind on several major problems because the evidence is overwhelming that he did. More important he explained his reasons for so doing—and in such reasoning lies continuity. In other words, the argument of this book is that Voegelin's early writing on law or on method was motivated by the same quest for understanding that is found in the rest of his work, including those reflective and meditative studies of what his own questioning consciousness was up to when it was actually engaged in the act of questioning. There is a consensus among students of Voegelin's work that he was a radical thinker in the old and original sense of the term. This book deals with the beginning of his quest for understanding reality.

In terms of subject matter, this study is not simply about the intellectual development of Eric Voegelin. It also deals with what might be identified, perhaps only tentatively, with the exhaustion of social science. From the beginning of his reflections, Voegelin was concerned with the inner logic of several branches of social science and of how to situate them in the context of contemporary spiritual and political disorders or even crises. We can see his lifelong concern with this problem of spiritual and political disorder in its infancy as he struggled to liberate himself from the restrictions, first of *Staatslehre* and the intellectual categories that sustained it. In the appendix we give a brief analysis of a confrontation between the later Voegelin and, as it were, the early Voegelin—or at least the position of his *Doktorvater* Hans Kelsen, from which Voegelin set out on his lifelong but incomplete, because endless, quest for truth.

Prefaces are also occasions to record one's debts and to thank institutions and individuals for assuming them. I am especially grateful to Jim Doak, to the Earhart Foundation, and to the Social Sciences and Humanities Research Council of Canada, for supporting the work I have done over the years on Voegelin's political science. I would also like to thank the Killam Trusts for a resident fellowship during the fall of 2007. Despite the inconvenience to students (and the shortsightedness of senior administrators at my university who see little value in such support) I am especially grateful for the teaching release provided by a Killam. Without it, this book would have taken much longer to complete.

Thanks as well to Mirja van Herk for her good-natured ability to transform my scrawl into processed words, and to my wife, Denise Guichon, for her good-natured tolerance of my distractedness while writing—and while not writing, too.

Voegelin's *Collected Works* are referred to in parentheses in the text, as has become almost conventional, as *CW*, followed by the volume and page numbers. The complete reference to the volumes of the *Collected Works* cited is found in the bibliography. The materials cited from the Voegelin Papers, housed at the Hoover Institution, Stanford, are also referred to in parentheses in the text, as HI, followed by box and file numbers.

Barry Cooper
All Hallows Eve, 2008

Beginning the Quest

Introduction

The title of this book needs to be accounted for. To be sure, it has a Voegelinian resonance. At the beginning of the last book he wrote, Voegelin provided an interpretation of the question, Where does the beginning begin? (*CW* 18:27). A couple of pages later he wrote of "the millennial process of the quest for truth" (*CW* 18:29), and of the many exemplars who have taken part in it. These are mature linguistic formulations that depend upon a meditative exegesis to be fully understood. Indeed, on occasion they have been taken to be formular, almost liturgical statements. Certainly by the time Voegelin came to write directly about these matters he had developed a precise vocabulary to describe the experiences of reality—including the experience of the beginning and of the quest or, as he sometimes said, The Question (*CW* 17:399–400). The deceptive attractions of such language and its mastery are well known (*CW* 12:7–10). It is important, therefore, to be careful and to be aware of one's focus, as well as what is not in focus.

One of the observations Voegelin made concerning the experience of the quest for truth, whether that of priests and prophets, or of Zoroastrians, Hindus, Buddhists, Taoists, witch doctors, or philosophers, is that: first, it takes place in the specific, or "concrete," consciousness of an individual human being; and second, such questioning people live in equally specific historical and social contexts, or milieus. Moreover, the textual expression of the quest for truth is almost always formulated initially as a resistance to, or criticism of, already existing formulations. Typically the new insights, or formulations, are met with indifference or resistance from adherents of earlier versions or visions. Finally, although Voegelin in his later work was concerned with what might be called the Big Questions—of consciousness, reality, language, and so on—his observations regarding the quest for truth also bear upon the narrower fields of legal, social, political, spiritual, and intellectual life considered in the present study.

Neither Voegelin nor anyone else who begins a quest for truth starts by declaring: "I am on a quest for truth." Rather, and particularly if they are philosophers as was Voegelin, they typically begin by considering specific problems or mysteries. We begin with an even tighter focus, on Voegelin the (political) scientist, the *Wissenschaftler,* and his intellectual formation during the 1920s and 1930s. There is continuity in Voegelin's work from the early 1920s to the mid-1980s, but as Sandro Chignola put it, this is because it had direction, *Richtung,* without an a priori goal, *Ziel.*[1] Even less was Voegelin's quest presented in the same language over a period of forty years. As Voegelin said, paraphrasing Toynbee, of his own work much later: "please do not hold me to anything that I have written previously, because science progresses and things change. Do not take seriously, or in an absolute sense, what I have to say today, because these problems as I present them today are again subject to change, and perhaps in two years I will have found other things which will demand a very different answer" (*CW* 12:95).

The argument of this book is that Voegelin moved beyond a legal approach to political realities (within which he had been extensively schooled) to a direct encounter and analysis of the mass political movements of the 1930s and of the language by which they expressed and understood themselves. For readers familiar with his later work, and especially for readers familiar *only* with his later work, the insights reached by Voegelin in, say, 1939, will have become familiar starting points for further reflection. To understand the origin of that achievement is not simply to indulge in nostalgic antiquarianism inasmuch as the achievement was actualized in the face of the resistance thrown up, inevitably, by intellectual conventions as well as by the uncongenial political realities of the day.

In recent years, the interest of scholars, particularly young German scholars, has turned toward Voegelin's early writings.[2] This does not mean there is a consensus regarding the importance of, for instance, Max Weber or Othmar Spann, Hans Kelsen or Carl Schmitt, on Voegelin's understanding of contemporary issues or how they are to be studied. There is, however, widespread agreement regarding *The Political Religions* (1938) that it was the result of his quest during the 1920s and 1930s and also that it marks the closing of a chapter, or phase, of his work, a closing made poignant by his forced emigration from Europe the same year it was published. For this reason, the following chapters are organized around the major steps Voegelin took between 1922 and 1938, many of which were marked by a significant publication, or occasionally an extensive piece of work, that remained unpublished at the time.

A final preliminary consideration can be introduced by a letter Thomas Mann wrote to Voegelin in response to *The Political Religions.* The book, he said, was a "stimulating work" that brings together a lot of material in a concise way. The disadvantage of this approach, however, was that Voegelin's "objectivity" was likely to give a positive accent to the National Socialist problem or even to be mistaken for an apology for the Nazis. He lamented Voegelin's lack of "moral resistance" and expressed his preference for a more aggressive stance as, for example, Hermann Rauschning provided in *The Revolution of Nihilism.*[3] In the preface to the second edition of *The Political Religions,* Voegelin explained why science is not in the business of supplying moral denunciations, a problem examined in detail below. But neither did it aspire to being a "value-neutral" or "value-free" description along the lines of a familiar (but simplified) version of Max Weber's reflections on method. The issue has resurfaced in recent years regarding Voegelin's understanding of and relationship to Christianity.[4] We must therefore say a bit more about "man the questioner" (*CW* 12:173–79). The example used to illustrate the problem is a recent (1997) one. The point of using it is to indicate that the continuity in Voegelin's philosophical questioning is more fundamental than the subject matter he addressed on any particular occasion.

In his article "The Vocation of a Scholar," Jürgen Gebhardt argued, as we noted above, that Voegelin was first and last a scientist, a *Wissenschaftler,* and not, to use Gebhardt's language, a prophet or a church father.[5] In support of his view and of the distinction he drew between scientific and other vocations, Gebhardt quoted a remark Voegelin made in 1976 at the Thomas More Institute in Montreal, in answer to a question regarding the adequacy of a Thomistic handling of the statement of Jesus, "before Abraham was, I am" (John 8:58).

"That's a large order," Voegelin began (*CW* 33:325–26). The problem, in summary form, was that the distinction made by Thomas between philosophy as the achievement of "natural reason" and theology that results from "supernatural revelation" just "doesn't hold water." Many Greek poets and philosophers have discussed their revelation experiences in the context of their account of the structure of reality, Voegelin said. Thomas, on the other hand, was concerned with salvation out of the structure of reality.

Voegelin then illustrated the problem with the example of a state-supported university housing a department of religious studies where students were taught every religion except Christianity because of concerns over the constitutional separation of church and state. "Everywhere," he continued,

> in such departments of religion you run into somebody who is bright enough to ask himself occasionally whether it is just a question of the Buddha having a conception of something, and Confucius having another one, and so on—or whether perhaps they have all experienced the same Divine reality and there is only one God who manifests Himself, reveals Himself, in a highly diversified manner all over the globe for all these millennia of history that we know. The mere fact that we now have in history a global empirical knowledge extending into the archaeological millennia all over earth requires a theology that is a bit less confined to Islam or to Christianity. It must explain why a God who is the God of some witch doctor in Africa is the same God who appeared to Moses as "I am" or to Plato in a Promethean fire. And that theology is unfortunately not yet in existence.
>
> **P. Coonan:** But wouldn't you have to use philosophy in order to try to understand the evidence and the formulation?
>
> **E. Voegelin:** Absolutely.
>
> **P. Coonan:** But it is a distinct job, you're not yet doing theology?
>
> **E. Voegelin:** It is a distinct job to develop a theology in the Platonic sense—to know all these various types of theologies, the various types of

> faith, and to analyze their structures—always with an eye to the problem that even the most exotic ones, ones that may appear primitive to us, are revelations that have to be respected. (CW 33:326)

It was clear from the subsequent questions Voegelin was asked that the more or less pious Catholics at the Thomas More Institute were distressed at the notion that the God who is the God of "some witch doctor in Africa" had anything to do with the Yahweh of Moses. It was also clear from the conversation with Patricia Coonan that she objected to Voegelin's implication that theology was no longer the queen of the sciences, as it was for St. Thomas.

Gebhardt concluded from this exchange that Voegelin had no intention of formulating any such "new theology" because his analytical understanding of the experiential sources of symbolic orders led him to conclude that "the language of the gods . . . is fraught with the problem of symbolizing the experience of a not-experientiable divine reality" (*CW* 18:83). As a result, because the language of gods tends to be misconstrued as referring to "a divine entity 'beyond' the experience of the [presence of the] Beyond," then the gods must die when a more adequate language is achieved. In this way, "the historical scene becomes littered with dead gods." On the other hand, if language is not misconstrued, "the succession of the gods becomes a series of events to be remembered" as the history of the presence of the Beyond. What has history, what leaves a historical trace, is not the Beyond, which is also "beyond history," but the presence of the Beyond "in the bodily located consciousness of questioning man." That is, "the experience of the non-experientiable divine reality has history," namely "the history of truth emerging from the quest for truth" that in turn occurs "in the bodily located consciousness of questioning man" and so constitutes an element of his (or her) biography. In this respect, "the serious effort of the quest for truth acquires the character of a divine comedy" (*CW* 18:84). In other words, there is no Beyond beyond the experience of the presence of a Beyond. And that being so, the focus of science is on the experience and its symbolization, not the imaginary hypostasis of a Beyond beyond experience. This is why Voegelinian political science is empirical in the precise, Aristotelian sense.[6]

A second piece of evidence, to which Gebhardt referred, was a 1953 letter Voegelin wrote to Thomas I. Cook, a professor of political philosophy at

Johns Hopkins. Cook had taken issue with Voegelin's "theological premises" in *The New Science of Politics* because, "being an agnostic with [respect to] religious sentiments," he could not share Voegelin's approach (HI, 9:28). In his reply, Voegelin set him straight:

> Your letter has been quite illuminating to me, because now I see—or I should say more cautiously, I believe to see—where the difficulties of our mutual understanding lie. The difficulty seems to be your conception of metaphysics or theology as a "premise" from which one starts in theoretical work; and you are worried about various such "premises." This attitude is so utterly strange to me that, I must confess, I am not even familiar with its historical origins or its principal literary manifestations, though I know that it [is] widespread in our academic environment. Let me outline what my objection is:
>
> The question whether anybody is an agnostic, or religiously inclined, or whether he is both at the same time, as it seems to be your predicament, has, in my opinion, nothing to [do] whatsoever with theoretical issues. I feel even unable to return your confidence on this point, for the good reason that I am not clear myself about my own state of sentiments in such matters. Metaphysics is not a "premise" of anything, as far as I am familiar with the works of philosophers, but the result of a process in which a philosopher explicates in rational symbols his various experiences, especially the experiences of transcendence. And the same goes for Christianity: theology is not a premise, but a result of experiences. As far as political science is concerned, we are faced with the fact that such experiences are constituent elements in social order. Insofar they are facts of political history. A theory of politics, therefore, must take cognizance of these facts and interpret them on their own terms, that is, as experiences of transcendent order, articulating themselves in metaphysics and theology. As a critical scientist I have to accept these facts of order, whatever my personal opinion about them should be. Their classification, not as facts of order, but as "metaphysical premises" etc., seems to me to express not a judgment in science, but a dogmatic misconstruction from the position of some ideology.
>
> Hence, I am not operating with a theological "premise," but with a proposition which certainly is empirically tenable, that is, the proposition that experiences of transcendence and their rational articulation in metaphysics and theology are ordering facts in history. In order to recognize this fact, to theorize it, and so forth, you don't have to be a

> theologian yourself anymore than you have to be a great artist in order to write a competent study on Rembrandt. Of course, in order to theorize these facts, your theoretical instrument must be adequate—and there comes the difficulty. For, the most adequate theoretical instruments of the treatment of these facts, happen to be (as might be expected) the theoretical articulations provided for such experiences by the men who had them. In brief: in order to interpret Plato or Christianity adequately, the theories developed by Plato or St. Augustine will prove considerably more adequate than the theories developed by such comparatively provincial thinkers as James or Dewey. But again, this should not be taken dogmatically, but as an empirical observation. As far as I am concerned, anybody is welcome to theorize the Platonic experiences of *thanatos* or *eros*, or the *hesed* of Hosea, by means of Humean skepticism or Jamesian pragmatism; I am quite ready to sit on the side-lines and to watch the performance. But nobody has done it yet; and I doubt that anybody could do it.
>
> Well, that should clarify certain points. Let me hear more from your side of the fence when it is convenient. (*CW* 30:187–88)

As with the remarks made in *In Search of Order* on the Beyond as cited above, the significance seems clear enough. The task of the scientist or scholar is to account for experiences of transcendence insofar as they are part of the reality he studies. And, in fact, those experiences happen to be a significant constituent element of the order of the political world. In addition, the scholar must reflect on his own experiences of philosophizing in order to understand the philosophizing experiences of others. Gebhardt then drew a perfectly sensible conclusion: that which "constitutes the intelligibility of the diverse civilizational processes is the historical equivalence of the plural modes of human participation in the one comprehensive reality of God, world, and human being. Voegelin expresses this common point of reference as the symbol 'universal humanity' that reflects the universal structure of human existence."[7]

Once again, however, as with the symbol, the Beyond, universal humanity—or "universal mankind," to use Voegelin's term—is not "a society existing in the world, but a symbol that indicates man's consciousness of participating, in his earthly existence, in the mystery of a reality that moves towards its transfiguration. Universal mankind is an eschatological index"

(*CW* 17:376). In other words, even though historical events are founded in the biophysical existence of human beings on earth, who live their lives in the time of the external world of plants, animals, and things, this biophysical existence becomes "historical" insofar as it is lived not in the external world but in the presence of the divine, which is not a "spatio-temporal given." There are plenty of complexities in Voegelin's formulation that remain to be clarified, but the general meaning is clear: what Gebhardt referred to as "the universal structure of human existence" appears in the world as specific and particular symbolizations of experiences of a truth that transcends the occasion of its manifestation. Gebhardt's focus, in short, was on the empirical.

Frederick Lawrence, in an article that immediately followed Gebhardt's in the same volume, took issue with him.[8] He began by referring to a paper, "Voegelin's *Order and History:* A *Civitas Dei* for the Twenty-first Century?" delivered by Paul Caringella to the second international conference on Voegelin, hosted by the University of Manchester in the summer of 1994.[9] As Caringella's title indicates, he argued that there were a number of parallels between Voegelin and St. Augustine. There are good commonsensical as well as textual reasons for thinking so. After all, Voegelin used as an epigraph for *Order and History* a passage from Augustine's *On True Religion.* In particular, Caringella drew attention to the meditative quality of the work of both thinkers, which Lawrence called the "mystical dimension" of Voegelin's thought. Whatever Lawrence meant by that phrase, it was to be contrasted with what he referred to as Gebhardt's "rationalism." Lawrence's argument was meant to show that "it is false to contrast his [Voegelin's] achievements in the restoration of reason in political science, with his meditative endeavor" (36). Lawrence, Caringella, and Gebhardt are all first-rate scholars, so it is important to discover whether they were simply emphasizing different aspects of Voegelin's text or whether they disagreed fundamentally about its meaning. I should add that the present analysis of the issue between Lawrence and Gebhardt does not assume that these are the only two alternatives to understanding Voegelin, that is, as mystic or as scientist. Even less is the purpose of the analysis to find some accommodating and conciliatory "middle ground" or to provide an opinion as to who was more "correct" in his interpretation, as if we were assigning grades on a term paper. Rather, we seek to illuminate a problem central to political science.

Caringella argued that Voegelin's "first *anamnesis*" was the "meditative unit," consisting of his anamnestic experiments of 1943, his paper "On the Theory of Consciousness," and his letter to Alfred Schütz of September 1943, on Husserl, all of which were collected in *Anamnesis* (1966) (*CW* 6:45–98). The background of this meditative unit was found in Voegelin's *Herrschaftslehre* of the early 1930s, which we will examine in Chapter 4, and also in a *"Privatseminar"* he gave in 1936–1937 at his apartment in Vienna.[10] On the basis of this first anamnesis, Voegelin was able to understand the importance of Vico as a kind of inoculation against the promise of Hegel that he had created a final and complete system of science.[11]

According to Caringella, Voegelin's "second anamnesis" took place during the decade after 1964 and found an initial expression in his paper "Eternal Being and Time" (*CW* 6:312–37) and a more complete formulation in the middle chapters of *The Ecumenic Age* (*CW* 17:229–339). The "third anamnesis" started with the 1977 paper "The Beginning and the Beyond" and ended with Voegelin's analysis of Plato's *Timaeus* in *In Search of Order* (*CW* 28:173–232; 18:103–4). From Caringella's presentation, Lawrence drew the conclusion that Voegelin's three anamneses corresponded to Augustine's *Confessions* and that his *Order and History* corresponded to Augustine's *City of God.* Accordingly, "Voegelin's career traces an anamnetic ascent not unlike that of Augustine" (42), the church father.

For reasons noted above, such a commonsensical conclusion is unobjectionable but not particularly insightful. The interesting problem emerges from Lawrence's analysis of Gebhardt. Unfortunately, he did not always provide a systematic commentary on the development of Gebhardt's argument. As a result, it is not always possible to compare the two commentators' texts with those of Voegelin. The present analysis of these two papers, accordingly, aims to indicate the logical structure of the problem Gebhardt and Lawrence were dealing with.

Lawrence began by retranslating Gebhardt's English back into German. Thus "The Vocation of a Scholar," Gebhardt's title, echoed the famous lecture of Max Weber, "Wissenschaft als Beruf," which could also be translated as "Scholarship as a Vocation."

Second, Lawrence noted that, according to Gebhardt, Voegelin "would have resented being elevated to a modern Church Father" but Lawrence neglected to add that this was because, in Gebhardt's view, Voegelin "would have preferred to have his work compared to Plato's, or to that of Bodin, who was his favorite among modern political thinkers" (Gebhardt, 13; Lawrence, 43). It is perhaps worth recalling that, so far as Voegelin was concerned, both Plato and Bodin could be properly described as mystics (*CW* 12:360–65, 6:393–96; see also *CW* 34:137–38 for Voegelin's understanding of the phrase *mystic philosopher*).

Third, Lawrence (43) quoted Gebhardt (13) that "the very nature of a modern scholar's search for truth" makes it an ongoing process that "resists being finalized in terms of a literary corpus," such as the Bible, "that will be transmitted and expounded by future generations." Rather, Gebhardt said, the modern scholar's search for truth exists "within the ever-expanding ecumenic horizon of empirical knowledge." Lawrence interpreted this observation of Gebhardt as referring to the modern "knowledge explosion" that "has made it virtually nonsensical to compare the situation for the philosophic integration of scientific results with that of premodern philosophy and theology" (44). He passed over in silence, however, Gebhardt's next sentence: "Voegelin characterized Augustine's work as 'the summa of the age that has laid the foundation of Western Christian civilization' and *Augustine's spirituality was undoubtedly a formative experience that shaped Voegelin's meditative efforts from the very beginning of his theoretical work*" (Gebhardt, 13; the quote from Voegelin on Augustine is from *CW* 19:206). Such statements by Gebhardt and Voegelin did not imply that Voegelin understood himself as a modern Augustine, or that Augustine was not as much a philosopher as an ecclesiastical statesman or church father.

Gebhardt then advanced the view that Voegelin considered philosophical anthropology to be the fundamental science for all the other "sciences of the socio-historical world" (14). He then explained the implications of this statement with reference to the changes between the position of Voegelin elaborated in *The New Science of Politics* and the first three volumes of *Order and History* with the position detailed in the fourth volume, *The Ecumenic Age.* To simplify somewhat: In the early works, Voegelin conceived the historical differentiation of human experience achieved by

Christianity and philosophy to be a "maximum" so that any retreat from "the revelation of the logos in history" constituted a "recession." On these grounds, Voegelin detected a "civilizational cycle of world-historical proportions" (*CW* 5:221–22). The first three volumes of *Order and History* were written on the basis of this essentially Vichian *corso.*

In the fourth volume of *Order and History,* however, Voegelin reflected on the limitations of such a cycle, world-historical or not, and concluded that the epochal events of philosophy and revelation, or of noetic and pneumatic theophanic experiences, occurred within the ecumenic age, to use the title of the book.[12] According to Gebhardt, this new interpretation was faithful to the theoretical interpretative principles that had guided Voegelin's inquiry from the beginning, namely the science of order based on a critical theory of human existence, a philosophical anthropology. Faithfulness to this hermeneutic accounted for why Voegelin abandoned the "history of ideas" approach to political order, and it explained as well the changes between volumes 3 and 4 of *Order and History.* Moreover, the application of this interpretative strategy to the ever-increasing material produced by the historical sciences—Lawrence's information explosion—has engendered a new theoretical perspective.

Gebhardt's formulation regarding this new perspective was that a "good part" of the institutional and intellectual heritage of Christianity was no longer "socially relevant," including a great deal of patrology (or patristics) and scholasticism.[13] Other parts of the Christian heritage, including faith formed in love *(fides caritata formata),* the psychology of concupiscence and pride, and certain theological formulations of Eckhart and Schelling, were "not yet ripe for falling into oblivion." Gebhardt interpreted the observation that Voegelin made in a letter to Karl Löwith as follows: "At closer inspection, the 'essence' of Christianity turns out to be a modernist, antitraditional, and antidoctrinal philosophical exegesis of the spiritual core of historical Christianity. Consequently, it is radically dissociated from the ecclesiastical establishment" (17).

If the allusion to Feuerbach's notorious *Essence of Christianity* were not sufficiently provocative, Gebhardt's inference regarding the implications of radical dissociation from the ecclesiastical establishment, that is, the church, certainly was. First, Gebhardt quoted an excerpt from Voegelin's

History of Political Ideas that, in its entirety, reads as follows:

> If we formulate somewhat drastically the deepest sentiment that causes the postmedieval spiritual tensions of the West, we might say: the bearers of Western civilization do not want to be a senseless appendix to the history of antiquity. On the contrary, they want to understand their civilizational existence as meaningful. If the church is not able to see the hand of God in the history of mankind, men will not remain peaceable and satisfied but will go out in search of gods who take some interest in their civilizational efforts. The church has abandoned its spiritual leadership insofar as it has left postmedieval man without guidance in his endeavors to find meaning in a complex civilization that differs profoundly in its horizons of reason, nature, and history from the ancient civilization that was absorbed and penetrated by the early church. In the face of this abandonment of the *magisterium* it is futile for Christian thinkers to accuse modern man who will not submit to the authority of the church of *superbia.* There is always enough *superbia* in man to make the accusation plausible, but the complaint dodges the real issue: that man in search of authority cannot find it in the church, through no fault of his own. From dissatisfaction at being engaged in a civilizational process without meaning stem the attempts at a reconstruction of meaning through the evocation of a new "sacred history" that began with Voltaire. And with Voltaire began as well the concerted attack on Christian symbols and the attempt at evoking an image of man in the cosmos under the guidance of inner-worldly reason. (*CW* 24:56–57)

Voegelin was clearly referring to a historical situation, namely the abandonment, in fact, of the *magisterium* by the church, and to the even more regrettable consequences that followed, starting with "Voltaire's attack," to use the heading of the next section in Voegelin's *History.*

Gebhardt then raised a question with which Lawrence took issue. Granted that the church had abandoned its spiritual leadership, where would modern or postmedieval men and women find it? Gebhardt answered his own question: "I suggest it is the philosopher-scholar who is called upon to accept the office of magisterium and defend it against intellectual usurpers." Indeed, he continued, Voegelin himself determined "the extent of his [own] magisterium by defining science as a truthful account of the structure of reality" (18). Gebhardt did allow both that *The*

New Science of Politics (1952) "may be called Voegelin's most Christian book" (15) and that the *History of Political Ideas* more or less conforms to the *corso* outlined in Vico's *New Science.* Starting with *The Ecumenic Age,* however, he agreed emphatically with what Gregor Sebba said even about the first three volumes: "Christian symbolism, however helpful in analyzing modern Western ideologies, provided no instrument for dealing with the problem of human (as distinct from Western) history."[14] Hence Voegelin's efforts, after 1960 or so, to develop a theoretical language adequate to the task of accounting for "an ever-expanding knowledge of the socio-historical world" that was unlimited by the specifically Western and Christian "language of the gods."

Lawrence indicated his understanding of Gebhardt's remark concerning the philosophical exegesis of historical Christianity as being necessarily dissociated from the ecclesiastical establishment by asking the following question: "is not Gebhardt invoking that distinction between philosophy and theology, between reason and revelation, that Voegelin ultimately deemed passé?" He then added a second question: "does this *translatio magisterii* from Church to philosopher-scholars imply the not-so-subtle and familiar post-Enlightenment position that philosophy, instead of being a *fides quaerens intellectum,*[15] is rather reason unillumined by faith, which, in the guise of the empirical human science of politics, has the task of sublating—in the sense of eliminating—faith in a manner scarcely distinguishable from the procedure of Hegel?" (45).

There are several things to be sorted out here. Most obviously, Lawrence accused Gebhardt, to employ the language of *The New Science of Politics,* of having regressed from the maximum differentiation of Christianity and philosophy in the direction of "the empirical human science of politics." Second, Gebhardt did so "in the guise" of this political science but in fact had another agenda, namely the promotion of a "familiar post-Enlightenment position" that, third, was operationalized by means of Hegel's procedure of *Aufhebung*—"sublation" being one of the technical words used in English to render Hegel's term. If the reference to *fides quaerens intellectum* was not simply a slip, Lawrence was indicating that philosophy as well as theology was faith in search of understanding, a position that was intelligible to Voegelin's understanding of science but one that is not self-evident (see *CW* 5:276, 6:168; compare with 15:290). Whatever one makes of these implications, it was clear that Lawrence was "arguing strongly" against what he called "this element of rationalist bias in Gebhardt's interpretation of Voegelin" (45). Of course, he conceded, Gebhardt may not have intended "such an interpretative twist," but nevertheless it stands in need of a "corrective," and, Lawrence said, one had been supplied by Caringella.

Clearly there is a disagreement between Gebhardt and Lawrence, though its precise contours are difficult to specify. Lawrence did not, for example, explain what he meant by calling Gebhardt a "rationalist." We can perhaps identify the issue more closely by questioning whether, or in what sense, Voegelin "deemed passé" the distinction between reason and revelation. As a practical matter it is not passé insofar as individuals can and do bolster their arguments on the priority of one or another of the two terms with a peppering of quotations from Voegelin. Again, as a practical matter there is a problem with what Lawrence called "an obscurantist dedifferentiation" among exegetes of Voegelin that would so strongly emphasize "the mystical element" as to eclipse the scientific argument (46). And finally, as a practical matter, the essentially Averroist position allegedly adopted by, for example, Leo Strauss, has much to recommend it.[16]

These prudential considerations do not however touch the theoretical issue contained in what Voegelin called "the problem of meditation." An investigation of this problem, naturally enough, begins from the present situation where, once again, the quest for truth is at issue. In the paper from which Lawrence quoted, "The Meditative Origin of the Philosophical Knowledge of Order" (*CW* 33:384ff), Voegelin discussed the two different types of search, which, to simplify, we shall refer to as reason and revelation—or, if one prefers, noetic and pneumatic experiences and symbolizations of a (or the) search. He also discussed the distinct ethnic communities, which, again to simplify, we can identify as the Hellenic and the Israelite, within which those distinct types of searches were undertaken. When these ethnic communities were brought together in the great ecumenic empires, particularly in the Mediterranean basin, the effort was made somehow to combine the previously existing searches for truth—a theology that combined the elements of revelation from the Bible with philosophical language. In this context Voegelin mentioned Philo and "a Christian theology strongly dependent on the theology of Philo" (*CW* 33:388; see also the discussion in *The Ecumenic Age, CW* 17:75ff). Today, however, Voegelin said, such an effort at systematizing or combining reason and revelation "is no longer needed." Why not? Because "today our historical knowledge is much greater," and we can describe the problem in precise detail.

> It would be senseless in the present ecumenic scientific situation to want to scientifically maintain this categorization. That does not mean that perhaps, in a larger theological context, it should not be maintained; after all, here we are dealing with a problem of a church organization that must deal with a large group of people. Here one must proceed circumspectly. In scientific contexts, however, one must be clear about how it has come to such things. (*CW* 33:389)

In other words, for Voegelin there is no scientific problem of reason and revelation, and Lawrence is undoubtedly correct to emphasize it, even though, so far as a church is concerned, which is to say, as a practical matter that involves a large number of people, not all of them scientifically inclined, "one must proceed circumspectly."

Let the distinction between uncircumspect science and the prudential administration of a church organization suffice to establish the context for the extensive quotation from Voegelin provided by Lawrence (46). With the awareness that both reason and revelation are concerned with the search for truth:

> Therewith the problem of meditation moves into the center of our consideration. From the one side, namely, from the human, the search can be accentuated. I would call that the noetic posture. From the other side, the revelatory side, one can emphasize the motivational factor. I would call that the pneumatic position. Both are present in the problem of meditation. The tension exists between being moved from the godly side and the search from the human side. Thus the godly and the human sides are assumed in a process of seeking and being moved [to seek]. Such symbols as I have used here—a godly reality that moves, a concrete human being who seeks, a process of seeking and being moved—I call a complex.
>
> Under a "complex" I understand the fact that this process of being moved and seeking, which is to be investigated here, should not be cut in pieces or fragmented such that, out of the concentration on the human

> side, an investigation into the human being, thus an anthropology, arises; or, out of confining [the investigation] to the godly side, a theology is formulated. Also impermissible is the isolation of the process in the form of a process philosophy that confines itself to an investigation of the process that exists between two poles and that would, thus, lead to a psychology. All three forms, "anthropologies," "theologies," and "psychologies," are deformation types and have no place in a meditative investigation. (*CW* 33:389)

Voegelin went on to discuss the significance of the meditative event and the language terms used to articulate it.

The only comment that needs to be made, it seems to me, is that Gebhardt stressed the importance of intelligibility as the defining feature of science (31). Even the "heart's subconscious love" that Lawrence invoked toward the end of his essay to balance Gebhardt's so-called "rationalism" needs to be made intelligible. Did not St. Paul himself require those who speak in tongues to be intelligibly interpreted?[17]

This consideration of the problem at issue between Gebhardt and Lawrence may seem to have taken us some distance from the purpose of introducing the study that is found in the following chapters. It seems to me, however, that Voegelin (along with Gebhardt, Lawrence, and Caringella, for that matter) remained a questioner rather than the recipient of answers. Not that his work did not clarify the structure of reality; on the contrary. Rather, clarity about the structure of reality included human being as questioner. Whether one begins from the position conventionally identified with reason or with revelation, from what Voegelin called noetic or pneumatic experiences and symbolizations, whether one appropriates a hermeneutic of faith or trust or one of suspicion, the result is still a search for intelligibility.[18] In this book we aim to make intelligible the beginning of Voegelin's beginning insofar as it is available in texts and to provide additional evidence, as was indicated above, to confirm Voegelin's character as a radical thinker. In short, Voegelin's search for truth was scientific even when it concerned the exegesis of mystic experience.

1
Methodenstreit

In his *Autobiographical Reflections* Voegelin remarked that the "atmosphere" of the University of Vienna, where he studied between 1919 and 1922, "was determined by the breakdown of the Austro-Hungarian empire at the end of the First World War. By its composition, the university was still the university of the capital of the empire and reflected in its scholarship and the personal attitude of the professors this cosmopolitan atmosphere." In the law school, the "great intellectual figures" were Hans Kelsen and Othmar Spann. Kelsen's reputation today as one of the great jurists of the last century overshadows that of Spann, an economist and a sociologist "who had developed a theory of universalism" and an economic theory far superior, in Voegelin's opinion, to the marginal utility theory of Eugen von Böhm-Bawerk (*CW* 34:21–22). Despite the greater historical and philosophical range of Spann, "the precision of analytical work that is peculiar to a great lawyer," Kelsen, held greater attraction to the young student (*CW* 34:48). Voegelin also mentioned that he put together a course of study leading to the degree of *Doctor rerum politicarum* because it could be gained in three rather than four years, the time it would take to obtain a law degree, one year less meant one year less to pay fees, and Voegelin was "very poor" (*CW* 34:33).

Voegelin said his degree was in "political science," a somewhat anachronistic use of the term (*CW* 34:33). Apart from the Hochschule für Politik in Berlin, there were very few political science departments in the contemporary sense of the term in the German-speaking academic world. In the words of Hans Maier, "to the universities, in fact, the whole discipline [of political science] was suspicious; too broad to the one, too narrow to the other, too overladen with materials or too vague in methodology and criteria of relevance to the third." Gregor Sebba, a friend of Voegelin both in Austria and America, made much the same point: "sociology, still an as yet undefined, unspecialized discipline, offered the greatest freedom for development, and 'government' offered him the only chance of a salaried professorial position. There was no 'political science' in the American sense; German *Staatslehre* was a much broader field, the right one for a theoretician of political order who was able to master constitutional law, if needed." As Sebba observed in another version of this essay, "Voegelin has always defied departmentalization."[1] However, described in retrospect, Voegelin's chief concern, experienced as a "strong but vague impulse," was that he would "embark on a career in science" (*CW* 34:33).

But what is "science"? We know most famously from the introduction to *The New Science of Politics* that, whatever it once was and again might be, it had been destroyed in the nineteenth century by positivism (*CW* 5:90). But this is a relatively late observation; we would like to know: what did *science* mean to the young scholar? We begin consideration of this question by making some general observations concerning the contemporary use of the term. In many respects, from the complex ambiguity of the language to the abstraction of the concepts, Voegelin's analysis of methodology in German social sciences during the postwar period resembles the discussion in American social science following the Second World War. This is one reason why Voegelin was impatient with the later American so-called scientific methodologies, the "unity of science" movement, and simpleminded behavioralism: He had already dealt with these issues at a philosophically more sophisticated level some thirty years earlier.

In the introduction to the first volume of the *Collected Works*, a translation of Voegelin's 1928 book, *On the Form of the American Mind*, the editors (including the present author) argue that a science of politics required an understanding of both philosophical anthropology and science of the spirit.[2] The context for Voegelin's reflections during the early 1920s was "the problem of a science of sociohistorical reality." At the time, this science was partitioned among several already existing sciences: *Staatslehre,* sociology, history, philosophy, to name the most obvious. There was also *Geisteswissenschaft*—literally the science of the spirit—to be considered along with complex combinations, the meaning of which is often not clear—*Staatslehre als Geisteswissenschaft,* for example, which was a term Voegelin used a decade later (*CW* 32:414ff).

The ambiguity of the conceptual language used during the 1920s reflects the historical context, the origins of which are to be found in the nineteenth century. As we have noted, *Staatslehre,* even in the twentieth century, did not mean "political science" in the contemporary sense, and *Geisteswissenschaft,* which has existed on its own terms since the mid-nineteenth century, was defined chiefly in opposition to *Naturwissenschaft,* natural science. Hence, the "problem of a science of sociohistorical reality" is both conceptually precise, because it clearly identified a subject matter, and entirely anachronistic, because at the time no one—certainly not Voegelin—used such language. The problem, therefore, is to indicate more or less precisely what Voegelin's language referred to, even though at a later date he would likely have called his own terminology "hieroglyphic" (*CW* 19:131–32), which is to say derivative. Even though it may be familiar within a universe of discourse, or a "school," it need not be part of a genuine theoretical argument or refer to any empirical reality. Thus, for example, the conventional notion that "man is a political animal" is usually uttered with great dignity and in equally great ignorance that when Aristotle wrote those words he meant that men (not women) could find fulfillment only in a polis, and not in some other kind of association such as a family or an empire. Much of Voegelin's writing during the 1920s, and even during the 1930s, was devoted to understanding the inadequacies of various hieroglyphic uses of ideas and of methods, which returns us to the question of "science," *Wissenschaft.*

According to Fritz Ringer, *Wissenschaft* refers to "any organized body of information," so that the best English equivalent would be "scholarship" or "learning."[3] Originally *Wissenschaft* was closely associated with the notion of *Bildung,* or self-cultivation, that Wilhelm von Humboldt introduced to Prussian university life in 1810 (*CW* 12:18–28, 31–32). Accordingly, the pursuit of *Wissenschaft* by scholars would produce the social figure of the well-cultivated citizen-pupil, the *Bildungsbürger.* From the mid-nineteenth century on, the argument was made (and accepted) that, broadly speaking, the *Geisteswissenschaften,* not philosophy, accounted for the truth about sociohistorical reality. Accordingly, the claims advanced on behalf of the *Geisteswissenschaften* entailed much more than an academic dispute; it exerted a claim to guide the formation of the German nation in a time of crisis (*CW* 1:xi). The burden of this self-appointed task for the *Geisteswissenschaftler*—the social scientist, broadly speaking—led to an intensive search for the theoretically adequate methodological foundations of his or her science. From this search came the *Methodenstreite,* the methodological controversies, indicated by the title of this chapter. Before analyzing Voegelin's contribution to this complex controversy, we will outline the major issues. Necessarily these preliminary remarks are somewhat summary.

In addition to the *Geisteswissenschaften* broadly speaking, which we have rendered as social sciences, there was a methodologically more precise meaning that was based on a distinction between the older practitioners of *Kulturwissenschaft* and the newer practitioners of *Geisteswissenschaft,* associated chiefly with the approach of Wilhelm Dilthey. Notwithstanding their methodological differences, briefly discussed below, both schools were anxious about their status as *Wissenschaften,* and both, therefore, were concerned about their role and purpose in German society. Moreover, because these "mandarins" were largely liberal Protestants, they were both mildly suspicious of non-liberal non-Protestants and, in the closing decades of the nineteenth century, were strongly attached to the new Bismarckian state, not least because the wars of unification were so successful. The task of the mandarins, therefore, was clear: to "revitalize the great traditions of the eighteenth-century German classics to which all humanistic scholarship was committed and [to] provide a sound moral and spiritual basis to the new nation-state" (*CW* 1:xiii). The *Geisteswissenschaften* were considered by their practitioners to be perfectly situated to combine the universalism of philosophy and literature with the specific needs of German society undergoing rapid social change. Social cohesion, it was argued, would be established when these allegedly universal verities were institutionalized in the culturally articulated legal state. The urgency of the task contributed to the sense of "crisis" noted above.

Combining, let alone synthesizing, the reality of German particularity in culture, literature, philosophy, law, *Geist,* or anything analogous, with the claims of universality, is a difficult, or rather, an impossible task. Indeed, claims to universality were in fact a particular expression of the German mind or *Geist* that was central to the speculations of Hegel and before him, of Kant and the thinkers of the German Enlightenment. Moreover, as we will see, one of Voegelin's early problems was to distinguish the question of the universalist aspirations of science from the particularity of its German expression.

Leaving aside that large issue, at least temporarily, the two schools—the older *Kulturwissenschaften* and the newer *Geisteswissenschaften*—adopted what they considered to be methodologically distinct ways of combining German particularity and scientific universality. On the one hand, an allegedly universal culture became the reference point for the *Kulturwissenschaftler,* and the "objective spirit" did the same for the *Geistenwissenschaftler.* Universal culture was understood to be the embodiment of a universal humanity formed by *Bildung;* objective spirit was the objectification of the historical life of humanity. We will clarify the meaning of these terms below, but clearly the accent for both schools was on the claim to ostensible universality.

The major problems with a position that claimed to be universal but that in fact was merely German, that is, was indeed particular, were apparent even in the nineteenth century. Voegelin provided an analysis of several works that dealt with this issue. His argument, which took several years to develop in detail, was simply that these claims to universality in fact did no more than reflect the political parochialism of both German culture and the legal structure of the German state. The problem was self-evident: to begin with, there was no connection between German culture (to say nothing of the universal culture that the *Kulturwissenschaftler* claimed it to be) and the universality of the state for the obvious reason that German culture, however understood, was divided between the Bismarckian, Prussian, or Hohenzollern state in the north, and the Hapsburg Empire, which in any event was multicultural, in the south. Moreover, the notion of the state was abstract because it was advanced independently of the specific political quality of human existence in a community, such as the fact that both states said to harbor German culture styled themselves either kingdoms or empires. Indeed, after the Prussian military victory over France in 1871, both the Hapsburg and the Hohenzollern lands styled themselves empires. None of this self-interpretation of German culture or of the German mind, *Geist,* seemed to matter to those who interpreted it in universalist terms.

Nor were there any arguments along pseudo-Aristotelian lines that human beings—all human beings, not just Germans—were by nature political for the obvious reason that matters pertaining to nature were the concern of the *Naturwissenschaftler.* As Ringer summarized the issue, the tradition of the legal state no less than the claims of *Bildung* led to the notion that the purposes of the state "were generally stated in moral and spiritual terms. The analysis of political realities was neglected. . . . Indeed the suggestion was that the details of everyday politics were ethically as well as intellectually beneath the notice of a cultivated man."[4] This attitude was reflected even in Bismarck's famous aphorism "to retain respect for sausages and laws, one must not watch them in the making." In short, a culturally elevated, spiritualized, or abstract and putatively universal notion of politics was understood to be institutionalized in the abstract legal structure of the state, which was also putatively universal where rule meant power imposed by law. This understanding of political rule eventually was questioned by Voegelin as well.

Within this general context of German academia, let us now consider, provisionally or in outline, the methodological and epistemological differences between the practitioners of *Kulturwissenschaft,* whom we may characterize as strict neo-Kantians, and the practitioners who followed Dilthey and the *Geisteswissenschaften.* The strict neo-Kantians began, not surprisingly, from Kant's epistemology, which was concerned chiefly with nature, and applied it to the realm of culture. In order to do so, they eliminated Kant's postulate of the "thing-in-itself" and concluded that valid knowledge was constituted, for both nature and culture, by the application of the categories of pure thought that, in turn, were properties of a "transcendental ego." In short, the objects of cognition in both natural and cultural or social science were generated by the intellect and selected for inclusion in the realm of science by concepts selected by the scientist. In contrast to the order of science, reality "itself" is chaotic, disordered, formless.[5] Only the scientific attitude of the scholar was able to ensure that from all the chaotic value-laden phenomena of culture, the leading aspects of culture could be described and accounted for. In this respect, the cultural scientist approximated the transcendental ego of neo-Kantian epistemology and produced a scientific, cognitively valid account of the cultural world.

In contrast, Dilthey's *Geisteswissenschaften* began not from the formal a prioris that, according to Kant, constituted science, but from the difference in content between nature and culture and the assumption that the two modes of being required different approaches, methods, and epistemologies. Within the world of culture, human experience confirmed the coherence of human life within any particular historical and cultural community, which Dilthey called "objective spirit." The world of the spirit was constantly in motion as a consequence of the interaction of individuals, communities, and so on. The task of the scientist of the spirit was to account for sociohistorical reality in terms of the structures created within the "objective spirit." By so doing, the world of the spirit grew aware of itself, and the scientist, who embodied this self-awareness, came to possess knowledge. As with the strict neo-Kantian *Kulturwissenschaftler*, reality was formless and chaotic, but by understanding the structures of the "objective spirit," the scientist gave an ordered and logical account, which was also the self-knowledge of the spirit or mind (that is, *Geist*). Accordingly, "in the course of the ongoing process of empirical research, the *Geisteswissenschaften,* as interpretative sciences of man, bring forth ever-expanding knowledge of the sociohistorical reality along with a growing understanding about man's position in the whole of reality. The *Geisteswissenschaften* disclose to modern man under the open horizon of history the common ground of all human life" (*CW* 1:xvii). This equally grandiose claim, the vaguely Hegelian provenance of which is evident, also did not say anything about actual politics or law.

The absence was felt particularly acutely after the defeat of 1918. There was clearly a crisis of some kind present, but it was not clear how it was to be understood. More to the point, the epistemological assumptions of both the strict neo-Kantians and the *Geisteswissenschaftler* had come under criticism from the newer approaches associated with phenomenology and philosophical anthropology. This context of change—where older forms of science were no longer entirely persuasive but newer ways of understanding and explicating the sociocultural world were not yet in place—greeted Voegelin on his entry into the scientific community.

Broadly speaking, Voegelin sought to combine the rigor and strictness of neo-Kantian science with an attention to the empirical contents of Dilthey's *Geisteswissenschaften.* Given the long-standing disagreements over method, it was not clear how this could be done.

As a final contextual observation, we may note that among the several social crises of postwar Germany was the "crisis of *Staatslehre*" brought on by the political changes between the Hohenzollern Empire and the Weimar Republic. Voegelin began his analysis of *Staatslehre* by way of interpretative (or, broadly speaking) Weberian sociology, but focused on the importance of symbols and ideas in the formation of the state as a political unit. This was *not* neo-Kantian a priori methodology but a kind of *Geisteswissenschaft.* Hence his concern noted above for a *geisteswissenschaftslich Staatslehre.*

When one reads the surviving fragment of his dissertation, "Interaction and Spiritual Community: A Methodological Investigation" (*CW* 32:19–140), the first thing that comes to mind is that it certainly *looks* like sociology, not least of all because the term is mentioned in the opening sentence. It is also, as the subtitle indicates, a methodological analysis. Voegelin began by noting the existence of disputes regarding the meaning of sociology as a science and resolved the issue into two questions: (1) What is the subject matter and method of sociology? and (2) What type of science is it? To answer these questions he provided a sketch of "our basic epistemological orientation," which he called "Critical Idealism." Voegelin said it followed the formulations and arguments of Edmund Husserl, the founder of phenomenology, and especially the latter's arguments, in *Ideas* and in *Logical Investigations.* Given that phenomenology aimed literally to give an account of the appearances—or, as Husserl said, we must aim at "the things themselves"—it is clear that phenomenology as a "strict science" was something other than the imposition of "scientific" neo-Kantian epistemological categories on a reality that was assumed to be chaotic.

The German title of Voegelin's dissertation, *Wechselwirkung und Gezweiung,* alluded to two technical terms as well. The first noun, "social interaction," is a basic concept in the sociology of Georg Simmel; the second, "spiritual community," was central to Spann's reflections on social reality, namely that spiritual life is necessarily communal or at least plural. In Voegelin's view, Simmel's concept of social interaction contained psychological constituent elements that meant it was not "scientific" in Husserl's sense of the term. A "more thorough analysis" of the problems associated with social interaction, Voegelin said, would expose the elements of truth in Simmel's account and indicate that, in fact, they were identical with Spann's theory of the spiritual community (*CW* 32:22). That is, an application of Husserlian analysis to Simmel's concept of social interaction would purge it of its psychological defects, render it compatible with Spann's arguments, and turn the two theories into "elements" or "material ontologies" of an "eidetic science," namely sociology. Voegelin's argument consisted of an elaborate discussion of the "sociological method" by means of which this task could be accomplished.

Scattered throughout this highly abstract argument were a number of concrete observations that "express" what sociology, as distinct from the sociological method, actually is. For example, Pierre Duhem's account of the difference between English and French physics (an example Voegelin analyzed in his first scholarly publication, discussed below) was such an expression. More generally, "the task of sociology is to grasp the phenomenon [it studies] in its social nature" so as to be able to account, for example, for why this painting was a *Dutch* painting or an *American* painting and not a good or bad, or beautiful or ugly, painting. The sociological method, Voegelin said, "provides us with a means of undertaking such an investigation" (*CW* 32:22). The "basic problem" in sociology "is expressed in the antinomy concerning the relationship of the individual to society. It is our task to resolve this antinomy." For instance, "the identity of a pile of sand is defined by the individual grains that compose it. The identity of the 'English nation' is not defined by the individuals who are members at any one time" (*CW* 31:2). That is, any society is to some degree independent of the specific human beings that make it up and so transcends the individual, even while society depends on individuals and exists through them.

More specifically or concretely, Voegelin discussed the example of a German engaging in social interaction, *Wechselwirkung*, with British people without thereby becoming British. He or she might simply be a visitor to the British Isles or perhaps an expat working in Britain for any number of reasons. On the other hand, a German could also become assimilated, which was a different kind of social interaction. In the second example, the social substance that made a German German would have changed along with the necessary condition for such change, namely a change in external social interaction between a German in German society and a German in British society. There is, moreover, a different meaning between assimilation in European societies as compared to assimilation in America, where it was possible not to remain an alien at all. In contrast, an assimilated German in British society would remain "an assimilated German" and so still alien—though not as great an alien as an unassimilated German. This, too, Voegelin said, involved a change in social substance, which was "the particular quality of the spirit by means of which an individual is recognized as belonging to a particular society and which renders him, and others like him, immune to alien influences." In terms of substance, the members of a society were all the same insofar as they thought and felt the same way about a wide range of cultural matters, from business mores to what constituted good art or good beer. This "sameness" was not identity but participation in a spiritual community. "Society," Voegelin wrote, "is a multiplicity of spiritual communities that are unified by virtue of the fact that the material content of their postulates, i.e., the concrete contexts of meaning, are the same" (*CW* 32:35–36, 55, 68, 72).

Prior to the completion of his dissertation, Voegelin published two papers, one on Frank Wedekind (*CW* 32:141ff), and a second entitled "The Social Determination of Sociological Knowledge" (*CW* 7:27ff). We consider only the second one here.[6] Voegelin began by delimiting the problem he wished to consider. Because the war was over, it was possible in 1922 to study foreign sociology; it was also then possible to see whether foreign research had deepened sociological insight or developed new points of view. This possibility of innovation and an increase in insight raised a more fundamental question: whether sociological studies undertaken in different countries complement one another. For those who understood sociology as a science, the question was absurd because science, as an objective activity, was necessarily independent of individuals and social contexts. Just as there was no German mathematics, the practitioners of this universalist understanding of science would say, there was no German sociology.

To which claim Voegelin made the obvious reply: There are hardly any examples of "objective" sociology, sociology untouched by "value perspectives." The reply to this objection was equally well known: Not yet, maybe, but "in the course of time the objective core of all these theories will work itself free and permit the formation of an exact science." What promised objectivity is the rigorous application of method; if it was not yet attained, that is only because the correct method had not been applied with sufficient determination or rigor. Voegelin then indicated that he would argue "that sociological knowledge is subjective in its essence." This may not have been the best language to use, because practically by definition *subjective* is not just distinct from *objective* but opposed to it. In any event, it is clear that, at the time, for Voegelin sociology could not be objective; but it is also clear that it could not be subjective in the sense of arbitrary or idiosyncratic, because then it could not count as knowledge of any kind.

From his account of British sociology and in particular the work of Graham Wallas, by "subjective," Voegelin meant something like participatory, and that among those participatory elements is nationality. Accordingly, the "overriding assumption," Voegelin said, was that even though British sociology, like all sociology, claimed or aspired to be science, in some sense of the term, it was also British, much as a Dutch or American painting aspired to be beautiful art without ceasing to be Dutch or American. A close examination of the work of Wallas, who served as a representative British sociologist, would thus define what is specifically British in his sociology. This analysis would contribute to the larger sociological enterprise in that it would help us understand what a nation is, and "modern sociology is as yet far from being clear on the meaning of this concept" (*CW* 7:29). The immediate practical significance of such an exercise, which was repeated on a larger scale in *On the Form of the American Mind,* was that it may contribute to postwar understanding between or among former belligerents. That is, without trying to understand the British or the Americans on their own terms, the only alternative was to see them and understand them in terms of one's own parochial, or provincial, approach. On the other hand, the effort to grasp the self-understanding of another—British sociology or the American mind—necessarily involved expanding the horizon of the scientist. From the beginning, one may say, Voegelin's motivation was, as he later observed, derived "from the political situation" (*CW* 34:118).

"Like all other sciences," Voegelin said, "sociology is to seek causes of events, and it is to do so in order, with the help of its acquired knowledge, to exert influence on the shaping of life." That is, the practical motivation we have linked to the postwar context was, for Voegelin, part of the purpose of sociological investigation. With Wallas in particular, what attracted Voegelin's attention was his argument that "social problems" were rooted in, or conditioned by, what Wallas called "dispositions." The methodological or perhaps theoretical problem with this notion, according to Voegelin, was that unlike the causing of bodily warming by the radiation of the sun, disposition "has a life of its own" and could be "baulked." That is, to the "natural" component of disposition must be added an ethical one, which makes both flourishing and a "baulked" disposition possible. This would appear to imply that the causal focus of sociology and thus its ability to influence life has disappeared, particularly because there was no mention of a "metaphysical personality" beyond the natural and the ethical that might have a bearing on causality. Nor, Voegelin observed, was there a "metaphysical personality" in puritanism or in Adam Smith's *Wealth of Nations*, from which observation he concluded that there existed a cultural community among British writers, at least insofar as that typically some things were missing from their arguments.

This initial observation was hardly a major insight since the particularity of British thinking had not been made explicit. Voegelin then reiterated his major assumption regarding sociological analysis, "that a mental [*geistig* (or spiritual)] phenomenon inherent in society must allow us to recognize the unique character [*Gepräge*] of a society, for a society is nothing but a totality [*Inbegriff*] of specifically characterized mental [*geistig* (or spiritual)] contents" (*CW* 7:40). Here Voegelin again referred to Duhem's analysis of the differences among British, French, and German styles of conducting physics (*CW* 7:46, 46n34) and observed: "what strikes us as odd is the uncommonly broad, and—for German sensibilities—irksome exemplification of this train of thought," namely its apparent lack of concern for philosophical grounding, such as the absence of a "metaphysical personality," noted above. "Wallas," Voegelin continued, "shares this peculiarity with a number of English writers: theory is immediately tested for its practical applications; a thoroughgoing systematic construction is much less important than a theoretical comprehension of individual phenomena. Fragments of theory are constructed as needed for shreds of reality" (*CW* 7:46). In other words, what was missing typically from the arguments of British sociology was a concern with what was central to German sociology, namely the (broadly speaking) Kantian and neo-Kantian arguments dealing with the metaphysical foundations of science. The implicit question therefore was: Is British sociology scientific? And if not, what is it?

Voegelin concluded his paper by revisiting the question with which he began: "namely, whether science is objective, and to answer a narrower question, whether a cooperation between the sociological investigations of various nations is possible." He answered by observing that, whereas a "general knowledge" is attainable as are "singular findings," there was no "transcendental sociology" unless the sociological practitioners were also "transcendental philosophers," which is to say, neo-Kantians, and drew the obvious conclusion: "whether we can find this type of philosopher outside Germany seems highly doubtful" (*CW* 7:48). The implication seemed to be that an adverse judgment regarding the scientific status of British sociology, if one were made by German sociologists, simply reflected the German approach to society and did not deal with British sociology on its own terms. That is, German sociologists did not find what they did not put into British sociology.

Voegelin revisited this question of the scientific status of British sociological thinking in a short 1928 paper, "Two Fundamental Concepts of Humean Sociology" (*CW* 7:336–43). German philosophical thought and sociological thought, Voegelin began, were different than their Western European, and especially their British, equivalents because of breaks in the German tradition. "One of the key causes of this peculiar [i.e., German] form of intellectual development may be sought in the political history of the German people." Unlike the British and the French, the Germans have experienced neither territorial nor state continuity over a long period of time. In the West, therefore, one finds a tradition that can be described in terms of the "continuous unfolding of problems," unlike the German tradition of "periods of intense brilliance shining forth from an embarrassing darkness that one can hardly comprehend." This was one reason why English philosophy, which took a few seventeenth-century problems and raised them "to even higher degrees of refinement" was "well-nigh impenetrable to non-Englishmen, and doubly so to Germans." Especially difficult for Germans to understand was the problem of "style" as distinct from "theory." The difficulty was methodologically significant, because today the Germans were dealing with problems that had been treated for years in England. Unfortunately, the presuppositions of the British approach were all but unspoken in contemporary British sociology, though once they had been explicit. Voegelin's point, very simply, was that, however great a problem the question of scarcely visible presuppositions may be for German sociology, it was not a problem for the British. In this context Voegelin proposed to discuss Hume's analysis of two of the currently unspoken or inarticulate presuppositions: the problem of identity of the person and the problem of sympathy.

For our purposes the significance of this analysis lies not in Voegelin's accounts of personal identity and of sympathy in Hume's philosophy, masterful though they were, but of his connecting these Humean philosophical categories to the contingency of Hume's British formation as a thinker. Indeed, it would seem that Voegelin's first essays in "sociology" all were concerned with a similar problem: how to integrate the particularities of the traditions of national consciousness or national spirit with the claims made by practitioners to be conducting a science that aimed at transcending the conditions of its origin or genesis. The problem recurred in his discussion of Max Weber, which we will consider next, but also in connection with his early legal studies, examined in Chapter 3.

Apart from a few remarks made *en passant* in book reviews (*CW* 13:12–15), Voegelin's next significant reflection on sociology and its methods can be found in his 1925 essay "On Max Weber" (*CW* 7:100–117). Voegelin began by drawing the by now familiar distinction between mathematical science and the other sciences where "personal participation" was more than minimal. We interpret mathematical arguments solely on the basis of their logical coherence. "Here the objective-material structure suppresses all personal content" so that it made no sense to examine a mathematical proposition or an equation in physics by considering the personal information concerning its author. That is, where mathematical science possessed clearly articulated laws, and thus meaningfulness, historical science—because of its fragmentary nature, owing to incomplete records, for example—"insists inexorably on the question of the reason for its being."

Thus the personal or participatory orientation of the historian, which Voegelin earlier called "subjective," was central to historical science.

But what, then, was historical science? And with respect to Voegelin's essay, where was it found in Weber's work? How did the great range of Weber's compilations and discrete analyses cohere? These may be legitimate questions to pose to Weber, though it would strike one as odd, to say the least, to ask similar questions of a mathematician. One would not, for example, ask Albert Einstein how his participation in the theory of relativity provided coherence to his equations; one would simply read his argument. This was not the case with a science based on fragmentary records that was also charged with making sense or bringing coherence to them. Such questions were above all legitimate with respect to Weber's work because "Max Weber posed this question to himself and answered it by means of a metaphysics of history." That is, according to Voegelin's interpretation of Weber, his historical science was in fact a coherent science on the basis of Weber's understanding of history, not on the basis of Weber's understanding of science. At first blush, this assertion also looked rather Hegelian.

The term used by Voegelin, "metaphysics of history," *Geschichtsmetaphysik,* which we might more conventionally call "philosophy of history," is not usually associated with Weberian social science. Voegelin began his explication by starting with Weber's well-known distinction between science and politics. According to Weber, science, especially historical science, was not in the business of justifying practical attitudes or specific decisions. On the contrary: According to Weber, science could advance toward the threshold of a decision, but the actual decision must be taken by a practical person, on his or her own, as it were. In Voegelin's words, "knowledge does not serve orientation in the world, if we wish to understand knowledge as a guide to right action" (*CW* 7:102). This familiar Weberian position led to an obvious commonsensical question: Why would anyone pursue knowledge if it did not serve to orient them in the world? Voegelin's answer was not clear until much later (*CW* 34:40), and it need not concern us here, where the focus remains on his exegesis of Weber's meaning.

Weber's answer, Voegelin argued, was itself historical, and hence a central element to Weber's philosophy of history. The modern situation, according to Weber (according to Voegelin) was the same in essential respects as the situation in classical antiquity. This is not, clearly, so much an empirical as a "metaphysical" observation, as becomes apparent when we learn the reason for it. In antiquity, humans might have sacrificed to the gods, but above human and divine quarrels "fate" held sway. Likewise today, human beings are governed by two "negative concepts" equivalent in meaning to that of fate in antiquity. They are the familiar Weberian notions of "disenchantment" and "everydayness." Today the fatal connection of antiquity that bound together man, nature, and the gods has been replaced with a more impersonal mechanism whereby human beings are more exposed and forced to rely only on their own devices. Likewise, people during classical times were (and for Weber we are) separated from the Middle Ages and the experiences of grace and religious prophetism that once reached toward an "immaculate holiness" beyond the world. Accordingly, disenchantment has been accompanied by everydayness: "It is the fate of our culture," wrote Voegelin, "after a millennium of exclusive orientation to the pathos of Christian ethics, to reenter religious everydayness" (*CW* 7:103). In other words, just as in antiquity fate governed the affairs of mortals, so too today "fate" has extinguished the pathos of Christian ethics and dealt us "everydayness." We may not like what fate has handed us, and we may prefer "immaculate holiness," but we do not, properly speaking, have access to it. Pretending that we do, pretending that the world is enchanted, or that immaculate holiness is at hand, can be no more than an escape for the bewildered or a "sacrifice of the intellect," as Weber called it. This was unquestionably Weber's attitude; once, when he was asked why he pursued his historical studies, he replied, "to see how much I can stand," which expressed an attitude that was the source of Weber's intellectual integrity, a virtue Voegelin admired all his life.

However that may be—and our purpose is not to analyze (even less to criticize) Weber, particularly not by introducing arguments made by Voegelin many years later, but to understand Voegelin's account of Weber in 1925: What bound disenchantment and everydayness together and constituted the core of Weber's philosophy of history was called by Voegelin "rationalism." Put negatively, the essential elements of rationalism were disenchantment and everydayness; positively, they were empirical science and individual responsibility. Unlike ancient rationalism however, the modern variant was not linked to virtue—hence knowledge only takes us to the threshold of decision and cannot guide us—or rather, cannot guide the decision maker—in making a decision.

Voegelin's focus was on the "positive aspects of rationalism, beginning with Weber's well-known distinction between the ethics of responsibility and the ethics of intention:

> if his subjectively pure acts have undesirable consequences, the ethicist of intention lays the blame on the world and its stupidity and rottenness [*Schlechtigkeit*], while the ethicist of responsibility operates with what is stupid and rotten in the world as factors that he takes into account and for whose consequences, to the extent they can be traced to a contact with his actions, he takes full responsibility. (*CW* 7:105)

Nowhere is Weber's intellectual integrity better exemplified than in his ethics of responsibility. But that, too, was Weber's personal fate, because, as he argued, responsibility also meant resignation to reality, to the historical situation that has been dealt modern human beings, namely disenchantment and everydayness. Indeed, resignation to reality—which was the opposite to renunciation of reality in favor of enchantment, "immaculate holiness," or the assumption of an attitude of aesthetic distance from reality—was the condition for the responsible and scientific apprehension of it.

If Weber rejected the notion that there were rational guides to conduct or a rationally formulated "order of values," what, then, was the source of the choice to accept responsibility as a scientist and pursue a course of resignation to reality? Weber's answer, as his discussion of "rationality" as the historical fate of the modern world indicated, was a kind of restatement of fate, only this time he called it his individual "daimon." The most famous daimon was the one that warned Socrates when he was about to do something wrong. In the present context, however, Weber's daimon seemed to be a somewhat Nietzschean way of referring to the neo-Kantian transcendental ego. However named, the task of the historical scientist was to marshal his will and ability to impress a concrete shape or form upon history. There was no party platform, such as Marxism, to do the job, nor, obviously, was religion (in the usual sense of the term) available. In other words, resignation to the reality of an everyday, disenchanted world turns out to be as willful or as passionate as escaping from it.

Voegelin concluded that Weberian historical science was a complex or "layered" phenomenon that combined his personal daimon with commitment to his national community—as expressed in his patriotic wartime essays, for example—as well as the existence of a European historical or cultural community that he qualified or called "rational." There was, therefore, a parallel between Weber's personal fate—his daimon—the fate of his being a German, and the historical fate of rational, everyday, disenchanted Europe. Likewise, for example, Weber's support for democracy was not based on the inherently redeeming qualities of democracy but existed because the political situation of his times (and so, of history and fate) indicated that democracy was the best way of selecting leaders.

Voegelin summarized the connection between the responsible practitioner of historical science and the fate of European history expressed in Weber's philosophy of history, namely rationality, as a combination of form and content. That is, "the content of his philosophy of history," namely resignation to the fate of European rationality, was "not only content, but at the same time the form in which the science of Max Weber achieves reality," namely as the consequence of the will of his daimon, which sustained his intellectual integrity as a responsible scientist. This did not, however, mean that there was only one form of rationalism, namely that of Max Weber, because, between the rational will of his daimon and the equally rational historical fate of Europe was the "layer" of the national community.

Weberian rationality was personal, which made it the rationality of Max Weber, but it was also modern and German and yet it also aspired to universality without falling either into abstraction or into an expression of megalomania. "There is," wrote Voegelin, "not *one* rational science, but every national community permeates this product of European cultural development with elements of the second—national—layer of value in such a manner that often the goals of the scholars of one nation become completely unintelligible to those of the other nations" (*CW* 7:111). What interested Voegelin, therefore, was how a specific, particular, or concrete "national character" exercised an influence on the sciences, whether in the natural or the historical and social sciences—and here Voegelin again mentioned Duhem.

National cultures, Voegelin concluded, influenced the historical sciences at least as much as the daimon of the individual in the selection of historical evidence, even when, as with Weber, they aimed to be "value-neutral." Obviously, "without the researcher's value ideas there would be no principle for choosing materials." The insight could be pressed further. Voegelin noted "a remark made by a prominent personality of the British scientific establishment, to wit, that one of the most important effects produced by the war was, as far as British scientists were concerned, their having been liberated from the nightmare of *value-free* science" (*CW* 7:112–13). That is, Weberian value-free science was not just a personal, daimonic idiosyncrasy nor was it science without qualification: It was the German form of science. It was, therefore, limited and so not universal.

To summarize Voegelin's account: Max Weber's own "value ideas" were based on a daimonic principle, which Weber called rationalism. According to Weber's philosophy of history, however, rationalism, and thus a rational science of history, was itself a product of history. "The content of history," Voegelin wrote, therefore "turns toward generating its own form and the form toward generating its own material, for 'history' comes into being only through the reference of some material to the form of value ideas" (*CW* 7:114). Moreover, all of this was but a reflection of Weber's personality and of his desire as a scholar to understand how this disenchanted, everyday world could be understood and how he could also be resigned to it. That is, he combined an understanding of history with an understanding of himself and of his time. In this respect, the loneliness of his scientific daimon was an expression of the loneliness of the neo-Kantian transcendental ego, a form of the human spirit that, as was noted in Voegelin's essay on Graham Wallas, could scarcely be found outside Germany.

Five years later Voegelin delivered a lecture in Vienna on the tenth anniversary of Weber's death (*CW* 8:130–47). On this occasion he reiterated some of his earlier remarks, often using strikingly similar language, but he also added to the account of 1925.

Voegelin began by recalling the earlier conclusion, that "reason" had dissolved "our belief in the rational justifiability of values," but at the same time, "we have difficulty acting with the required force of conviction in the absence of such belief." There existed, accordingly, a tension between reason and action. This was true existentially for Max Weber who, Voegelin reaffirmed, was a man of action (*CW* 7:107–8). As a result, "the demands made on the strength of belief have been pushed to their limit" (*CW* 8:131).

The separation of rational, scientific cognition and faith had developed to a much greater extent in Germany than in "the national communities of the West," namely France, Britain, and America, which had been living within a tradition that existed continuously from the seventeenth century. In France, for example, the national community was formed by the creation of a national language that has been defended by a national academy and polished through the life of the salon, literature, and the philosophical cultivation of "internal temporality" from Descartes to Bergson and Valéry. The well-known, but not always appreciated, result was "the chosenness of the French nation to realize the value of the human being within its cultural community."

Likewise in Britain, the ideal established by Cromwell's Protestant revolution, which was given philosophical form in the work of Locke, maintained a vision of "man in community that is based on the universal, voluntary consent to leadership by suitable persons." And in the other Anglo-Saxon country, America, political ideas have served the pragmatic purpose of assimilating foreigners. The consequence is "rough-hewn theories that lie far beneath our [German] rational professional standards" even though they were entirely adequate for the purposes for which they had been developed. As a result of the American commitment to democratic equality, "the spiritual capacity to cultivate intellectual tools has been lacking" or, where not entirely absent, has been overlooked or ignored.[7] In both the United Kingdom and the United States, reason has been considered instrumental for the actualization of social values that were themselves not questioned. "Thus it never penetrates to the core of human and state activity in a reflective, paralyzing way," as it had done in the development of German science.

The spiritual traditions of the West and the shelter they have provided to the corrosive and paralyzing effects of "reason" provided a context for the history of the particular German spirit and the place of Weber within it. The history of the German spirit fluctuated between periods of aridity (the seventeenth and the late nineteenth century) and of flourishing (the age of classicism and romanticism). Voegelin was filled with hope that Stefan George would be the prelude to a flourishing new era. On the other hand, images of political unity were nonexistent. There was simply no way to tie German citizens to one another and to the leaders of the state, no image "that would have impressed itself on the individual existence so thoroughly that it would have seemed an unquestionable aspect of human nature, as it did in the West." On the contrary, individuals in Germany have been exposed to the insecurity that inevitably follows from uncertainty and the absence of a meaningful tradition.

The external absences and uncertainties of the German mind found most obvious expression in the "encyclopedic and fragmentary character" of Weber's work. The range of his work was enormous, but seldom were any but the most focused essays brought to a conclusion. In part, Voegelin said, this resulted from his "abstract, withdrawn" neo-Kantian "logic of history" but equally from his forming his understanding of history not on the basis of "the pallid, anonymous values invented by some philosophical system or other, but the values that are at hand in the cultural tradition of his time." But because Weber lived within German culture, without a living tradition of education, he had to establish new values on his own and create an image of history on the basis of his own personal resources.

Voegelin then returned to the question of Weber's philosophy of history discussed above. "The work of understanding does not destroy values," Voegelin said, "it only destroys the belief that absolute values can be recognized by understanding." We may be able to grasp the meaning of French or German, British or American values, but, because they were irreconcilable, we could never reach a decision to prefer one to another. And yet we must decide and bear responsibility for our decision. Hence the importance of the daimon that somehow steers the fate of a life; hence as well the conflict between the necessity of action and choice and the inability of reason and understanding to direct it.

As we saw in the previous section, the contemporary Western human being lives in a world that reason, science, and understanding have disenchanted. This unenviable condition "is intensified to the utmost for the Germans" precisely because of the absence of forms of community. Max Weber's relentless intellect and great passion for understanding made visible, Voegelin said, our common destiny. In this respect it may bear a comparison with the experience of Nietzsche, who equally suffered the disillusion and disenchantment of the failure of Germany to create a new form of political life following the external achievement of unity under the political leadership of Bismarck.[8] For Weber, according to Voegelin, Bismarck's legacy was a nation lacking in both political education and political will because "Germany had grown accustomed to the statesman at the helm taking care of politics." When Bismarck was dismissed, not least of all because of "the uncommon political tactlessness of the last monarch," there was no political tradition, and there were no politicians who might have cultivated one. Indeed, Bismarck had created a constitution that made an enduring political class next to impossible because in order to function it required "a great statesman of the kind that emerges once in the course of a century." As a consequence, whatever the achievements of Bismarck as a political leader, he failed at a leader's greatest challenge: ensuring a worthy successor within an enduring regime.

Voegelin's closing few pages provided strong testimony to his admiration of Weber, but they also identified his own intellectual tasks to lie in the area of *Staatslehre* and political science, not Weberian sociology. Weber's praise of objectivity and of the capability of acting, which Weber described as indicators of the German national mind, were, Voegelin said, also descriptive of Weber's situation: "a great, naked human force living in the everyday world of understanding without the mediation of a form in which it believes." In contrast, "the West takes pleasure in the good fortune of its traditional forms." Weber's political realism, which we noted above was expressed as a qualified support for democracy, was also that of Voegelin: "The influence of power must prove itself on the given materials, and it must not go beyond those givens," especially not in the direction of belief in the superiority of particular German state forms, ideas, or, worst of all, a world mission.

Voegelin's analysis of sociological and "socio-historical" method clarified for him the importance of participation in both the aspiring universal and scientific community and in the actual particular community of one's time and place. The perspective of participation was simply a given for all social science, including political science. The context of participation included an awareness of one's nationality but also, as with Max Weber, of one's daimon and one's "fate." That is, scientific analysis was always conducted within political, historical, and, indeed, a personal context. As science, however, it could not be reduced to that context, which posed additional questions that Voegelin had to confront in his subsequent work.

However that may be, one conclusion seems clear: Even before Voegelin left the German intellectual milieu for the United States and experienced the great break in his early life as a scholar, he sensed an inadequacy in the methodological quarrels of his contemporaries. His great admiration for the life and work of Max Weber was tempered by an awareness that the aim of his work exceeded its achievements. In his encounter with the American *Geist,* to which we now turn, the limitations of the German understanding of science became more apparent. Moreover, his direct experience in America also then informed his response to the decadence or *Schlechtigkeit* of the German spirit that was more evident to him upon his return.

2
America

During its brief period of operation, from 1918 to 1929, the Laura Spelman Rockefeller Memorial, according to Robert M. Hutchins, "did more than any other agency to promote the social sciences in the United States."[1] It was not until 1921 that a modest amount of money, well under 1 percent of the funds of the memorial, was directed toward "scientific research and investigation." Social welfare, support for religious organizations, and emergency relief absorbed over 80 percent of the funds available from the memorial. By 1924, 86 fellowships were available, chiefly for "able young American social scientists," to provide them with "time for research at a crucial time in their careers." By 1928, 165 out of 450 were available for foreigners; assuming the same ratio for 1924, about 32 fellowships would have been available for non-Americans. Along with Oscar Morgenstern and Denis Brogan, Voegelin received one of them, which paid him $1,800 a year—as compared to $30 a month, which he received in 1927 as Hans Kelsen's assistant in Vienna.[2] It was, therefore, a highly competitive and generous award.

Voegelin arrived in New York on October 4, 1924, and started a well-thought-out program of study. He began his work at Columbia, studying sociology with F. H. Giddings, educational theory with John Dewey, and public administration with A. W. Macmahon, as well as biology in the lab of T. H. Morgan (who won a Nobel Prize a decade later), and economics with John Wesley. Voegelin moved on to Madison for the 1925 summer session at the University of Wisconsin and first met John R. Commons and Selig Perlman, who introduced him to American political history, populism, and labor history as well as the achievements of populist institutions and forms of government in the upper Midwest. In the late summer and early fall of 1925, Voegelin and Heinrich Pollak, a Rockefeller fellow from the German University of Prague, undertook an extensive tour of the western states (*CW* 1:xxxviii *et seq.*). He spent the late fall of 1925 as a research fellow in economics at Harvard but spent most of his time studying American jurisprudence with Roscoe Pound and attending Alfred North Whitehead's philosophy lectures. After Christmas he returned to Madison and then spent the summer of 1926 studying with Arthur Corbin at the Yale Law School. During the entire twenty-four months, Voegelin informed the Rockefeller Foundation, he would be undertaking research on his own of "the irrational elements in American social sciences applied to social psychology, philosophy, legal theory, economic theory, and legal philosophy." In the late fall he returned to Europe and spent a year in Paris. Given Voegelin's interest in what might be called comparative sociology and jurisprudence, the exchange program supported by the memorial seemed tailor-made for him.

In retrospect, and notwithstanding a few minor discrepancies between Voegelin's recollections and his reports to the Rockefeller Foundation, it is clear that his American experience strongly influenced his personal and scholarly outlook. Before analyzing Voegelin's 1928 book, *On the Form of the American Mind* (*CW* 1), let us consider his recollection of his time in America (*CW* 34:56ff). "These two years in America," he said, "brought the great break in my intellectual development." As with many scholars, "the most important influence came from the library" and from the leisure and solitude of reading and reflection. With the help of Dewey and Irwin Edman, also at Columbia, he began "working through the history of English philosophy and its expansion into American thought. . . . I discovered English and American common sense philosophy" and "got the first inkling of what the continued tradition of classic philosophy on the common-sense level, without necessarily the technical apparatus of an Aristotle, could mean for the intellectual climate and the cohesion of a society." On reflection, he concluded that common sense was just what was missing from German intellectual and scientific life.

At Wisconsin, Voegelin recalled, he encountered "what I considered at the time, with my still limited knowledge, to be the real, authentic America. It was represented by John R. Commons, who took on for me the shape of a Lincolnesque figure." It was also at Madison that Voegelin learned of the importance of the U.S. Supreme Court "as the source of political culture in America." In contrast, Whitehead's lectures at Harvard introduced him to the wider cultural context of "Anglo-American civilization." In the work of Santayana he found "a man with a vast background of philosophical knowledge, sensitive to the problems of the spirit without accepting a dogma, and not interested at all in neo-Kantian methodology."

Again in retrospect Voegelin remarked that his book on America did not provide a full understanding of the importance of those two years. "The great event was the fact of being thrown into a world for which the great neo-Kantian methodological debates, which I considered the most important things intellectually, were of no importance." What mattered was the political and legal culture developed on the basis of the American founding and the background context of classical and Christian culture that was rapidly fading in Europe, the last glimmer of which was constituted by the methodological conflicts among varieties of neo-Kantians. "In brief, there was a world in which this other world in which I had grown up was intellectually, morally, and spiritually irrelevant. That there should be such a plurality of worlds had a devastating effect on me." It destroyed his "European provincialism." He "gained an understanding in these years of the plurality of human possibilities realized in various civilizations, as an immediate experience, an *expérience vécue,* which hitherto had been accessible to me only through the comparative study of civilizations," which is to say, mediated by the texts of others—chiefly Max Weber and Oswald Spengler. Accordingly, when he returned to Europe, certain phenomena—and here Voegelin mentioned Heidegger's *Sein und Zeit*—which to his European colleagues seemed to be important, "no longer had any effect on me. It just ran off, because I had been immunized against this whole context of philosophizing through my time in America and especially in Wisconsin."

It is probably an exaggeration to claim that he had been "immunized" against Heidegger, who was in any event not a neo-Kantian, but it was accurate enough to claim that common sense did provide Voegelin with a new epistemological basis for his interpretative analysis of sociohistorical reality. This did not mean, however, that the language Voegelin used in *On the Form of the American Mind* was modeled on that of Dewey or Commons, let alone the older commonsense philosophers, Ferguson and Reid.

In place of the neo-Kantian understanding of culture as the object of a specific science of cognition, Voegelin said that the subject matter of his scientific inquiry emerged from his analysis of what he called "intellectual [or spiritual] formations," *geistige Gestaltungen,* a term that is self-evident in its meaning neither in German nor in English. The sense can be apprehended from the examples of American philosophy, law, or economic theory, all of which are understood, as American, to be expressions of a common form and style. In the previous chapter Voegelin raised this question in the context of considering what made any given painting a typical example of Dutch or American art and not merely an exemplar of beauty or ugliness. In turn this common "form" was understood to bind together the otherwise disparate subject matter (or intellectual formations) into a meaningful unit and unity *(Sinneinheit)* that could then be described. *On the Form of the American Mind,* among other things, provided a more precise and occasionally a new conceptual vocabulary to account for this problem of particular styles of culture. These epistemological issues constitute the subject matter of the introduction to Voegelin's book and provide a sequel to the issues raised in the previous chapter of this book (*CW* 1:2–22).

There are, Voegelin began, plenty of studies of American institutions and intellectual life, and they have fulfilled their purpose and "steered interpretations of the American mind to a point that calls for new methods if the task is to be mastered." These new methods may be needed, he said, but they have yet to be found. One can say with some confidence, however, that the old methods of neo-Kantian a priori categories and "generalized slogans" were no longer useful; what was needed must be intimately connected to the materials, but the materials, in this instance those pertaining to the American mind, were unfamiliar to Voegelin's readers. So the problem involved presenting the (unfamiliar) materials at the same time as the "instruments of interpretation." His introduction was an effort at justifying this procedure. It was also, incidentally, the procedure Voegelin employed in writing *The History of Political Ideas* and the one presently being used in this analysis of Voegelin's work in the 1920s and 1930s, which, it is fair to say, is unfamiliar, at least as compared to his postwar work or to the *History.*

Looked at externally, the contents of the book, from the discussion of time to American labor policy or the federal reserve system, appeared quite distinct, which would make the book a collection of essays rather than a coherent whole or "meaningful unity." In fact, however, all these subject matters dealt with a single class of phenomena that were focused on language concerned with matters of "a theoretical nature," where theory referred to "an attempt claiming to order a field of problems rationally and thus to render it comprehensible." Natural sciences were eliminated, along with history and philology, leaving a selection of theoretical works in philosophy, law, politics, economics, political science, and sociology selected as being suitable to the study of form and as examples. All, he said, were "self-expressive" linguistic-theoretical phenomena *(sprachlich-theoretische Ersheinungen).*

The principle of selection could not be based on a priori principles, and even though Voegelin had no wish to discuss methodology, "something will have to be said concerning the method employed here." The method, very simply, was that "the rules grew out of the material studied." Or rather, the rules were not so much followed as "found." Specifically, every "intellectual formation," which included everything from political institutions to the color of Hudson River tugboats, "reveals traces of its origin in its form." In other words, interpretation of phenomena must follow from an understanding of the material, of its inherent meaning, and of the most appropriate method to clarify it. It must proceed "immanently" and must "never be subject to a transcendental value system." The similarities with Husserlian phenomenology as well as with Cassirer's modified understanding of *Geisteswissenschaften* have been noted (*CW* 1: xxii–xxv). Later, in *The New Science of Politics* (1952), Voegelin called this method of analysis "the Aristotelian procedure" because it began from self-expressive phenomena of the actual self-understanding of individuals and communities (*CW* 5:110ff).

Of equal importance was that the linguistic theoretical phenomena selected be "self-expressive." This attribute enabled the scientist to reflect upon them as well as upon his own act of reflection. Thus the subject matters—the self-expressive phenomena—were also the media in which they were studied by the reflection and self-reflection of the scientist. Accordingly, one can philosophize about philosophy, but one does not normally write music about music or poetry about poetry. Such "self-expressive" phenomena have conventionally been assigned to different disciplines—economics, law, philosophy, and so on—but in fact they were interconnected in terms of form.

Voegelin was fully aware that such an approach can be persuasive not in terms of a priori arguments but in terms of results, namely the insight that emerged after the argument and the illustrative examples were understood. The task of reflection, which is the task of the scientist, was to get the material to speak on its own terms, which was why Voegelin said his approach was "purely empirical" rather than a priori. For Voegelin, "empirical" also meant experiential so that reflection or self-reflection was also "personal" or participatory. Other aspects of the subject matter were not directly personal but "peripheral" in the sense that they were not experienced immediately but by way of institutions and other anonymous or quasi-anonymous processes.

The question of form was tied both to the individual or the personal—because even an impersonal or institutional expression of mind was empirically bound to an individual whose experience it was—and it was tied to anonymous processes. This double connection meant that "the form is not an inflexible boundary for a subject" and so was not subject to precise definition. Hence Voegelin's reliance on "a broader description, fleshed out with specific examples." The reason for adopting this interpretative strategy was not simply because the categories of personal and peripheral "summarize the results of studies that are in essence historical" but because the choice of a historical subject matter followed the events of history. Here Voegelin introduced a striking image, to which we return below, to express his meaning: "The historical line of meaning runs like a rope across the abyss into which everything that cannot stay on the rope plunges." This did not mean that history was a single continuum or accumulation of meaning, for things were lost, were forgotten, and failed. Thus "it does not seem useful to treat such a tangled web with short formulas and all-encompassing definitions." Instead there were careful descriptions that indicated a uniform style common, for example, to administrative institutions and social mores or to the intellectual biography of a philosopher and the account of the life and work of a man of action.

This presentation may seem abstract—as abstract, in fact, as the neo-Kantian methodologies Voegelin sought to replace. Voegelin's intent, however, was to describe how to interpret the *form* of the American *mind.* So it is time to ask: What do those terms mean? An answer can be formulated only by comparison, so that the common elements can be distinguished from the differentiating ones. Moreover, the accumulations of personal and impersonal history also have to be considered—youth and old age, for example, or the position of the foreigner in America, or New England Calvinism. What was novel in Voegelin's approach to these matters was that the historical forms of the American mind were brought into existence by history itself. In a sense Voegelin was simply reiterating the point made in the previous chapter regarding Weber's intellectual integrity—that such integrity was entirely apposite in an age of disenchantment and everydayness because it was the form taken by an ethics of responsibility for a scientist concerned with a rational account of sociohistorical reality. The difference between Voegelin and Weber on this score was that Weber's account, being retrospective, conveyed a powerful element of necessity; hence Weber's extensive use of the term *fate.* In contrast, for Voegelin history contained a greater sense of contingency. Hence the image noted earlier of a "line of meaning" that "runs like a rope across the abyss." Before introducing that rather Nietzschean image, Voegelin observed that only one contingency ever is chosen "not by the historian, but by life itself." Accordingly, each successive "intellectual formation" along a line of meaning was connected to preceding moments and to prior intellectual formations. The sequence of intellectual formations articulated the movement of—in this instance—the American mind in both its individual and personal, and its institutional and peripheral, forms.

The sequence of intellectual formations, the line of meaning, was the articulation of the primary and inarticulate problems of life: "sorrows of loneliness, yearning for the company of others, for intimacy and love, and emotional adventures of youth, the disillusionment of old age, the expectation of death." These problems were "primary" because they were inarticulate; Husserl once described them as belonging to an antepredicative "depth." That dimension of reality, prior to interpretation, had few enough emotional and temporal structures—sorrow, longing, the sequence from the adventures of youth to the expectation of death—but they were responsible for the richness and detail of the form of the mind: They were primordial experiences that instigated the articulation of the intellectual formation.

From an evocation of the emotional and temporal structures that undergird the methodological considerations of the introduction, Voegelin moved on to a comparative philosophical analysis of British and American articulation of those structures in terms of "Time and Existence" (*CW* 1:23–63).

The skepticism of David Hume, Voegelin said, was both a contrast and a model for American thought. On the one hand, his "cool doubt" contrasted strongly with the "warm trust" of the Americans Peirce and James; on the other, Santayana, for different reasons, "finds himself adopting a solipsistic stance that comes very close to Hume's skepticism." Even so, there existed an intelligible sequence from Hume to the common sense of his contemporary, Thomas Reid, and to later modifications of common sense and skepticism in America. Voegelin was not, however, interested in a history of the idea of Humean skepticism. Rather, his concern was the form taken by skepticism in America, namely, a lack of respect for the development of European philosophy. Europeans might understand this attitude as amusing or deplorable, but for Americans it was, on the contrary, "very resolute and only slightly at a loss in the face of matters that have no significance for them." A lack of concern for European philosophy, by Voegelin's interpretation, was part of what it meant to be a member of a democratic community. William James, who was undoubtedly also a philosopher, but an American one, strongly agreed, and Voegelin quoted him at length in support of the distinct styles and forms of American philosophizing. Even so, this difference "cannot easily be described clearly, even if all-encompassing definitions are forsworn." Such definitions were in any event typical not of philosophy but of European philosophy. In keeping with the argument regarding methodology presented in the introduction to the book, Voegelin's task was to illustrate by example the self-interpretation and self-reflection of philosophizing in the American style or form.

A start was made with James's own *Pluralistic Universe* (1909), where the author argued that philosophy was first of all a matter of vision and not the logical coherence of a "system." In Platonic language James stressed *noesis* over *dianoia.* For the Europeans, including the British, the focus was on "dialectical" problems that arose from considering the relation of consciousness to the external world and from the problem of temporality in consciousness, both of which derive from skepticism. In contrast, the Americans—Peirce and James—did not regard the unity of consciousness and its transcendence into the external world as problems but as givens from which other explanations could be developed.[3]

However described, the consequence was that the "quarrels of the various [European] schools are merely external, seemingly more a badly adapted European habit than something inevitably connected with American thought." Accordingly, a philosopher such as C. S. Peirce may be inconsistent in his elaboration or account of his vision, but that did not touch his greatness, whereas "in Europe, and especially in Germany, the intellectual apparatus is so extensive and the elaboration of problems is carried to such length" that the concern with the details of the logic of the system was more important than the adequacy of the vision. This did not mean that American philosophers were somehow inferior to European ones because they may have overlooked things that the Europeans found to be important, nor that, in the example of James, could he be criticized simply for writing clearly. Instead, Voegelin said, it would be more advisable to assume "a new experience, essentially different from the European tradition of skepticism."

Voegelin discussed this "new experience" by analyzing the "emotional motive," which from the introduction was understood to be primary, in James's *Pluralistic Universe.* The traditional Christian doctrine of "monarchic theism" discussed the divine creation of the world in a way that was obsolete even though it may still be affirmed and "confessed at church in formulas that linger by their mere inertia." But, James said, "the life is out of them." Instead of an "alien" relationship between Creator and creation, a more intimate symbolism, which did not first emphasize the difference between the two, was needed. According to James, the needed symbolism would be more intimate and organic, "more like a federal republic than like an empire or kingdom." In short, James and Peirce abandoned "the attempt to structure a rational image of the world." Rather, several images might be invoked and, depending on the context, may be equally acceptable or adequate. Even polytheism was a possibility.

Corresponding to the contrast between European imagery of divine being in terms of monarchy and the pluralistic hierarchy of James was a similar difference in the understanding of human being. For James (and Peirce) human existence was open to the gods or God, the friendly powers that stretch above us away into a limitless beyond. Following Bergson, Voegelin called this understanding of human being the open self. In contrast is the European tradition "with its mania for conceptualizing the mystery of the person rationally," which Voegelin called the doctrine of the closed self. For the American philosophers "the contraction of time and existence to the present moment of the self and the problem of the origin of the world no longer have much meaning."

We noted above that Voegelin informed the Rockefeller Foundation that he proposed "on his own" to study the "irrational elements" in what he came to call the American mind. It is evident that he meant Peirce and James; it is also evident that by identifying their philosophizing with "irrational elements" he was not dismissing them by adopting even provisionally the perspective of European rationalism, the closed self, and the mania for conceptualizing a mystery. This did not mean that Voegelin was adopting a position on the side of "irrational elements" in some general sense but only that he (as James) rejected the "reason" of the closed self and the neo-Kantians for whom mystery was indeed conceptualized into science. We should also bear in mind that Voegelin was not concerned with what might be called the dogmatic attributes of divine being but with the expression of the divine in European and American philosophy insofar as that expression, that "meaningful unit" or "intellectual formation," helped constitute the form of the American (or European) mind.

In other words, a balanced appraisal of American "irrationality" as distinct from European "rationality" pointed to the difference between American and European self-consciousness that had attained great clarity in the self-reflection of European and American thinkers. The open self that characterized the American mind was the center of meaning from which all other intellectual formations radiated into society: the basic principles of the democratic community, economic life, the understanding of God, the devotion to practicality in science, and the deprecation of theory as abstract and empty intellectualism.

In the chapter that followed, on George Santayana (*CW* 1:64–125), Voegelin found elements of both European and American forms of philosophizing, as befits a thinker with Santayana's biography. Voegelin began his discussion by raising explicitly a question discussed incidentally in the previous chapter: Why is there no progress in philosophy as there is in the natural sciences? And what is to be made of the contradictory claims of philosophies? Santayana replied that they contradict one another only "when they cling to the word and try helplessly to catch the unknown. But they agree and supplement one another when they are symbols, thoughts wrung from the experiences of the hearts of poets." Then all philosophies were equal, and the issue of "progress" evaporated. In principle, that is, philosophy accounted for the "experiences of the hearts of poets," which is to say, experiences of self-expressive reality *par excellence.* In contrast, because natural philosophy was *not* self-expressive, it was possible to gain increased insight over time into the structure of natural phenomena, which is called progress.

Voegelin compared Santayana's philosophizing to that of Brentano, who wrote on similar subjects, in a way analogous to his previous comparison of Hume and James. As in the previous analysis, the aim was to show that even though Santayana and Brentano were both philosophers and both were concerned with, generally speaking, the same philosophical problems, they each had different styles of philosophizing.

The focus was then drawn even tighter as Voegelin considered "the genesis of Santayana's world" in his poetry of the 1880s. Santayana, Voegelin said, was a "man of letters," a term, he added, that was as impossible to render in German as the word *gentleman.* "At best we could compare the rank of the latter [the gentleman] in society with that of the former [the man of letters] in the realm of the mind. *Literat* would be to diminish the concept, *Dichter* would be going too far. To connect them with *Geisteskultur* is too reminiscent of shirtsleeve professionalism; *Bildung* of the academic.

All these terms touch on essential traits of the 'man-of-letters' without hitting his essence." Voegelin's characterization of Santayana's poetry, no less than his philosophical reflections, showed great sensitivity to language, not least of all because he understood it to be an index of historical-cultural reality. And with Santayana, as with James and Peirce, the emphasis was on the importance of vision and the limits of logical coherence. "It is surely true," Voegelin wrote, "that philosophical systems contain structures that can roughly be described by the idea of concretion and its rational evolution; but in a large system the rigidity of logical coherence is no more than a line of order drawn through a field of points, where each point could as easily fit along another line. The elements in one system could be elements in another and still retain the aura of possibilities no matter where they are organized at the moment" (*CW* 1:120).

But it was just this concern of Santayana with "logical coherence" in his "philosophical system" that made him more difficult to interpret than James or Peirce. According to Voegelin, this was "because Santayana's person stands at the frontier where the European and the American mind abut." Specifically, Santayana's status as a skeptic and a lonely stranger was unlike the position of James or Peirce, where even the gods were friendly. And yet, Voegelin said, "in the United States, the 'foreigner' is a typical phenomenon, and standing-at-the-border is every bit as much an American problem as unquestioned membership in an older tradition." Moreover, the newly arrived—especially when they arrived in great numbers, as had happened during the later nineteenth century—"had no less influence on the formation of political institutions than did the previously settled, assimilated population." As one historian of American culture (and student of Santayana) observed, his teacher may never have become an American, but he certainly ceased to be a European.[4] This ambivalence of Santayana, akin to that of other immigrants of the late nineteenth century, raised the question: In what way was his thought linked to that of James and Peirce? Voegelin's answer was that through the use of terms such as "pure experience" and "essence" all three were linked to the older form of Puritan mysticism (*CW* 1:126–43).

In the early eighteenth century, with Jonathan Edwards, "the separation of dogma from mysticism begins in the United States. According to the dogma, God is an arbitrary, threatening, absolute Person who deals with believers as a king deals with his subjects, who can claim no rights. In mysticism, the perilous superiority disappears, and the religious life is dissolved in the immediate relationship to divinity, in a sequence of ecstasies that do not require dogma." Accordingly, the connection between, for instance, James's view of the divine and the growth of American democracy was anything but accidental. The eclipse of the dogma of a Royal God by the community of believers was itself an expression of the form of the American mind. No wonder, then, that even in the twenty-first century American religious practices remain essential to the meaningful unity of American life. "The systematic structural relationship," Voegelin concluded, that tied Edwards to Peirce, James, and Santayana, "is indisputable." Not just the absence of "systematic conclusions," akin to the European mania for conceptualizing mystery, united them, but so too did their understanding of history as an adaptation to God and a gradual victory of the good. This positive, one might say optimistic, element was present in Edwards's understanding of the elect, in James's pluralistic universe, and in Peirce's evolutionary love. "And even Santayana's philosophy believes in the historical growth of reason in the world, so that the original Calvinist dogma is preserved in these forms of rational skepticism." In the intellectual formations of all these thinkers, evil remains as an inextinguishable element that can be overcome only by cultivating what was good and reasonable, which in turn was an endless temporal task.

Before turning to Voegelin's analysis of Anglo-American jurisprudence (*CW* 1:144–204), let us gather together some of the themes Voegelin has developed. The "guiding principle of this study," Voegelin said, "that every intellectual formation that arises in a social body reveals the traces of its origin in its form—illustrates my method." As noted above, by "intellectual formation" Voegelin referred to such obvious phenomena as political institutions or art and philosophy, but also everyday matters such as theater tickets and the color of construction bricks (*CW* 1:15). The form of the American mind bound the several intellectual formations into a meaningful unit, which Voegelin connected to the development of democracy in America. The apprehension of the forms, however, is not a matter of imposing transcendental categories on an otherwise chaotic and disordered external reality because (1) the reality is not external and (2) it is not chaotic. On the contrary, the reality that constitutes the form of the American mind appears as "self-expressive" linguistic-theoretical phenomena. Moreover, these phenomena have a history that is sustained by continuity of spiritual formations—not in any sense of retrospective necessity imposed by a storyteller but by the influence of "style." Thus one form of earlier thinking in the realm of religion can, generations later, influence philosophy or poetry.

The intellectual formations can also be understood as articulations of the primary or primordial experiences of life, from sorrow to adventure to joy. Because they are articulate, they will be influenced by previous self-expressive forms that, in turn, articulate, in this instance, the basic forms of America—crossing the ocean, the encounter with the land and its inhabitants, the "social contract," beginning with the *Mayflower* Compact, that sustains the enterprise of self-government.

The general influence of English law on American law is well-known, though knowledge regarding the details are often somewhat hazy, and the distinctiveness of American law, which is widely assumed to exist, is but obscurely accounted for. Voegelin began by considering English analytic jurisprudence.

After John Austin gave his famous lectures on jurisprudence in the late 1820s, there was no successful effort in the United Kingdom to establish any systematic jurisprudence until the 1870s and 1880s, when conflict between the common law traditions of civil rights and the courts of equity provided an opportunity to deal directly with the systematic characteristics of the law. Voegelin praised Austin's work but noted that, for want of interest, his chair in jurisprudence at Oxford was discontinued. A half century later jurisprudence was revived in the form of casebooks and maxims as well as more systematic treatments. Most of the structural elements of the legal problems that could be found in English analytic jurisprudence were also found in the American version, "but all are reshaped and arranged in new intellectual contexts that distinguish them sharply from the way they appear in the English formulations" (*CW* 1:165). The main addition and modification of the English tradition was provided by the eighteenth-century doctrines of natural law.

"The Declaration of Independence and the Preamble to the Constitution," Voegelin wrote, "indicate the purpose of founding a state," namely "to guarantee human rights and to establish a system to secure justice." The United States may not have originated the notion of "the administration of justice" (it is found in Hume's *Essays*), but in America was found its most thoroughgoing institutionalization in the Supreme Court. The absorption of natural law principles into statute law and judicial decisions, however imperfect, provided an epistemological model of jurisprudence practically unknown to contemporary legal theory in Europe. "Knowledge of rights," Voegelin said, "is communicated through acts of intuition: concepts of rights are axioms of the human mind" that have arisen spontaneously and allowed human beings to make sound judgments concerning right and wrong. "They are intuitively perceived like any other truth of the metaphysical sciences," a method adopted from Scottish commonsense philosophy and justified by religion. In accord with the intellectual formation articulated by Edwards, "the unalterable principles are given us by God; it is he who has furnished us with 'rights' and given us the ability to know them unmediatedly and without thought" (*CW* 1:170). The rules of the state, "jural law," derived their validity from divine law.

In order to deduce rights by intuition, certain principles were nevertheless required. Instead of developing systematic jurisprudence, however, American law accumulated accounts of precedents. This response had its own problems: "The system of precedents results in the mass production of reports of decisions. The decisions of every court are reported to a central collection point, which indiscriminately sends them out for publication," the trivial and local decisions along with the important and national ones. The physical bulk of such cases was enormous and the principles embodied in them all but impossible to determine. The federal organization of the states meant there was no national control of decisions as in England, which has a single, homogeneous court hierarchy. Finally, the unsatisfactory and unsystematic nature of American jurisprudence was a result of law school training by case law. "Only a very few law schools pay even the slightest attention to the history and philosophy of law." Partly in response to this almost chaotic accumulation of materials, just prior to World War I the American legal profession commissioned an ambitious program of translation so American lawyers would have access to the works of European jurisprudence.

The result was not a wholesale importation of a European "science of law" but a typically American effort to create categories and concepts that would be pragmatically useful, not theoretically elegant. More specifically, jurisprudence had to be useful not for law professors and legal scholars but for their students, who became ordinary lawyers and judges. That is, the Americans were not concerned about the scholarly integrity or originality of their work. "It is a way to step out of the river of action for a moment in order to find a more effective mechanism to deal with reality. But the thought that theoretical values exist for their own sake and go through an evolution in their own sphere remains alien." Analytic jurisprudence was accordingly considered to be little more than an interesting intellectual exercise, the value of which lay "in facilitating and improving the solution of legal problems," much as if organic chemistry existed to assist in solving problems encountered by chemical or petroleum engineers.

In this context of focused practicality, the point of analytic jurisprudence as an instrument was presented as a "message" to the legal profession: Analytical jurisprudence is a tool no properly trained lawyer can ignore. Voegelin's attention was drawn to the implications of the term *message*, the origins of which were in religious discourse. "Today it can be used in its original meaning in the revivals of the Salvation Army, when converts are called upon to tell the story of their conversion and bring to their listeners the message of salvation." It is a term more generally used in the context of popular education "and in particular the lectures arranged by women's clubs." Those who deliver messages were usually linked to "the business of university education: the president, the 'noted educator,' and the football coach." Voegelin's point was not just that message delivery was something entirely different from scholarship or the practice of science—though he must have enjoyed poking fun at the "noted educator" delivering the message that students can benefit from a year studying Greek culture without the tedium and bother of learning Greek—but that it was connected to another term expressing the common purpose of academic enterprise in general: It makes a "contribution."

A contribution, Voegelin said "expresses an attitude toward intellectual endeavour that does not see such an achievement as the work of the person, the expression of personal philosophical stature; rather it democratically reduces the individual to a number in the mass of cooperating minds." In short, "making a contribution" was less a personal act than an activity of cultural significance far removed from any German notion of *Bildung.* "Greece, Rome, the Middle Ages, Europe, all are seen from the aspect of their 'contribution' to the height of American civilization. (If the writer believes in gestures of humility, he will reverse the relationship and speak of 'our debt to Greece and Rome.')" This unquestioned faith in progress brought by delivering "messages" and making a "contribution" by turns amused and irritated Voegelin. "'Progress' is accepted as somehow structuring itself, while the 'messages' and 'contributions' come from no place or time and seek their progressive position in the process according to an unknown law." The result is the sentiment that "we're all in the same boat" and that the ensuing cooperation ensures the march of progress over chaos. "This attitude eliminates the problems of adopting a tradition, of originality, of theoretical connection, and of the growth of a culture." Unfortunately, it also results in "outbursts of the intellect unlinked to the structure of the subject matter," namely analytical jurisprudence as a coherent discourse.

The result was the production of volumes dealing with examples rather than principles so that, even if one did have faith in the existence of progress, there would be no way to measure it. Moreover, by confining discussion to examples, the importance of the argument is of little theoretical significance. The impression left by reading Voegelin's analysis of American efforts at producing an intelligible legal theory is that the products were incoherent and amateur. This, too, was an intellectual formation that helped constitute the form of the American mind.

The final chapter, "On John R. Commons" (*CW* 1:205–82), reflected both Voegelin's close personal relationship with the man and his significance for the social, economic, political, and spiritual or intellectual formation of American democracy. Commons's life, Voegelin said, "overlaps the shaping of the American nation, and his work is woven into this process," but its beginning lay in the pre–Civil War expansion of the country to the Midwest, where he was born, and beyond. He had been influenced by his Quaker upbringing and by Josiah Warren, "the American anarchist," but especially by the experience of pioneer life, which confirmed existentially the doctrine of self-sovereignty proclaimed by Warren.

Voegelin made a useful distinction between Warren's "individualism" and that of J. S. Mill. Mill's defense of individual liberty grew from the British version of the natural rights tradition that conceived the individual as being equal to others as a result of membership in humanity. Such beings had a right to the development of all their faculties and were to be protected, as a right, from encroachment by the state, which was the organized form of the collectivity, namely society. Such individuals were essentially isolated, which was why Mill's scheme of proportional representation seemed a sufficient mechanism to ensure they received a fair share of influence upon government. In contrast, Warren did not see the individual as an atom of humanity in need of protection from the state. "He identifies the individual as a member of a concrete community," and so related to others despite any personal differences by means of service and labor (and division of labor). Warren's "idea of the individual is derived from the model of the American pioneer" and from life on the frontier, which combined individual labor and community cooperation. "Commons' origins lie in the same social surroundings as Warren's," so it was no surprise that in Warren's writing Commons initially found what he was looking for. Or rather, "the experience of the pioneer community" was the basis for all "his practical and theoretical work."

In Commons's work the pioneer experience was accepted directly, immediately, or as a matter of course, whereas in Voegelin's East Coast sources of the intellectual formations he studied or studied with, "it was made the subject matter of separate observation." Thus Franklin Henry Giddings, whom he met at Columbia, began with the "elementary subjective fact" that Giddings called "consciousness of kind."[5] This referred to a sense of membership in a group that may be at odds with one's individual interest—for example, in maintaining the solidarity of a strike over the individual economic benefits of strikebreaking. Santayana, in contrast, was skeptical as to whether the pioneer experience could be generalized to larger, industrial groups. Citizens, he once famously said, would have to be "plebeian in position, patrician in spirit," a society inspired by strong patriotism akin to that of Sparta, which he thought would soon turn into fanaticism.

Dewey, perhaps reflecting the native-born American experience directly, agreed with Giddings. He used the term *likemindedness,* not consciousness of kind. Voegelin was aware of the biblical origins of Dewey's term (*CW* 1:219n23) and recalled it many years later as highly significant (*CW* 34:57–58; 8:233–34). In the context of Voegelin's initial understanding of America, "likemindedness" referred to "the obligating power behind all specifics of social action." Also, as Giddings had argued, Dewey proposed a progressive widening of likemindedness to sustain larger or wider levels of a democratic community by means of commerce and division of labor. Likewise "in Commons' concrete investigations and philosophical formulations, the pioneer society is always the first premise, and it is only on this basis that the special problems he addresses have meaning." But unlike Warren, for example, he did not postulate utopian solutions and social experiments. In Commons's work "one can see a linear increase in a sense of reality" compared to his predecessors.

For example, Commons added to the doctrine that "all men are created equal" the provision that all must be in a position to make use of their opportunities for there to be genuine democratic government. The great exception to equality of opportunity was provided by the condition of African Americans. In this context Commons remarked that the "greatest injury" inflicted on the United States was

> the stimulation given to the spirit of suppression which, in the end, brought anarchy to Europe. For we are by history a nation of frontiersmen and rough riders. We make concessions only to our equals. If to our population is added negroes, we do not fraternize as do the French, but we keep them in the place which we think fit for them, and lynch law repeals the Fourteenth Amendment. If we add successively Irish, Chinese, Slavs, Italians, we use the later races as "hunkies" to displace the children of the earlier races who have begun to aspire, and, if they too demand an equal voice in their treatment, then, forgetting how we used them, we denounce them as foreigners, aliens, un-American, led on by anarchists and revolutionists, and reach for our guns.[6]

Voegelin commented that Commons's words "describe a historical situation as inevitable, and they do so without sentimentality." There was no "metaphysical doctrine of superiority" (based on "race," for example) introduced in order to justify the position of African Americans but only a "consciousness of responsibility." Commons was likewise a realist in his view of immigration and the need to order it in such a way that "the new arrivals are given enough time to acquire experience and enjoy education in self-government."

The most important event in Commons's life was the process by which industrial workers were integrated into the democratic community of equals. The chief problem was caused by the increased immigration after the Civil War and the end of the creation of pioneer communities that attended the closing of the frontier. The individual who represented or symbolized the effort to bring equality to the industrial laborers was Samuel Gompers. Gompers's leadership was as realistic as Commons's research. His goal was to ensure the participation of workers in American democracy; his distrust of intellectuals who tended to get carried away with their own grandiose ideas was, in Voegelin's view, what preserved the union movement from collapse. He sought "higher wages, shorter hours, more liberty," all of which were goals of mainstream America.

Gompers's biography, Voegelin said, was not so much a "source book" as the story of how a European worker became an American worker. Moreover, the politics of the American Federation of Labor (AF of L) was not "behind the times" in any sense compared to the intellectually driven class politics of Europe. Rather, the rejection by Gompers of socialist and communist theories and his refusal to politicize the labor movement simply reflected the reality that the American trade unions developed their own self-understanding indigenously, from the experiences of the antecedent pioneer communities, as well as from their own understanding of "likemindedness." The AF of L had no need to deal with the alien notions of intellectuals such as Karl Marx—and Gompers was suspicious of such people precisely because they were not laborers. As Voegelin put it, Gompers was "more radical and more class-conscious than Marx" and so excluded bourgeois intellectuals and other social reformers from union leadership. Accordingly, the "antitheoretical tactic of bargaining over concrete problems of the worker's situation" reflected a view "that the rational-active sphere of thought encompasses merely a small and superficial sector of the total life, that it is merely an intellectual annex to life, not a world with its own origins."

Commons's thinking took a similar form. For example, "he finds it incredible that thinkers develop certain views on metaphysical problems or arrive at conclusions in the theory of law without studying the development of common law and American labor law." Compared to his own study of the law at the feet of Hans Kelsen, Commons's approach, which was based upon thirty years of studies of American legal and economic history, was indeed a major revelation to Voegelin. Always Commons's concern was commonsensical and practical: Developments in industry had destroyed the pioneer community. This change gave rise to another practical problem: how to create a new democratic community, which meant integrating recent immigrants while maintaining the structure of American society as one of equals? In practice this insulated Commons and American labor leaders from the seductive appeal of Hegel and Marx, but also from Adam Smith. There was no preestablished harmony or unseen hand either in the present or in the future. There were just day-to-day conflicts that must be resolved "without historical pathos" and without any ultimate ideals coming into play. "It is not an exciting drama in which masses wrestle each other. It has no utopian goal of ultimately reconciling all contradictions. Murkily it rolls along, without an end in sight." The form of the American mind, Voegelin emphasized here, was that it entailed the rejection of ultimate goals as abstractions. Commons was concerned with "the concrete"—a term that Voegelin adopted for his own analyses for the rest of his life.

The difference between Commons on the one side and Giddings and Dewey on the other were, Voegelin said, metaphysical. For the latter two, the end of the frontier democratic community meant that the "democratic ideal" had receded, leaving a historical divide between "current concrete individual actions" and the ideal. For Commons "there is a metaphysical tension" that "cannot be resolved by any historical objective in concrete actions at any time." Commons's historical research and his speculative reflections originated in that tension. It could only be endured, along with the desire "to help those who, through a historical accident, are externally handicapped in the unending chain of overcoming it." Commons's attitude, therefore, was relentlessly pragmatic and practical and his theoretical and historical research explained why this was also the height of realism.

Commons's concern for the practical was anti-intellectual only to the extent that intellectuals were alien to social life. "The 'genuine democratic spirit,' to which Commons refers occasionally, knows only one class of equals, who must get along with each other." From this attitude followed his skepticism regarding authority, particularly bureaucratic authority, which subverted the "genuine democratic spirit." When conflicts arose, as inevitably they did, the expectation that they would be settled by compromise rather than by removing the opposition by force was based on Commons's notion that life was essentially self-healing because of "the necessity of getting along as well as one can."

Commons's understanding was the final consequence of the history of the development of the American mind. "The equality of the pioneer community was materially conditioned by a shared predicament; such a community represented a fighting unit in hostile territory." Today it was an "intellectual value and a requisite for its own sake" that "in Commons' writings . . . has turned into a philosophy of life, thus obtaining its metaphysical significance." In this respect it differed from the European egalitarianism of Simmel or Bergson: Commons developed his ideas "without any significant prior philosophical education." As a result, his "typically American approach to problems" began not with a system but "in its tangibly experienced everyday events." The results were comparable to those of the Europeans, but the genesis was far different.

> The same philosophy of life that presents itself in Europe as the final product of individual philosophical culture, seen by selected people and aimed at an intellectual elite, is discovered in America by an exceedingly modest and amiable man who, coming from a farmers' and workers' environment, spent decades working through his historical and political experiences. His perspective was so astute that, almost without being aware of what he was doing, he needed only to say what he saw in order to give the highest philosophical expression to the significance of the society in which and for which he lived. His technical flaws are part of his being: in a society of equals, the perfection of the apparatus—to which every European philosopher worthy of the name aspires—is considered improper and merely an attempt to be better than one's neighbor.

Voegelin closed his analysis of John R. Commons by reproducing a quote from Commons's essay "Utilitarian Idealism," where "idealism" referred more or less to European philosophy in general. Commons said that there was as much idealism present in the breeding of a fine ear of corn or an instrument designed to measure the ratio of casein or butterfat in milk as there was in a *Venus de Milo.* "Of course," he said, "a cow is just a cow, and can never become a Winged Victory. But within her field of human endeavour she is capable of approaching an ideal. And, more than that, she is an ideal that every farmer and farmer's boy—the despised slaves and helots of Greece—can aspire to" (*CW* 1:282). For Voegelin, Commons's "philosophy of the concrete life" most fully expressed the lasting effectiveness of the open self in all areas of American social, economic, political, and cultural life.

If we recall Voegelin's original methodological concern, that the *Geisteswissenschaften* be an empirical philosophy of reality based on experience, it would seem that in the life and work of Commons, in his intellectual formation, Voegelin found a splendid example that combined the personal and the collective or community. That is, Voegelin saw in Commons's experience of life the harmonious combination of the personal and the cultural, social, and political. No wonder his admiration for him was so apparent, particularly when it is recalled that the German philosophy and jurisprudence in which he had been schooled seemed, in fact, to have no implications for economic, social, political, or cultural life—for the public sphere generally—despite airy pretensions to the contrary.

Between 1926 and 1930, Voegelin published several additional papers and book reviews on various aspects of the United States. Some of them reiterated points made in the America book; others made explicit comparisons between similar phenomena in Europe and the United States. Some, indeed, were highly technical legal and economic analyses.

The first dealt with the constitutionality of the Eighteenth Amendment, ratified on January 16, 1919, prohibiting one year later "the manufacture, sale, or transportation of intoxicating liquors" (*CW* 7:149–74). Voegelin's report dealt with the process of judicial review though he was quite cognizant of the fact that "even the serious judicial investigations" are "in some cases diminished by emotional indignation" (*CW* 7:150).

The constitutional problem with the Eighteenth Amendment resided in allegations by litigants that it was improperly introduced and that it was direct or popular legislation, even though legislative power was reserved exclusively to the institution of Congress. Moreover, by directly intervening in the police power of the states, it eroded federalism by undermining state sovereignty. "As a result, the essential limits of the separation of powers in the American system would undergo a shift, and these limits are the very ones for whose protection the adoption of the first ten amendments has been made the condition of the entry of the states into the Union" (*CW* 7:158). The U.S. Supreme Court, however, simply declared the Eighteenth Amendment constitutional and provided no argument as to why. And if the Eighteenth contradicted, for example, property rights as found in the Fifth, the latter prevailed on "political" grounds. One matter was very clear: Voegelin was entirely comfortable discussing the often recondite arguments put forward by politicians and litigants regarding the constitutionality of the prohibition amendment and the legislation drawn up to enforce it, chiefly the Volstead Act.

In "Economic and Class Conflict in America (1926–7)" (*CW* 7:175–81), he elaborated a point discussed above in connection with Gompers. European socialists had found that American workers to be backward as compared to those in Europe; European entrepreneurs found the antirevolutionary nonclass conflict in America to be ideal, and they praised the "solidarity of interests between entrepreneurs and workers." What was, in fact, different about America "is the existence of economic conflict without class conflict." In Europe, class was both an economic condition of insecurity and a part of a tradition where nonindustrial workers had more assured places in the existing order than they did in America. In contrast, in America there may be economic insecurity and bloody industrial strikes, but they were confined chiefly to unorganized and usually "foreign"—that is, unassimilated—workers. Among English-speaking workers there was no "class" difference, in contrast to the "foreign" workers.

The educated and assimilated workers in Gompers's AF of L certainly engaged in economic struggles with entrepreneurs, but it was not class-based and not socialist in its inspiration. Instead, the norm was "peaceful negotiation." "The prerequisite for this kind of relationship is mutual trust and the indubitable feeling of equal entitlement." The purpose of such negotiations was to obtain wages sufficient to permit savings and to provide for retirement. Moreover social mobility made class categories next to meaningless because they need not refer, as in Europe, to more or less static occupational demarcations. In the language of *On the Form of the American Mind,* the open self and the heritage proceeding from New England puritanism to the transformation of the frontier in twentieth-century industrial society consistently sustained social mobility practically as a corollary of immigration.

In "La Follette and the Wisconsin Idea" (1927) (*CW* 7:192–205), Voegelin explained that the "Wisconsin idea" was both a historical development and the crystallization or endpoint of it. It began in 1908 and was constituted by a social movement around the slogan "Restoration of the Government to the People." It was not called the "Wisconsin idea" because populist measures were enacted only in that state, but because La Follette was governor of Wisconsin when the most extensive measures were enacted. But it was part of a broad American movement whose beginnings antedated the Revolution.

Here Voegelin recapitulated some of the themes and intellectual formations of the America book. First and most fundamental was the "experience of the democracy of equals that had its origin in the frontier situation." The social order it implied was less "a stratified society of free personalities," than "a mass of equal individuals." This was a social reality in the early periods of the settlement of America but, as we noted above, it changed with the closing of the frontier and the growth of industrialization and became overlaid with economic and party stratification that eclipsed or excluded frontier equality.

At the same time, those who were latecomers, and those who were forcibly brought from Africa, were not integrated into the ideal of American life but rather existed side by side with the society of equals, only without rights or with only diminished rights (see *CW* 1:225–26). Even so, it has been in the American West, where the memory of the frontier was still strong, that the concern for equality against the big shots, the bosses, and the trusts was most strongly felt. A sense of injustice, of inequality for both citizens and sections or regions of the county had been exacerbated by the railway, and by the influence of the railways in politics. The "Wisconsin idea," or populism, was a response to this new circumstance and clothed itself in the garb of reform, anticorruption, returning government to the people, and so on. "The causes lie in the sectional clashes of interests that were superimposed upon the older stratum of the 'people' experience." Hence La Follette's failure in 1924 when he ran for the presidency showed the limits of his regional as well as his experiential appeal. This limitation was linked to a second change: The end of the frontier experience was followed quickly enough by urbanization. Historically, prior to 1910, cities played little political role; after that period, one found "the flowering of an urban culture and intelligentsia with ideals different from those of the puritanically hidebound hinterland." Sophisticated urbanites were not easily tempted by populism then and are not so tempted now.

Two papers published in 1928 dealt with the Federal Reserve system, a matter about which he disagreed with Commons (*CW* 7:255–73; see also *CW* 1:244–45, 245n51). A discussion of "Research of Business Cycles and the Stabilization of Capitalism" (*CW* 7:274–84) is interesting not simply because of its discussion of Daniel Defoe, whom Voegelin treated as a serious economic thinker and not merely the author of "utopian" South Seas escapist literature (*CW* 13:69–70; *CW* 7:276–79; *CW* 10:200), but also because Voegelin criticized Marx's economic doctrine: the capitalist order had stabilized itself about the same time as he and Engels were writing the *Communist Manifesto*—a point first made by Commons (*CW* 1:258–59; *CW* 7:280). Indeed, in Voegelin's view, research on the business cycle was the most recent evidence of the long-term stability of capitalism. Voegelin then reiterated a point emphasized above, but one that must have astonished his European readers (along with Americans enchanted by the form of the European mind):

> We can see here one of the principal differences in the development of European and American capitalism. In Europe, the improvement of the situation of the workers often had to be enforced by the state against the will of a group of entrepreneurs. Classes in our sense have never existed in America, and a psychological attitude has endured since the time of the pioneers to consider special relief for a group of the population as somehow demeaning: To be sure, the group receiving public welfare would be helped, but it would be stigmatized as a class of people that does not know how to help itself.

In America capitalism was stabilized not through the intervention of grandiose Bismarckian state activity but in a series of small settlements and agreements made between capital and labor with the objective of cooperating—and here Voegelin included the Federal Reserve system. "All the examples drawn from the American experience," he said, "have their origin in an intellectual [or spiritual] attitude that is fundamentally different from the one that led to the development of European theories of crisis." In fact, as Voegelin noted in his America book and reiterated here, there was not much concern for economic theories at all in America and no concern with classes or estates that must be protected or raised for the simple reason that none existed: "The whole nation is an economic body, and the stabilization efforts aim at the calming of economic life in the concrete case—with no systems of national economy to be consulted." Despite bitter and sometimes violent strikes in industries such as coal mining, sectoral agreements—all the way up to the Federal Reserve Bank—were concerned "to secure the general stability of price levels." None of this activity was designed to benefit one particular class, as in Europe (as described by Defoe and then Marx), "but an ideal image of a democratic economic subject who is on the same level as all the rest, and which the community, the commonwealth, must protect equally from undeserved profits or losses, and to whom it owes justice as to everyone else. The American stabilization of capitalism is possible only in terms of a stabilization of society." It is probably fair to say that Voegelin reiterated arguments made in *On the Form of the American Mind* because he considered them to be striking discoveries that were bound to surprise his German scholarly audience. This did not, however, turn him into a Social Democrat, as has occasionally been suggested.

Nowhere among his early essays was the comparison between Europe and America more forcefully and wittily made than in his analysis of "The Meaning of the Declaration of the Rights of Man and the Citizen of 1789," published in 1928 (*CW* 7:285–335). In America, Voegelin began,

> equality in possessions and in way of life permits the use of egalitarian phraseology, while in European society, which is stratified into estates, its consequences are inconceivable. This is the same characteristic that fundamentally distinguishes American democracy from its European forms even today: European society has achieved at best an equality in the right to vote, while its American counterpart offers equality at a very

high niveau of equipping with material goods. In these two societies, the declarations of equality that are identical in their wording have virtually nothing in common in their meaning.

Thus the French, impressed with the external similarities of the American and French revolutions—namely that both were innovations—thought that, like the Americans, they too must make a declaration of some sort even though the liberation of a colony was much different from an internal revolution overthrowing an ancien régime. So, enchanted by words and brimming with enthusiasm, they "make a declaration of rights we actually do not want to make" for the obvious reason that someone "might take human rights literally and view the term *man* as something other than a bourgeois [*Bürger*] enjoying a comfortable existence."

As for the speeches that allegedly discuss the *Declaration of the Rights of Man and the Citizen,* they were so cut off from reality, not to say filled with clichés, as to be little more than the expression of the mediocre personalities of those who spoke then. And they were boring, because they seemed endless. The speeches, Voegelin said, need to be understood as "a declamatory idea fulfilled by a person playing a theatrical role, not a well-considered idea based on and aiming at realities." In this respect they compared poorly even with such examples of partisan argument as are contained in *The Federalist Papers.*

In 1929–1930, Voegelin wrote three relatively short articles for the *Archiv für angewandte Soziologie,* all of which dealt with aspects of the American understanding of social justice, particularly as concerns the notion of liberty and property (*CW* 8:53–88). His focus was on a number of Supreme Court decisions and the theoretical context within which they were decided, namely the political theory of Locke. In *Race and State* (1933), Voegelin described property as a pre-legal, pre-economic, and "existential" reality grounded in human nature (*CW* 2:3–4). As a consequence, the judicial and economic understanding of property needed to be supplemented by political theory. That is, neither legal nor economic science was adequate by itself—nor is the contemporary "law-and-economics" approach—to account for the complex and composite phenomena. Both, Voegelin said, are "imperfect." The economic understanding of a property transaction examined only the market but ignored the state and the possibility of coercion necessary to ensure compliance. The legal understanding ignored market realities that have a coercive effect on those undertaking the exchange (*CW* 8:53–54).

Voegelin illustrated his point with an exegesis of a nineteenth-century Supreme Court decision, *In Re Slaughter-House Cases.*[7] The facts are as follows: Several New Orleans butchers were put out of business when the state of Louisiana established a slaughterhouse monopoly in the city. They brought suit against the state because its legislation had rendered the slaughtering capacity of the butchers worthless, and they were compelled to pay the monopoly to do a job they were perfectly capable of accomplishing by themselves. The Supreme Court ruled that the monopoly neither threatened their property, in the sense of their knives and equipment or their butcher shops, nor did it threaten their ability to enter into contracts. Accordingly a majority held that the monopoly did not violate the Thirteenth and Fourteenth Amendment rights to liberty and property.

The non- or pre-judicial context for this ruling, Voegelin said, was provided by Locke's "dogmatic" teaching on natural right. Property, by this interpretation, consisted simply of the material and labor of the solitary individual. Locke's famous remark, "in the beginning all the world was America" was approximated by the frontier experience.[8] In Voegelin's words, "the economic form of the early American settler was in fact the family farm," and it was of limited size and productivity owing to the limitations imposed by the frontier economy. "It was not until the course of the nineteenth century that the last remnants of this natural condition in which property was originally created died out" (*CW* 8:57). As a consequence, Locke could not account for a modern, complex, and highly stratified economy (*CW* 8:63–65).

The majority decision reflected this obsolete understanding of property. The minority, however, was more in tune with the realities of the situation of individuals in complex industrial societies where a change in the economy, as permitted by the Louisiana monopoly legislation, could have catastrophic consequences for individual citizens such as the New Orleans butchers. "The precondition of the minority opinion was thus a new concept of property," namely that property was not so much a concrete thing, such as a butcher knife, but "the individual's entire sphere of action, a sphere ensuring him of a certain quality of life in a particular social situation" (*CW* 8:65). By this understanding, the butchers were injured "even though they kept their equipment" (*CW* 8:67). Eventually, the constitutional position of the minority in the slaughterhouse cases became accepted by way of the "due process" clause of the Fourteenth Amendment, even though that amendment was initially intended to deal with arbitrary state action and slavery.

The contrast between the majority and the minority position in the slaughterhouse cases (and the later development of the political principles involved in the "due process" interpretations) also raised for Voegelin questions of philosophical anthropology. There were two aspects to this problem. The first is that Locke's notion of property was so indeterminate that it received its actual content only from historical practice, such as the family farm on the frontier. But, as was clear from the slaughterhouse cases, when those historical circumstances changed, the principles of social justice could easily be violated.

More basic than Locke's reliance on historical circumstances, however, was the argument that "man must 'labor,'" which meant that human beings must allow their bodies to bind with natural objects

> in order to produce the new unities that serve to preserve life and procure food and shelter. Thus, the ultimate causes of the origin of property are to be found in human corporeality: in the threat of death against which the human has no defense besides his work, his influence on nature. At the base of Locke's theory of property lies recognition of the fact that the human is an existential center [*Lebenszentrum*] endangered by death. From this simple recognition proceeds the demand to preserve life. (*CW* 8:55)

The focus on property, for Locke, was thus a focus on things associated with, or pertaining to, bodies, including the fear of death. For Lockeans, the interpretative move of the Supreme Court by way of the due process argument to a more adequate understanding of property has always been seen as illegitimate. For Voegelin, however, it reflected a more comprehensive understanding of the person or, so to speak, a more adequate philosophical anthropology than can be found in Locke. In his America book, Voegelin quoted Giddings on "consciousness of kind" and Dewey on "likemindedness" to indicate the more comprehensive understanding of human being (*CW* 1:217–19). So far as the Supreme Court is concerned, however, it

> does not press toward full clarity of thought on the matter. It contents itself instead with making decisions from case to case, and because the general principles themselves do not admit of any clear conclusions, the court's attitude changes with its composition and with the nature of the particular case. (*CW* 8:87)

The way the court has gone about its business does not lend itself to clear and principled analysis in terms of "normative logic" or *Normlogik,* to use Kelsen's term. It does, however, provide occasions for education and for the exercise of statesmanship, as Voegelin indicated in *On the Form of the American Mind* (*CW* 1:168–69, 34:58–60).

There is one other category of publication from this period that deserves notice. Having returned from America and published a book on his experiences and his research there, Voegelin was pressed into service as a book reviewer, which also, no doubt, augmented his return to a meager European salary. Between 1928 and 1930 he published half a dozen or so reviews of American books or of books by Europeans on America. By and large the latter "penetrate to principled insights only with difficulty; perhaps they do not even want to penetrate to them, where such insights are not very pleasant for Europeans" (*CW* 13:24). Many, he said,

> have in common a certain attitude toward American problems. None wants to explore phenomena of American history, economy, politics, or the American mind for their own sake, but only for the significance these matters may have for Europe. In all these writings, America *per se* is in fact wholly unimportant. They all seek either to ascertain only Europe's part in American history, or to extract theories from it. All the books were written in the shadow of an upheaval that has shifted the center of gravity of the world economy to the West, and in almost all one can sense a more or less veiled *ressentiment.* Even the most outstanding among them in terms of cultural history [*Geistesgeschichte*] . . . still do not seek to explore a strange world with unreserved affection. Nor do they concern themselves with the meaning of this strange phenomenon for its own

> sake, and a style of *l'Amérique pour l'Amérique,* which would be the first prerequisite for first-class cultural history, is missing. (*CW* 13:19–20)

In addition, many of these works were based on secondary sources, not archival studies or firsthand experience.

Voegelin was equally critical of a number of texts on social science written by Americans. Some were little more than propaganda tracts less concerned with scientific objectives than providing, for example, a summary of "Catholic educational work on social questions" including evolution and birth control. "If we also mention that the existence of God is convincingly proved, there remains nothing more to say" (*CW* 13:25).

In a review of a book on the methods and objectives of research in the social sciences (*CW* 13:26–28), Voegelin made several still pertinent observations. First, "everyone assumes that 'science' means adopting the particular aspiration of a natural science that discovers laws." But second, since such a science would have little to say about social, political, cultural, or historical reality, the implications have generally been ignored, and the scholars proceeded about their business anyway. Third, most social science research has been justified because it dealt with practical matters so that, fourth, it has become an activity that is both widely subsidized and conceived essentially as a collective enterprise. Voegelin found this last aspect most interesting because it led to a social hierarchy with the following layers:

> (1) Clerical assistants—scientific assistants, stenographers, graphic artists, secretaries, etc. (2) Routine or average men—persons who have had the benefit of a scientific education and are also employed as "teachers" at universities, but who cannot properly be called scholars because, to put it crudely, nothing scholarly ever occurs to them. These people are suited to undertake follow-up work where the major problems have been solved. (3) Investigators—researchers, scholars of rank who, in addition to the conventional knowledge of their specialty, have a capacity for the creative and insightful development of their science. (*CW* 13:27–28)

This hierarchy was somewhat dysfunctional because, if the "advancement of science" were entrusted to the "routine men," unfortunately "they can produce nothing significant." On the other hand if an "investigator," a genuine scholar, were commissioned as the director of a collaborative enterprise "he himself runs the danger of both losing contact with research materials and losing the leisure necessary for his own work. Thus he ends up wasting his talent" (*CW* 13:28). Some aspects of academic life in North America have remained unchanged since Voegelin observed them.

Let us draw a few conclusions regarding Voegelin's initial visit to the United States. In his *Autobiographical Reflections* Voegelin said that the experience of America occasioned the "great break" with his European intellectual formation because it introduced him to a new world that was simply beyond the horizon of European scholarly concern. There is no reason to doubt the importance that his American experience had; in retrospect it could hardly have looked otherwise. It is clear from this brief account that Voegelin stressed the differences between American and European experiences and between the American and European mind, whether the latter be French or German. Moreover, looking ahead to his escape from Vienna to America after the Anschluss, the gratitude of an immigrant and then of a new citizen also shaped his recollection of his first time in the United States.

His experience was not, however, a kind of conversion so that, henceforth and forever, he would put the cares and tribulations of Europe behind him. Even prior to his voyage of discovery, as was indicated in Chapter 1, Voegelin was fully aware of the importance of the "other" and of other peoples' ways of conducting scholarship. The concept of "German science" meant that science, however understood, was greater than its German variety. His articles published prior to his first removal to America showed the development of a critical attitude toward a neo-Kantian understanding of the law and of sociology. It continued to develop after his return, as we discuss in the following chapter. His American experience confirmed his dissatisfaction with received methods; his analysis of the American materials provided an example, in practice, of what an alternative might be. It is also clear, if for no reason other than the sheer density of his prose, that Voegelin was still in the midst of a reformulation of the principles of his science of sociohistorical reality.

It is always easier to say what is wrong with a received approach than it is to construct something better. Moreover it was clear to Voegelin even before he went to America that the pretense of neo-Kantian social science, that the scientist was "outside" social reality, was a fundamental error. Hence his interest in Husserl and his own, admittedly somewhat opaque, efforts at reformulation of a more adequate method, which is to say, a method adequate to the sociohistorical reality he studied. Instead of an a priori imposition of categories by the positivist, neo-Kantian ego of the social scientist, Voegelin discovered the importance of the self-articulation or self-interpretation of linguistic phenomena as the elements that constitute the historically meaningful unity of any given political society.

So far as *Staatslehre* was concerned, as we discuss in the following chapter, the alternatives turned out to be either the analysis of an a priori formal legal structure or the description of the internal articulation of the political community. However deep his admiration of the intellectual power of neo-Kantian *Staatslehre*, Voegelin came to the conclusion that it was not "empirical." The alternative to the postulate of a Kantian (or neo-Kantian) transcendental ego that postulated both values and concepts was that of a situated scientist who mediated the empirical materials, including the grand methodological issues, as they arose in the process of history. Granted that his American experience instructed him in the importance of participation—hence the significance of Commons—it was still necessary to give an account of the modes of participation with the same rigor that the neo-Kantians accounted for the nonparticipation of the transcendental ego. In the following chapter we will examine how Voegelin deepened his criticism of the neo-Kantian "science of the law" and continued to move, somewhat haltingly, toward a more adequate science of sociohistorical reality.

3

Beyond *Staatslehre*

The next book Voegelin published, in 1933, was *Race and State* (*CW* 2). As we shall see in the following chapter, it was written in part as a response to political discourse in Germany after 1930. In terms both of its subject matter and of its rhetorical style, it reads like much of Voegelin's postwar writing. It deals with what are recognizably "political ideas" in the sense that the term was used in his *History of Political Ideas.*[1] The introduction to *Race and State* provided an account of Voegelin's understanding at the time of the relationship between the subject matter of that book and *Staatslehre.* Most of Voegelin's writings in the late 1920s following his return to Europe from America—and despite the importance of his experience of America—dealt with questions and problems within the German tradition of *Staatslehre.* This present chapter deals with the arguments made by Voegelin that clarified the limits of *Staatslehre* as well as what a more comprehensive science of sociohistorical reality would entail.

It would be an exaggeration to say that Voegelin was "groping" for an approach more adequate to his concerns. His arguments, however, did not lead directly to an obvious conclusion. As Voegelin said of Augustine, there was "direction" to his thought "but no rational notations with which to describe its goal" (*CW* 32:227). As a result, Voegelin's characteristic incisiveness in critique was accompanied by a tentativeness regarding what was to replace defective approaches and formulations.

Recall that in Chapter 1, we noted that, following the successful conclusion of the wars of unification in 1871, *Staatslehre* developed as a method and a discipline to deal with the inconsistencies of heterogeneous German legal systems by harmonizing their provisions within a governing constitutional order. To the extent that any philosophical reasoning was needed to justify legal and constitutional norms, this was accomplished by neo-Kantian arguments. The goal was to order all laws and government regulations within a logically consistent system (or "ideal system") that would then form a "normative sphere" independent of historical contingencies and everyday political phenomena. In Voegelin's view, his teacher Hans Kelsen had produced the most consistent version of a *Staatslehre* in his "pure theory of law."

Voegelin never lost his admiration for Kelsen's analytical achievement even while he was concerned with its limitations. In Chapter 1 we examined a few of the methodological issues involved in the area of—for want of a better term—comparative sociology. As we saw, even prior to the existential confirmation of a "pluralistic universe" in his experience of America, Voegelin had serious reservations about Kelsen's approach. Let us review the evidence.

In a 1924 article on the pure theory of law and *Staatslehre* (*CW* 7:49ff), Voegelin began by noting again that the epistemological principle of the pure theory of law was established by neo-Kantian norm-logicians. "Knowledge does not portray an object given in reality" by way of understanding its several facets with the aid of various sciences. Rather, "a priori forms, antecedent to all modes of experience, determine the character of the judgments and thus the structure of the objects that are contained in these judgments." In Kelsen's words, "the object of knowledge is determined by the aim of knowledge." As we saw in the first two chapters of this book, such an approach was antithetical to Voegelin's concern with accounting for units of meaning that were to be found in social self-understanding. In his first article on Kelsen and in others written around the same time, Voegelin approached the problem of neo-Kantian social science from the inside, as it were. The result was, first of all, a virtuoso demonstration by

Voegelin of his mastery of the formal, almost scholastic, language of the pure theory of law. But it was also a sustained critique.

What made his theory of the law "pure" was its independence from what Kelsen called "social events." He was concerned entirely with the normative logic of the law, which was susceptible to analysis and thus could constitute a body of knowledge and science, rather than with the social or political conditions that may have generated the law or within which it operated, which were mere contingencies. The eventual result was a "formal determination of an order of norms" detached from "the pulsating life of law" and in fact from historical and empirical considerations of any kind (*CW* 7:66–68).

Voegelin contrasted here, and in several other articles and reviews, the pure theory of law and the historical theory of the state. "The means for transforming historical facts into a theory of the times is the identification of the essential elements in the construct of a state; the fundamental forms are elaborated on the basis of the historical material, whose forms participate more or less clearly and more decisively or less meaningfully in the construction of every state." Hence new elements could enter into the historical construct of the theory of the state. "The essential elements are no longer the logical forms of a scientific formation of judgments" but instead "possess characteristics of content; they are not pure forms of logical genesis of objects; they enter with their fullness of content into the reality 'state'; once so incorporated they are capable of gradation, of a more or a less [degree] . . . and become more intensive or weaker images of their core content" (*CW* 7:80–81). From the perspective of "pure theory," the chief problem with "content" and with the historical variability of content was that it did not lend itself to precise, analytic, scientific treatment. It was inherently variable so could not be the subject of a priori logical investigation.

On the other hand, the historical account of the genesis of a particular configuration of "content" did have the inestimable superiority of being connected to "historical events," from which Voegelin drew an important conclusion: "the definition of law cannot be accomplished within the scope of the 'pure theory of law' because this theory consciously ignores the problems of social reality . . . and limits itself to an investigation of the fundamental concepts of legal norms" (*CW* 7:92). "The path that leads to the 'pure theory of law'" was questionable because it "avoids the problem of the state form; the 'pure theory of law' attempts to eliminate all sociological and speculative concepts and to reduce their object of cognition to the logical elements of a complex of problems." In fact, however, this "path" led either to a dead end where one simply ignored legal as well as social and political reality or to a point where the problems posed by "content" were allowed to reenter the theory in "logicized" form.

The implication Voegelin drew from this argument was clear: It was always possible to practice "norm logic" because norms were postulated objects of cognition. By the same token one could not practice legal logic because the formative elements in the latter were not objects of cognition but "symbols, ideas, fragmentary acts, and the founding elements" of the polity—all of which demanded imaginative participation, not scientific, neo-Kantian cognition in order to be apprehended. In short, the criteria by which law was to be distinguished from other social and political realities was found not in the formal structure of its norms but in its content (*CW* 7:96–97). And content, as Voegelin had stated on several occasions, appears in "a particular manner of givenness" and not as an a priori cognitive construct of a transcendental ego or anything similar. This remained a major limitation to *Staatslehre.*

If one looked upon Kelsen's pure theory of law as itself a "content," which is to say as a "historical event," then the direction of analysis would aim to bring to light the "internal" connection between the pure theory and the experiences of defeat in the Great War and the enormous social, political, economic, and legal disruption associated with the replacement of two large empires with one medium-sized and one small republic. This problem was explored by Voegelin in his 1936 study of Austrian postwar politics. He ended this 1924 essay on the pure theory of law and *Staatslehre,* however, on a rather different note.

The "purity" of Kelsen's theory was achieved at the end of a lengthy history of criticism of the historical theory of law and the state. With Kelsen, legal theory had become almost entirely formal and systematic. The "problems of the state," and of *Staatslehre* concerned with "historical events," lay almost entirely outside the concerns of the pure theory of law. The externality of the pure theory to the reality of historical events thus provided an opportunity to begin "the reconstruction of a complete *Staatslehre.*" That would entail bringing together the "symbols, ideas, fragmentary acts," and so on noted above with a logic that accounted for how these phenomena were connected to one another within the "idea of the state." Moreover, Voegelin concluded, "with this final anchoring of *Staatslehre* in the theory of ideas, we have reached a point of departure for other cultural objectifications; we may set beside the theory of the idea of the state a theory of the idea of art, of language, of religion, of the economy." This is precisely what Voegelin undertook to do in *On the Form of the American Mind.* Finally, "with a demonstration of the connection between these ideas we stand at the highest systematic level of a system of the philosophy of society; the structure of the *Staatslehre* outlined here reaches [or aspires, *reicht*] directly to this level" (*CW* 7:99). In other words, by 1924 Voegelin had concluded: (1) that a pure theory of law needed to be significantly supplemented by "ideas" to constitute a "complete *Staatslehre*" and (2) that even a complete *Staatslehre* would be subordinate to "a system of the philosophy of society," which was indicated in Chapter 1 above by the phrase "science of sociohistorical reality."

In terms of actual content, "The Pure Theory of Law and *Staatslehre*" just discussed was, to a significant extent, a series of analyses of the legal arguments put forward by several authors—Kaufmann, Schreier, Sander, Gierke, Laband, Jellinek, Hatschek, Dahlmann, Waitz, Roscher, Schmidt, and Verdross—other than Kelsen.[2] Some of their books were also reviewed by Voegelin (*CW* 13, *passim*), and some of the arguments reappeared in other analyses of legal questions, as we will see. Because of his importance both personally for Voegelin and because of his preeminence among legal thinkers, Kelsen remained a center of attention. Nowhere was this more obvious than in Voegelin's first publication in English, which introduced Kelsen's theory to American readers through the pages of the *Political Science Quarterly.*

"Kelsen's Pure Theory of Law" (1927) dealt chiefly with the first edition of Kelsen's *Allgemeine Staatslehre* (1925) (*CW* 7:182ff). This book, Voegelin began, "is likely to be the standard treatise on the subject for some time" in the area of "the sciences of law and government in Germany." Kelsen was given high but obviously not unqualified praise. Voegelin added that he would deal only with "the underlying principles of its legal philosophy" beginning with the pure theory of law, "with the accent on the word *pure.*" As has been noted, Kelsen sought to distinguish his "pure" legal theory from a host of other problems thrown together under the heading of *Staatslehre.* And *Staatslehre* acquired its somewhat eclectic nature because of the complexities associated with amalgamating diverse public law traditions in the single, postunification constitutional order. The creation of "a magnificent legal structure" from a mixture of unsatisfactory and distinct legal systems drew the attention of legal scholars—Gerber, Laband, Jellinek, and then Kelsen—to the question of positive law, as distinct from preunification, eighteenth-century speculations on natural law. For the first time, Voegelin had (1) situated the importance of Kelsen's theory in the political and intellectual history of Germany and (2) indicated that the focus on positive law was undertaken for pragmatic purposes, namely to bring order to an unsystematic collection of legal codes, decrees, and practices that were inherited from the era of "German particularity" prior to the wars of unification (see *CW* 21:194–200, 316–17).

At the heart of Kelsen's improvement over his predecessors—Jellinek and others—was the application of neo-Kantian epistemological theory to a diverse collection of legal materials. Kelsen argued that law belonged to the category of a normative essence *(Sollen),* not existence *(Sein),* of a priori postulates, not temporal or spatial phenomena such as political or judicial institutions, or even traditions. The "elemental structure" of the pure theory of law was "governmental enforcement machinery," not rights or duties, privileges, liabilities, disabilities, and so on. These latter were existing "legal relations" to be sure, but their existence was itself "subjective" and so changed with social conditions. The content of what was enforced was distinct from the essential attribute of enforcement. That is, ethical purposes, which changed, were distinct from the legal means, which did not. Government was thus always government *by* law, whatever the law happened to be. The implications were somewhat different from (and perhaps antithetical to) the Anglo-American notion of government *of* laws (and not of men). Likewise the category of causality, which was also tied to existence, had no meaning within Kelsen's theory.

Toward the close of this comparatively short article, Voegelin made two additional observations. We postpone consideration of one of them,

Kelsen's most important practical achievement, drafting and commenting on the Austrian Constitution, until Chapter 5. Voegelin's first observation dealt with the question of sovereignty and international law.

For Kelsen, sovereignty indicated "the independence of an internally coherent legal system from any superior set of legal rules." Accordingly, a corporate charter was not sovereign because its validity depended upon its having been issued by a state; likewise a statute was not sovereign because its validity depended upon its conformation to the law of the constitution. State sovereignty meant there was no superior legal order upon which the legal order of the state depended for its validity. But what, then, was to be made of international law? Voegelin argued that the process of international recognition among states, with the implication that a state be accepted as a member of the society of nations only if it obeyed "certain rules of international intercourse," was a prima facie indication that "the international legal order rises above the legal orders of the individual states." Thus, "there is good reason to name this highest order as the truly sovereign one and to consider the states entirely devoid of sovereignty."

That the status of international law is not entirely a formality is indicated by the phenomenon of revolution: New postrevolutionary institutions may be internally disconnected from the old ones by the new legal order, but if a new government, for example, refused to acknowledge the debts of the old, the usual remedy has been for other states to bring sufficient pressure to bear on the new regime to reestablish the legal connection between the pre- and postrevolutionary orders. That is, "the stratum of international law produces unity in the legal history when otherwise ruptures would have occurred" (*CW* 7:187–88). Voegelin's point did not deny that the *effective* cause of a postrevolutionary regime restoring the legal connection to the prerevolutionary one was political pressure brought by debt holders. Rather it was that the connection between the two regimes had to be formalized as a *legal* one.

Further light is shed on this issue when, a couple of years later, Voegelin returned to the question of sovereignty and international law in an essay that compared Kelsen's theory with that of John Dickinson, a Princeton law professor, whose theory "is unquestionably defined by the Anglo-American tradition" (*CW* 8:27ff). This "tradition" extended back to Hobbes by way of Locke, Bentham, and Austin, and several minor thinkers. In the postwar Anglo-American legal world, Harold Laski's *Studies in the Problem of Sovereignty* (1917) and C. H. McIlwain's 1926 article in *Economica* brought the issue of sovereignty again into focus. In particular, Dickinson's merit (and his novelty) was to have attempted to develop a theory of sovereignty that was close to "German attempts to purify both the legal sphere and legal concepts of nonlegal elements," rather as Kelsen had done, though without relying on neo-Kantian epistemology. Dickinson argued, first, that sovereignty was a "logical postulate" or assumption the meaning of which existed in the context of legal logic; second, the legal system was coherent so that legal logic could in fact operate; and third, such unity could exist only on the basis of an assumption that there was a single source of law that endowed subordinate tribunals and officials with authority.[3]

Notwithstanding the similarities of their objective—to provide an account of sovereignty—"a difference reveals itself in the expression" that comes from "a variation in the style of thought," not from "a variation in intent." For Kelsen, sovereignty expressed the unity of the legal system *and* of the knowledge of that unity. Dickinson was concerned, as the title of his two articles indicated, with a "working theory" that is, first of all, a pragmatic, useful, and institutional account of sovereignty. Moreover, as Voegelin had already noted, Kelsen's formulation followed from his neo-Kantian epistemology of which Dickinson was completely innocent. Indeed Dickinson was entirely pragmatic in his account of the predictability of the law, as compared to Kelsen's deductive analysis based upon the "basic norm." This was entirely in keeping with the American understanding of law as discussed in Voegelin's book on America.

Another significant difference between the two was apparent with respect to the treatment of international law. For Dickinson, the apex was the "supreme organ of a legal system," however described in terms of institutions; for Kelsen, as we have seen, international law incorporated the legal order of the state within a higher norm-logic. International law for Dickinson was merely empirical, and he tended to ignore its "norm-logical significance for the unity of the legal system." For Dickinson, the content of international law is ultimately determined by the sovereign states. For Dickinson international law may be a norm and even a law, but it was akin to primitive state law because there existed no norm-enforcing institution. Such a "higher sovereignty" was "thinkable" as an "ought" *(Sollen)*—the League of Nations, for example, might be a sovereign organ—but in fact a sovereign league did not exist. On the contrary, international law was binding on a state only if the state agreed. In contrast, for Kelsen, the formal norm that constituted the "basic norm" of international law was that agreements must be kept—*pacta sunt servanda,* a deal is a deal. For Dickinson, the contrary Latin tag, *rebus sic stantibus,* was more important: You keep an agreement so long as the circumstances remain as they were. And when circumstances change, as in fact they do and, more importantly, as any state can claim they have, then the obligation to keep an agreement evaporated.

The contrast between the two "styles" and "attitudes," Voegelin said, reveals "an unexpected, deep insight into the nature of law in general." Kelsen's basic norms in the absence of any account of historical institutions led to an infinite regress that could be closed only by the inflexible and so arbitrary maxim *pacta sunt servanda;* institutions without norms lead to the primacy of *rebus sic stantibus,* and "above the state [there] remain only institutional stumps, first attempts at the formation of law," such as the League of Nations and associated institutions such as the International Labor Organization.

An alternative formulation, particularly well adapted to Dickinson's argument, concerned the "regime of law" that aimed to reconcile law and justice. The security or predictability of law could be assured by reducing the flexibility of legal formulas, but inflexibility would widen the gap between law and justice, perhaps to the extent that there were no juristic means to close or bridge it, in which case "those who are subject to the norms will overturn their legal system through revolution." On the other hand, an exclusive preference for justice over law "would be tantamount to the destruction of the legal order." Instead of the irresponsibility of invoking "the mantle of impeccable ethical conduct," something akin to Max Weber's ethics of intention, Dickinson (and, it would seem, Voegelin)

> wants the principled peculiarity of law, its contrasts to the ideal of justice, its compromises with this ideal, and the necessity of a fundamentally unjust legal order to be recognized as the lot of the cultural community as such. He [Dickinson] hopes thereby to avoid vague, idealistic prattle [*Geschwätz*] in this matter and at the same time to show how ideals of

justice can influence the legal order without endangering its security. (*CW* 8:48)

We noted above that Dickinson's title, "A Working Theory of Sovereignty," carried implications of pragmatic flexibility rather than normative finality. This was one reason why, Voegelin said, "this term is not easy to render into German." From the foregoing reflections, however, it is clear that by "working" Dickinson did not simply mean useful, which would find an exhaustive justification in the ever-present *rebus sic stantibus* maxim. Rather, there was an element of improvement, of closing in a principled way the gap between law and justice. In the domestic American example, the Supreme Court was the state institution that controlled the content of the norms of the law, but it did so (as was indicated in Chapter 2) by subordinating itself to them. This was a concrete rendition of the notion of the rule of law as a governing expectation. At the same time reform as implied in a "working theory" required a "realistic recognition of the limits of legal order, of its contrast to the ideal of justice, and of its character of compromise." This meant "that ultimate control of a legal order is a meta-legal affair, a question of the personal, statesmanlike qualities of the highest organs." This is why, in his *Autobiographical Reflections,* Voegelin said that, with respect to domestic law, the Supreme Court is "the source of political culture in America" (*CW* 34:58–59). There was, however, nothing remotely analogous to the U.S. Supreme Court in the area of international law. On the contrary, the central elements were not institutions—the court at The Hague, the League of Nations, and so on—but the "personal statesmenlike qualities" of political leaders. When Voegelin tried to formulate a more adequate *Staatslehre* in his unpublished *Herrschaftslehre* written during the early 1930s, he began by discussing "personal" qualities by way of philosophical anthropology.

Before we consider Voegelin's *Herrschaftslehre,* there are two additional writings to consider. The first is "On the Theory of the State Form" (1927) (*CW* 7:206–54). Here Voegelin began his argument with the observation that Jellinek's remark of 1892—that "the theory of the forms of a unified state" was among "the most neglected problems of the general theory of the state"—remained true. That is, the accounts of why some states were democracies and others were monarchies or dictatorships of various sorts were generally unsatisfactory. The reason for Voegelin's severe judgment was the by now familiar one: the tradition of *Staatslehre,* and especially of the pure theory of law, did not take "sociological" elements, which in fact conditioned the form of the state, into account. As a consequence, sometimes the question of the form of the state was "dispatched as if it were a postscript, more a matter of tradition" than a reality of first rank importance. In fact, however, writers in the *Staatslehre* tradition were fully aware of the "difficulties" involved in integrating the theory of the form of the state into a general theory of the state as such. In this article Voegelin proposed to survey and analyze five fundamental "ideas of the theory of forms [of the state] currently in vogue."

He then provided a critical analysis of these different schemes of classifying the form of the state, which is to say, the kind of regime. He came to the provisional conclusion, because the classification was essentially external or elemental, to use a term from the *New Science of Politics* (*CW* 5:112–15), that the "historical significance" of these "pseudo-constructions" was that they revealed that "the problems themselves" were a result of a "system-creating power" that was sufficient only to bring the need to replace them into focus. "The question of a theory of state forms therefore comes to a head as a problem of the formulation of state concepts," the only possible basis of classification being "the one based on the right to governance" [*Herrschaft*], a term the significance of which Voegelin did not develop on this occasion.

The great defect of external classificatory schemes, whether based on criteria such as the number of rulers, whether they are real or artificial persons, whether they possess a temporary or permanent right to govern, and so on, was that they all followed a peculiar technique of abstraction or "emptying" [*Entleerung*]. As a consequence they were able only to identify the problems "without, however, penetrating to the subject-matter [*Gegenstand*] itself." They took their bearings not from reality but from prior textbooks, "word combinations clinging to handed-down thoughts," which is to say, they amounted to a commentary on traditions.

Voegelin's analysis of the defects of these external, formal, or "emptied" theories of state forms led him to conclude—on grounds familiar from Chapter 1 of this book—that, if the subject matter of the science of the state in general existed, it did not follow the model of mathematical or quasi-mathematical natural science because, precisely, such a model was empty of content, abstract, and so on. What was needed was a focus on "material determinations" because they would become manifest "in a type of form all its own, which is the 'idea' of the historically meaningful unit [*historischen Sinneinheit*] of the state." The "emptied" theories were empty of meaning.

Nor, for reasons given above, is the pure theory of the law much help because it, too, is empty of "political contents." This meant, Voegelin said, that "the theory of state forms," or what we have called the theory of the types of regime, was distinct from "the theory of state law as a juridical discipline." This is why the classification of states as monarchies, democracies, and so on was meaningless—"the state has only one constant element: the idea of the meaningful unit, and this idea is the same in all states." What remains to be done is examine the problem of "symbol-constructing principles" that determine the historical construct of meaning. Although Jellinek began such an analysis, he did not sufficiently consider the motive, principle, or fundamental experience that lay at the core of every symbol. As we saw in the previous chapter, Voegelin undertook just such an analysis in his book on America, linking for instance the experience of equality on the frontier and the necessities of self-government to such externally unconnected phenomena as the mysticism of New England Puritans and the practical purposes of American legal education. They were connected internally, as a unit or unity of meaning *(Sinneinheit).*

Before turning to the argument of his *Herrschaftslehre* or "theory of governance," we must note one additional constituent element in Voegelin's legal formation: the theory of Carl Schmitt, to which we will return briefly toward the end of this chapter. In 1931, in the midst of his work on the *Herrschaftslehre,* Voegelin reviewed Schmitt's *Verfassungslehre,* which was highly critical of Kelsen (*CW* 13:42–66).

"German *Staatslehre,*" Voegelin said at the outset, "has not produced a constitutional theory." The constitution existed—and here Voegelin followed Schmitt—because of a "general decision" by which the regime was constituted. It began existence with an "ought," which placed Schmitt in opposition to Kelsen's normative theory of law for which the distinction, as noted above, between is *(Sein)* and ought *(Sollen)* is fundamental. Schmitt argued that what *is,* namely the existence of a constitution, began with an *ought.* "Schmitt," Voegelin said, "uses the formulation" of beginning with an ought "in connection with his criticism of Kelsen's theory of law, which appears to me to be important as a principled counterformulation to the neo-Kantian principle of methodological purity." As we saw in detail in Chapter 1, for Voegelin, "methodological purity" in connection with the entire sphere of the *Geisteswissenschaften,* including *Staatslehre,* was not feasible, because the field that served as the subject matter of scientific research constituted itself outside the context established by science. "Thus the scientific account of the subject matter cannot be executed independently and solely according to its own principles, but rather has to follow the contours of source material."

In this context, Schmitt was "undeniably" correct to argue that constitutional norms were "dependent for their content on the political and social situation of the time of their origin. Accordingly all talk of an order of law, the normative context of which culminates in a basic norm, is empty of meaning." Of course, the great achievements of the pure theory were untouched by this criticism; it remained a technically elegant intellectual structure. Schmitt, however, as Voegelin, wanted "to escape the dead end of neo-Kantian methodological purity," and for that alone Schmitt's work deserved praise. In Voegelin's opinion, however, Schmitt did not go far enough. Neither he nor Kelsen were able "to withdraw from juridical categories in order to discuss the problem of the constitution of society, even though his [Schmitt's] program aimed at referring the validity of law to social being."

To undertake a proper analysis of sociohistorical reality, it was necessary, Voegelin concluded, to work outside the conventions of *Staatslehre* entirely. This is what he attempted to do in his *Herrschaftslehre.*

Let us summarize the argument in the first section of this chapter. First of all, there is the empirical observation that much of Voegelin's work in the 1920s, both before his voyage to America (as indicated in Chapter 1) and in his report on his time in the New World (as indicated in Chapter 2), led him to the conclusion that "conceptualizing the world," to use an apt phrase of Stanley Rosen, was radically deficient.[4] What was needed was not a more refined *Staatslehre* or even a "complete *Staatslehre*" but a deeper understanding of the problems and of the limits of the sociohistorical reality of which *Staatslehre* is a manifestation. Voegelin on several occasions alluded to this deeper understanding by his references to symbols, ideas, or political contents. A preliminary task was thus to discover the kind of language that would allow him to think "beyond *Staatslehre*" rather than to consider completing or perfecting it. It seems to me that Voegelin was clear in his own mind about the problem.

In one of the few commentaries on this period of Voegelin's scholarship, Sandro Chignola called his concern with symbols, rather than with the logical-formal order of legal propositions as found in Kelsen's pure theory, a "methodological device."[5] It is true that shifting his focus to symbols and what he was starting to call "political ideas" was a methodological alternative to neo-Kantian epistemology. The more important point, it seems to me, was that his attention to symbols, political ideas, and so on not only was an alternative to Kelsen's pure theory but, by building from the ground up, as it were—that is from fundamental experiences and "working theories"—he was eventually enabled to enter upon a more comprehensive and realistic account of sociohistorical reality. This may be a "methodological device" in some sense; more important, it turned out to be a methodological device *superior* to the neo-Kantian one.

There is no implication that Voegelin came to this conclusion all at once and then embarked upon the practice of his superior science of sociohistorical reality. On the contrary, in essays and articles written during the late 1920s, Voegelin was still prepared to devote a great deal of energy and attention to German legal writings. He repeated on several occasions, perhaps in different words, his by now well-developed criticism of the *Staatslehre* tradition and especially of the pure theory of law. He did not, however, simply repudiate the *Staatslehre* tradition. How could he? What would it be replaced with? Rather, he used the language of *Staatslehre* to indicate what lay over the horizon. Sometimes this took the form of adding modifiers, as when he spoke of a "complete *Staatslehre*," for example. By the start of the 1930s, Voegelin was ready to attempt to write his own "theory of governance" or *Herrschaftslehre*, of which mention has previously been made.

Until the publication of his *Autobiographical Reflections* in 1989, the sole mention of the *Herrschaftslehre* was in the introduction to *Race and State*. (The balance of the latter book will be discussed in Chapter 4.) It is clear from Voegelin's remarks that although he had good reason to compose his account of "race ideas" independently from his *Herrschaftslehre* (which, as noted, he did not publish), he had by no means abandoned the project, which seemed to have had several different titles.[6]

Race and State, Voegelin began, grew from his work on "a system of *Staatslehre*" one section of which would be devoted to "various ideas about the state" including "body ideas" (such as race) that gave meaning to political communities. These ideas were "of comparatively minor significance in the overall system"—that is, his projected "System of *Staatslehre*"—but in order to make them "comprehensible," he would have to undertake a presentation of the materials followed by an analysis. To do so adequately would "lead to a serious quantitative disproportion among the parts of the system." To deal with this problem of "disproportion" as well as the familiar one of combining the presentation of relatively unfamiliar materials with the analysis of them, Voegelin separated out his analysis of body ideas and especially the race idea, "which is of paramount importance at the present time," from the legal arguments that would constitute the "System of *Staatslehre,*" the "complete *Staatslehre,*" the "*Herrschaftslehre,*" or whatever Voegelin eventually might have named the finished project.

Voegelin's remarks in *Race and State* are important in the present context because they indicate how he understood the limited purpose of *Staatslehre* and what a more comprehensive argument would entail. First of all, his explanation of the genesis of *Race and State* indicated both its "systematic intent" and its connection to "the fundamental idea of the system of *Staatslehre,* namely, that the roots of the state must be sought in the nature of man." Thus the great challenge for *Staatslehre* was to develop the argument "on the basis of a philosophical anthropology" that would deal with four major topics. Voegelin then provided a "cursory overview."

First he considered the phenomenon of law. The origins of law were found in the moral experience of the individual and also in the experience of the community. From the former came the sense of what ought to be done, and here Voegelin referred to his article on "the ought" (*das Sollen*) in Kant's system (*CW* 8:180ff), which is discussed below. From the latter came the "universality of the norm that renders it obligatory for a majority of persons." From these two experiences arose the "norm," which was "an anticipatory design for future actions" that pervaded the whole legal system.

Second, therefore, was the question of the norm, which became particularized in any one community through other fundamental experiences, "namely those of ruling and serving," the most obvious subject matter of *Herrschaftslehre.* "Systematically speaking," Voegelin said, "the *Herrschaftslehre* is the second part of a *Staatslehre,*" the first being the elaboration of a philosophical anthropology. The *Herrschaftslehre* "serves to delimit the specific action by which the community constitutes itself as having political existence (Carl Schmitt)." Here Voegelin referred to his review essay of Schmitt's *Verfassungslehre* just discussed, and to contemporary sociologists for their "significant contributions," but, he added, "a complete restoration of this great theme" of ruling and serving was possible only by "returning to Nietzsche and Fichte and especially to the *Herrschaftslehre* of antiquity," by which he meant Plato and Aristotle and also Augustine.

Third was the "legal order" that arose at the intersection of the norm and the governmental organization of the community. It had two dimensions: (1) the regulation of community members with each other and (2) the regulation of the community as a political body. Historically the former was handled by the natural rights tradition with the emphasis being on liberty and property. However, the dogmatic form taken by the natural rights tradition, in the texts of Hobbes and Locke, for example, needed to be transformed into "an analysis of existential experiences" that would explain why the regulation of liberty and property was part of any legal order. Regulating the actions of the political community involved "the problems of the idea of the state and the form of the state." These "ideas" helped to constitute the reality of the state and were derived from these same "existential experiences." Some of these experiences, in turn, were developed from Christianity—equality, for example. Others, which Voegelin called "Germanic ideas," were not. One way or another "body ideas" were involved in the constitution of the community as a *body* politic, whether in the form of a dynasty, blood lineage and kinship, the mystical body of Christ, or race.

Finally, he said in this introduction to *Race and State,* a system of *Staatslehre* must describe the structure of the legal system, its legal principles, institutions, and constitutional documents, which explained how the principles upon which the state was founded were translated into positive law. This was the most external or elemental understanding of law.

Voegelin's "overview" of his system of *Staatslehre* was in some respects the antithesis of post-1871 German thinking on the question which, as we noted, considered *Staatslehre* to be a tributary of constitutional law. By that traditional account, the "systematic center" of *Staatslehre* was found not in the fundamental experiences, and thus in philosophical anthropology, but in the final product of those experiences, the positive or elemental law, which presupposes all the other parts—the theory of norms, *Herrschaftslehre,* and so on. The critical argument Voegelin made in his 1924 article on the pure theory of law and *Staatslehre* discussed above was thus being reiterated in a more pointed way. "The basic problems are dealt with," he said, "not on their own ground but only as they are reflected in the contents of positive law, and therefore they are *of necessity* seen in a distorted way." Jellinek's *Staatslehre,* which Voegelin admired because of its contents, nevertheless was unable to account for *why* the purpose of the state or the problem of evil had to be included—except on the traditional grounds that they had previously been included in prior works of the same general type. That is, Jellinek developed his *Staatslehre* in the absence of a philosophical anthropology.

Voegelin reiterated that the clearest example of the problem was Kelsen's pure theory of law. It provided a good account of the theory of law, of its validity, and of its content, but it grew progressively less satisfactory as it tried to deal with the form of the state or with its animating ideas, to say nothing about the origin of the "normative sphere" in human nature. By purging *Staatslehre* of everything other than positive law, Kelsen was consistent, and this consistency brought the other aspects of *Staatslehre* "into view with a clarity they never had before." Kelsen's consistency thus had the unintended consequence of drawing attention to what he did not do—namely develop a comprehensive "system of *Staatslehre*" on the basis of a philosophical anthropology.

While developing the arguments of his *Herrschaftslehre,* in 1931, in a contribution to Kelsen's *Festschrift,* Voegelin discussed Kant's "ought" (*CW* 8:180–227). As many commentators have remarked, for Kant "ought is not a random philosophical topic beside others, but the one phenomenon of our existence that aroused him so profoundly that his entire philosophizing welled up from the ground of this arousal" (*CW* 8:217). Voegelin gave a thorough account of the twofold content of the moral law, namely the duty to act in such a way that suprasensory or intelligible nature comes into view and to respect the ends in oneself and one's neighbors as members of a community. Three points in this analysis were significant for our present purposes.

First, if legal theory were just the science of positive law and nothing more, there would be no need to take obligation or the "ought" into account. The ought matters only "when we expand the idea of legal theory beyond that of a theory of science and seek to understand the phenomenon of law in the context of the totality of our experience of the state." And that, of course, was just what Voegelin sought to do. With respect to the "phenomenon of law" it was necessary to approach it first of all in its "primary constitution" as a product of the spirit, and not by way of the "synthetic and secondary constitution" as a product of science. The conclusion, which has been encountered before, is that a proper analysis of the ought "is possible only within the purview of an all-embracing philosophical view of the essence of man," that is, a philosophical anthropology. And apart from Nietzsche, there had been no serious philosophizing since the early nineteenth century. Hence a "return to Kant" may expose the problem of the moral law and of the ought, which may indicate it to be a problem independent of Kant's time and place and thus may serve as a basis for what is absent in contemporary legal theory. Voegelin then provided an exposition of Kant's teaching concerning obligation and concluded that contemporary legal thought was so deeply connected to natural law—of property, for example—that the connection between a Kantian ought and the foundation of human or civil rights had not yet been made.

Second, and notwithstanding the elegance of Kant's theory of obligation, it was combined with "the extraordinary poverty of Kant's image of man and society. Corporeality, nobility, political reality, and history are not regarded as essential contents of existence but are collectively dismissed with a derogatory gesture as sensuous being and contrasted with a nearly empty core of existence" (*CW* 8:224). Kant simply ignored "blood and lineage" and thus "the essential foundations of society." He ignored body and blood as conditions of the noble life and thus he provides no place for their laws in his ethics. Partly as a consequence, the relations between the individual and the community, as members of the community went about internalizing the moral law, were rather insipid.

Somehow the contents of the moral law evoked both the outline of the ideal state and the typical features of the kind of human being for whom the idea would be a guide to the kind of action that would bring him closer to the ideal.

> This person is "well-disposed," with a slightly commercial tinge to his convictions, because in assuming the idea of freedom, he does so well aware of "his true advantage," but also with his "heart" in this practical interest. Disinclined to adventures, he cannot be satisfied with floating in the infinite regress of conditions "with one foot in midair at all times." He prefers a secure beginning in order then to move straight ahead, accompanied by the comforts of leisure and the feeling of having his back covered. As we have already heard, these people do not amount to much; Kant occasionally says of them that they are cut from such crooked wood that it would be difficult to make something entirely straight from them. (*CW* 8:219–20)

Such people did not move toward the ideal as individuals but apparently only as part of a collectivity, "bound together within a community with specific laws."

Finally we note what Voegelin called the "almost impolite haste" with which, in *The Critique of Pure Reason,* Kant moved from concern with "the primordial mover of the world" to human being. The standard for such a discussion was provided by

> the meditations of Saint Augustine on the relation between *creator* and *creatura.* Just as Kant does, Augustine also investigates the cosmological question of the beginning of the world, of the entire *creatura* together with its time, even though for him, too, human beings are the most important of the *creatura*'s parts. Yet with what devotion does Augustine delve into the details of the relation between the eternal creator and the temporality of the world, continually seeking and finding ever new and pertinent formulas by which to capture *aeternitas* and *permanere* in their persistence beyond the flux of time. How suffused with the experience of creaturely lowliness is his talk of the *distentio animi,* the disintegrated state of the spirit from which he must return in *intentio* toward the divinity. Compared to this modesty, the impulses behind Kant's thought

> become clearer. When Kant, having only just alluded to the puzzle of divine spontaneity, quickly returns to his little god, the spontaneous man, we sense an obsession with the this-worldly spontaneity of human action and its obligatory law.

In other words, Kantian philosophical anthropology, for all its merits and for all its importance *in absentia* from legal theory, is less comprehensive than the account of human being and of the "cosmological question" found in Augustine.

When Voegelin turned to his account of the relationship of the primordial mover of the world to human being, his first task was "To Determine the Concept of the Person." To a considerable extent it consisted of a detailed discussion of passages from St. Augustine (*CW* 32:226ff).

Voegelin observed in his study of the ought in Kant's system that "the informed reader will easily notice the close affinity of my analyses to those of others, especially those of Scheler" (*CW* 8:181n1). Moreover, as William Petropulos has argued persuasively, "Voegelin's reading of Max Scheler in the *Herrschaftslehre* is intimately involved with his reception of the thought of St. Augustine."[7] Finally, because the ostensible subject matter of the *Herrschaftslehre* is command and obedience, and because command and obedience includes the spiritual existence of the individual person, then "a fundamental form of philosophical thinking" is needed to account for the person and the relationship of the person to the theory of governance (*CW* 32:226). St. Augustine's *City of God* can also be read as an example of *Herrschaftslehre* in the ancient Western world that, Voegelin indicated, was more comprehensive than contemporary efforts. Perhaps most importantly, Augustine undertook the "fundamental form of philosophical thinking" that, following Descartes, Voegelin called "meditation." Voegelin proposed to indicate "what takes place during a meditation and what its essential characteristics are" by providing an exegesis of "the classical model that has been praised and followed for investigations into the essence of the person and time," namely books 10 and 11 of Augustine's *Confessions.* The purpose of a meditation is not to develop a superior concept of God or of time or anything similar, but to experience divine or temporal reality. Necessarily that experience will include the discovery of the meditating individual as a "person," to use Scheler's term.

Let us then follow Augustine's argument as recapitulated by Voegelin. To begin with, Augustine did not start by postulating a concept of the soul or of God, but with the experience of seeking a direction in the absence of rational indices or argument. He was searching not for a conceptual account of God but for the much more concrete experience of peace in his soul. So meditation is the "step-by-step elimination of all that is unsettling, all that is merely world-immanent." The sought-for "place" of tranquility was defined only by what has been passed through, that is negatively in the sense that the soul has passed beyond unsettling places. The "things of the world" are negated—and yet, as Augustine said, the world is still the creation of God and not an alien thing.

The course of meditation is neither subjective nor "an arbitrary wandering but strictly determined by the structure of being." Indeed the strictness and the discipline of the meditative experience must persuade the person doing the meditation that the path was the right one and the goal found was the one sought. "The meditation proceeds from the world of the senses and passes through all of its levels upwards toward the soul, where it penetrates to the soul's core. From the core of the soul follows the crossing over [*Überschritt*] to God." Voegelin then summarized Augustine's formulation of the meditative context within which God was sought, from the body to the memory of memory and the mind that remembered that it remembers. "The meditation comes to a provisional end in a definition of the core of the person [*Personkern*] as the reiteration of memory."

Even awareness of the *Personkern* was not, however, the genuine goal of the meditation but was rather a world-immanent and changeable reality that in turn must be transcended in the direction of what is permanent and has "no place," because it is beyond all places and all things that are predicable. In book 10 of the *Confessions,* which Voegelin was discussing, the imagery was spatial; in book 11, it was temporal. The result, however, was the same—the soul seeks not a place (or time) of repose but an eternal sabbath. And just as the place of God is beyond all places, so is the time of God beyond all time, even while God creates both the places and times where humans act. That is, the meditation led to a consideration of creature and creator and gave rise to a consideration of the relationship between the two that, Augustine remarked, was possible only if certain "idle questions" were avoided. These include the puzzles of the village atheist: What did God do before he created the world? Why did God create the world when he did? One can think of others. These questions merely emphasized the distinction between creature and creator even as they illustrated the clever silliness of the questioner. The reason is obvious: God's duration for Augustine was not subject to temporal extension and neither was his "place" anywhere.

Thus would the meditator come to understand: "I am not with Him, but immersed in becoming, in moral decay, and in time." He also would understand that the person was "the point of intersection between divine eternity and human temporality; in the person finitude is revealed as the essence of the world. The person is the experience of the limits demarcating world-immanent finiteness from the transcendent infinite." The procedure whereby world-immanent concepts such as space and time lost their intuitive meaning when applied to the infinite Voegelin called "dialectical." This loss of intuitive meaning was expressed verbally (and paradoxically) "by the simultaneous positing and negating."

Voegelin then compared Augustine's meditation and theory of the person with more modern ones exemplified by Descartes, who, at least with respect to "the personal existential character" of the experience, attained "greater clarity" (*CW* 32:239).[8] Augustine, Voegelin said, was searching for a point where the soul might find peace; Descartes sought a point of certainty from which knowledge might be constructed concerning the world. Augustine's concern was the relationship between creator and creation; Descartes' between the subject of cognition and the world. As with Augustine, Descartes' "skeptical meditation" followed a rigorous path as well, only not with respect to the structure of being but with respect to "the structure of being that is to be exposed to doubt." Likewise Husserl clarified certain aspects of Descartes that were unclear in Descartes' understanding of the person by focusing on the intentionality of consciousness.

> All consciousness is essentially the consciousness of something; a perceiving is a perceiving of a thing, judging is a judging of a predicatively formed affair-complex; valuing of a predicatively formed value-complex; a wishing of a predicatively formed value-complex. Acting bears upon action. Doing bears upon the deed, loving bears upon the loved one, being glad bears upon the gladsome. (*CW* 32:246)

Finally, Voegelin undertook a highly technical analysis of Husserl's phenomenological argument and its connection to that of Descartes, the conclusion of which was to emphasize the importance of "an existential, philosophical process on the part of a concrete human being" that began with the actual concrete life of the individual and ascended to the intelligible meditation of the thinker. That is, for Voegelin at this time, Husserl's great achievement was to have restored the centrality of the actual or of the concrete experience of the individual thinker.

This first chapter of the *Herrschaftslehre,* "To Determine the Concept of the Person," was unfinished; it broke off in mid-sentence. Even so, it did both provide an argument about what a fundamental form of philosophizing with respect to the person would entail as well as exemplify what such an argument might be by the exegesis of St. Augustine's texts. The second chapter, "The Powerful and the Powerless Person" (*CW* 32:255), raised the question: What can rationally be said about "the phenomenon of governance [or rule] by human beings over other human beings and about the corresponding acts of obedience?" On the basis of the arguments regarding the person in the first chapter, especially the notion that the person "is the experience of the limits demarcating world-immanent finiteness from the transcendent infinite" (*CW* 32:236), some kinds of government are to be excluded: for example, force and the threat of force to motivate obedience on the grounds of fear holds the person in contempt, much as a rule by custom or ideology or even traditions is indifferent to the person. The central problem for a theory of governance, therefore, was to reconcile the theory of the person with the self-evident necessities of command and obedience, of ruler and ruled.

To deal with this question, Voegelin first looked at the arguments of the sociologist Alfred Vierkant and his notion of an "instinct" of subordination. This might explain subordination based on fear, he said, but not on law, which must be based on "respect" and thus belongs to the realm of the spirit rather than causal instinct. That is, the follower obeys a command because he is convinced of its value and necessity. One component of the spiritual content of governance, Vierkant said, was subordination to the "law of meaning" and the agreement of the subordinate to abide by the order of this law. Unfortunately, Voegelin commented, "the very delicate ethical problem," namely the concrete meaning involved in this law, was not discussed by Vierkant.

A second argument was provided by Eduard Spranger, for whom the life of the man of power was manifest as (1) "the vital self-assertion of his own nature in the form of a primordial drive" because (2) the powerful person desired "to have the validity of his will acknowledged." However, he said that (3) "true power" was "based on a genuine source of value." Voegelin concluded that this third attribute dealt with the concept of the person as elaborated in chapter 1.

> When a person is at one with himself [*ganz bei sich selbst*], he is simultaneously open to a super-personal [*überpersonale*] sphere. When one is in possession of one's self, one possesses simultaneously more than oneself. In manifesting one's self, one also manifests what transcends the self. Those persons are powerful who manage to live in self-possession [*bei sich*] and thus transcend themselves. Personal power is a fullness of personal being [*das Person-sein*]. This content of the experience of the person [*die Personserfahrung*], which can only be formulated dialectically, appears to me to be the utmost that we can say in the analysis of power. (*CW* 32:261)

This formulation introduced another issue: if the essence of power were found in the fullness of personal being, then there could be no place for command because the one in command could not know what was the right thing for the powerless to do. If he could have such knowledge, he would be essentially identical with the powerless. This would mean that the pair—the commander and the obedient—together constituted the "value-whole" because the obedient one would already know what to do without being ordered. Readers of Hegel can detect in Voegelin's argument an early criticism of Hegel's famous dialectic of Master and Slave.

Voegelin looked to Scheler to supplement Spranger's argument, which did not specify how the obedient would understand what to do, by arguing that "it is not necessary that the individual attain autonomous insight into good and evil himself." Rather, insight may be mediated by tradition, authority, and so on. One way or another, we must gain insight into the moral superiority of another and follow him. As a consequence, "we can say that a relationship of governance that is founded on personal power may be characterized as a relationship between persons of different existential fullness, such as the existentially weaker person adopts the law of his or her conduct from his model, or the direst command he receives from the existentially stronger person." But how could a superpersonal moral authority, into which a genuine ruler has insight, be compatible with the personal individuality of both ruler and ruled? The answer, said Voegelin, "will remain obscure, for here lies the seed of evil that clings to all power." With that enigmatic remark, chapter 2 abruptly ended.

Voegelin discussed to this point the notion of the person and the "superpersonal moral reality" of the community to which the person was related. Governance required cooperation between ruler and ruled or between commander and obedient in order to exist. Because the person was open to the full range of experience, including the experience of divine presence, and because the person interpreted himself and his situation within a common world of symbols, governance therefore appeared to involve a spiritual as well as an institutional or "mechanical" hierarchy. That is, governance had to take into account the different spiritual gifts of all members of the community. To anticipate slightly, "good governance" would accord proper respect to those who most fully actualized the "core of the person." Voegelin's argument was essentially that of Plato's *Republic.*

Chapter 3, "Basic Types of Theories of Governance," combined several pages on Max Weber that were originally to be part of chapter 2 plus considerable additional material not included in the original outline (see *CW* 32:268ff and 225 as well as the editors' introduction, 8ff). This chapter combined the chief insight of chapter 1, regarding the person, with that of chapter 2, regarding a moral or spiritual hierarchy.

For Weber, commands originated in the will of the commander, but obedience followed because "there apparently exists between the person who commands and the person who obeys a relationship of legitimacy and recognition of legitimacy." Legitimacy did not depend either on the insistence of the commander or on the "personal view" of the obedient. Given the importance of the person as established by the philosophical anthropology outlined in chapter 1, Voegelin returned to an earlier observation: It would not be acceptable to say that the obedient one (B) absolved himself or herself of responsibility by granting the commander (A) moral authority. "This amounts . . . to an expansion of A's action radius at the price of absorbing and instrumentalizing B's person," which could not be legitimate. Moreover, it was "a specifically legal way of looking at things" by constructing a chain of command whose whole purpose was to instrumentalize. "But in the sphere where human beings actually exist [*Dasein wirklichkeit*], there is no 'extinguishing'" of the moral person. Every human being existed in all modes of being, including moral being, even if he were in a command-and-obedience relationship.

Because all human beings are moral persons, obedience must also be an act of moral obligation. That meant that both A and B were part of a moral community where both experienced their respective actions as the realization of a moral whole. The existence of the moral whole required a "legend" that created a justification of the difference between A and B that allowed both to see that difference as legitimate. But this argument introduced additional questions regarding the "moral whole." What is it? To what extent is it held in common? How does power fit into this moral whole? Above all, what are the essential constituent elements of humanity?

Voegelin found an answer in the arguments of his teacher Othmar Spann. "The human being is a spiritual being [*Geistwesen*] open to a super-personal spiritual reality" that Spann called "the world of ideas." Humans were open to this world through the gift of intuition, the basis of which is mysterious. That is, Spann assumed the openness of existence to a superpersonal spirit. It was a "known fundamental" of existence. From this assumption he proceeded to a metaphysical one that "existence is historically concrete and continues through time." Any reservations regarding the reality of this superpersonal spirit derived from an "object-oriented theory of society" for which there no evidence. Indeed, daily experience indicates just the opposite. Because we must consider a superpersonal spirit in any theory of governance we can be persuaded of the validity of the metaphysical assumption of an "objective spirit." As was discussed above in Chapter 1 of this book, we do so for the same reasons that natural scientists adopt the metaphysical assumption regarding the reality of "nature."

Here Voegelin summarized a methodological insight that he borrowed from Spann and retained for the rest of his work: "Of course we cannot view the objective spirit that is present in the historical world as real and continuous becoming, as timeless [being] in itself; but as scientists [we can] only approach it through the scientific treatment of it in historical reality." That is, the "objective spirit" is not akin to a phenomenal object—it is after all a mode of *Geist.* The reality of the objective spirit thus belongs to its historical appearances; it is, accordingly, both superpersonal *(überpersonale)* because it is independent of the individual person, and personal in the sense that it exists in human consciousness (*CW* 32:289–89; *CW* 1:17).

Voegelin then provided a straightforward account of the "liminal experiences" of finite consciousness opening toward the outside and the meditative elucidation of such experiences along with the accompanying moods of hope, anxiety, heroism, calm, and so on. These experiences could never be exhaustively accounted for using subject-object perceptual terminology or an "object-oriented" language even though, grammatically, we may have to use words that way. "We must remain conscious of this aporia," Voegelin said, "which belongs to the essence of existential thought, in order to understand why the problem of power has not been satisfactorily treated up to now." The reason was relatively simple: Unlike the objective spirit of a work of art, for example, the creative center of the state did not exist externally but only "in the variety of the realizing acts between ruler and ruled that are coordinated with one another." That is, with a work of art, one can distinguish the superpersonal spirit (for example, romanticism) from the openness of the artist as well as from the artist's product. In contrast, since the spiritual structure of governance included the openness of the commanded or ruled existences as well as that of the ruler, the question of openness itself necessarily must come into focus. The reason, quite simply, is that, unlike a work of art, "the state . . . is never finished." It is also why the *threat* of the use of force is evidence of successful governance, not its application, which is purely physical or mechanical, not spiritual. That is, internal command or rule is by authority, not force.

Voegelin illustrated this stage of his argument in an analysis of the position of Jacques Necker's *Philosophical Reflections on Equality,* a polemical and reactionary critique of the French revolutionary ideas of liberty and equality. In the language of Spann that Voegelin was using, Necker rejected "the thesis that all human beings participate directly and equally in the objective spirit." Voegelin also argued that no one is sufficiently distinguished that "next to him, all other human beings can only participate in the objective spirit through obedience." Notwithstanding differences in spiritual, intellectual, or even physical gifts, the problem of determining the content of government was not an academic exercise that followed certain procedures but a matter of "intuition" on the part of social and political participants.

> It is not the scholar who knows what is objectively valid, but those participating in social reality at concrete points in the course of history. Because of the fact that, in an act of intuition, all participants are principally capable of grasping what is objectively valid, [and because of] the impossibility of that intuition being either proven or refuted, differences of opinion over the correctness of the ruler's action are in principle always possible. This can occur because among the ruled there are persons who insist that they know better than the rulers what is valid and right, or because there are persons who though they themselves do not know what is right, nevertheless believe that, judging by the consequences of the rulers' actions, they can say with certainty that the rulers do not know either. (*CW* 32:313)

Accordingly, the validity of any government can, in principle, be questioned by people with their own valid insights who disagree with the rulers, by others who agree with the rulers but seek a more perfect actualization of what the rulers only imperfectly have achieved, and by the "rabble," who constitute a special category to be discussed below. Moreover, at any one time there may be several potential actualizations of the objective spirit. There can be only one that is in fact actual, which means it has suppressed other possibilities: There were possible poets at Sparta but no actual ones. "Suppressed discourses" as Michel Foucault might have said, are inevitable. Historical realizations of the spirit "are no less impenetrable than bodies in space—where one has established itself, there is room for no other." As with Aristotle's discussion of *politeiai,* there can be but one regime at a time. As a result, even a perfect realization of one particular spirit could not entail everlasting peace and harmony, because it existed only by the suppression of people who bore witness to another spirit. And those who lived by another spirit would see in the realization of the dominant spirit nothing but evil, and so a spirit to be resisted, perhaps to the point of revolution, the risk of life, and death.

Of particular importance were the spiritually disoriented rabble who could see nothing in the rulers but the threat and use of force and so would always be ready to rebel. The spirit that the rulers actualized, whatever it may be, would always be antithetical to those whose spirit was disordered because "the notion of governance as inner governance is incomprehensible to them." Thus they must be controlled externally or mechanically, and so by force. The rabble, for Voegelin, were Plato's *demos,* the persons ruled by ever-changing desires. Politically speaking, they constituted a bottomless reservoir for change and revolution because they embodied nothing beyond the potential to be other than any given order, whatever it may be. For the rabble, any rule was evil.

The intractability of the rabble provided a genuine appeal for leaders who would follow the reactionary program (in this case of Necker) and shoulder the burden of morality and spirituality on their behalf. This "escape from freedom," as Eric Fromm later called the problem, cut off the individual from responsibility for his own decisions regarding good and evil. For Nietzsche, Voegelin argued, the entire issue of morality was rendered superfluous; in Dostoyevsky's "Legend of the Grand Inquisitor," the same result was obtained by a deliberate betrayal of moral choice and responsibility on the part of a leader who claimed superior knowledge and insight. But as was just noted, it is not a question of a superior knowing "what is objectively valid" because "all participants" are equally capable of such insight or "intuition," as Spann and Voegelin called it.

At the end of chapter 2 of the *Herrschaftslehre,* Voegelin spoke of "the seed of evil that clings to all power." With Nietzsche and the Grand Inquisitor, we find illustration of that remark: Physical force seems to be a necessary accompaniment of political power because of that aspect of human nature most vividly expressed in the rabble. In this respect, the Grand Inquisitor was the paradigm of the totalitarian ruler insofar as he claimed to improve or correct the religious or spiritual predicament of human existence.[9]

> Herein lies the "mystery," as Dostoyevsky calls it, which must remain obscure; here is the source of evil in governance that becomes evil at the very moment when it tries to do its best for the weak by giving them the happiness they are capable of receiving. Here we reach the theme at

> the root of the problem of governance: the ultimate fact of the closeness to or distance from God, which is ours by no action of our own; or, in our terminology, to the human being's closeness to or distance from the spirit. (*CW* 32:330)

Granted that "the problem of evil clings to all power," we must not lose sight of the fact that it does not cling as tightly or as extensively or in the same way to all regimes or all forms of power. Some regimes are worse than others. Or, as was noted above, good governance must be founded on "the fundamental state of the human being," namely "the human being's openness to divinity." This, too, was not a mere academic argument. Voegelin claimed that such a regime was actually described in Frederick Wolters's pamphlet *Governance and Service* and that it referred to his experience and understanding of the poet Stefan George and his circle. By Wolters's argument, the servant in communion with the spirit of governance in the ruler would be transformed "into a member of the empire and [would bring] his entire internal and external being into a deep, unshakable relationship with the ruler." In this way the servant attained the height of enduring service. At the same time, "any type of revelation or dogmatic secret doctrine is energetically rejected." Instead, all one could say was that the moment of communion—between the servant and the ruler as between the ruler and the divine—"is followed by the enduring state of being moved and inspired by the law of the spirit that orders one's life." The ruler, who has the exceptional constitution that allowed him to commune with the divinity, was filled with a love for his fellows and a desire to let them participate so far as is possible, in his condition. Accordingly, the

> extension of the ruler's power over the servant and the creation of an empire is not achieved against the individual's will, but is the result of loving communication and an embrace that touches the essential core of the weaker partner and wakens his powers and inspires him with a burning passion to attain the highest goals he can reach. Service is not subjection to an incomprehensible external power, but an opening of the soul and spirit in piety and understanding to the point of surrender in which the servant wins back himself, strengthened, inspired, and able to let the best in him come to fruition. (*CW* 32:341)

Voegelin was fully aware that his discussion of rulership was unlikely to find a favorable response among current practitioners of *Staatslehre.* He was also aware that post–French revolutionary fantasies of "the society of equal citizens without the need for rulers" would make his more ample and spiritual theory of governance seem both impossible and undesirable. In fact, as he had indicated early in his study, modern *Herrschaftslehre* had to be augmented by classical *Herrschaftslehre.* To simplify somewhat, Voegelin was reiterating the argument of Aristotle: Men are both equal and unequal, and governance must take both aspects into account. If equality only were emphasized without the greater spiritual insight of the ruler, and thus his inequality, then the result was bound to be not peaceful equality without governance, the liberal and bourgeois dream, but mechanical dominance by the ruthless and physically unequal. "The noble life and knowledge of the science of the state characterize the ruler. Overflowing with love he bends toward the less gifted human beings in order to give their lives purpose and meaning through example, that they may imitate in service." The governor governed in splendor while taking the burdens of rule upon himself, serving the servants, who in turn piously attempted, fully aware of their weaker constitution, to be happy in a life that was gained when they surrendered the empty freedom of life without governance.

Voegelin's conclusion was essentially Platonic. Governance was understood to mean "the leadership of those with less understanding by those with superior understanding" and thus became "salvation from the state of servitude and mutual destruction" (*CW* 32:354). His reflections were clearly neither those of an "academic" elitist nor those of a dogmatic liberal democrat so much as those of a character he later would call a "spiritual realist" (*CW* 21:70ff), that is, a person who understood that the search for despiritualized happiness would gain nothing but despiritualized brutality, which is to say, the reduction of the entire political community to the level of the spiritually disoriented "rabble."

Moreover, the many references to Plato's *Republic* and especially to his "Phoenician lie," which contained the myth of equality and inequality (see Voegelin's later treatment in *CW* 16:158ff), were an indication that Voegelin sought to recast the Classical teaching into contemporary German *Geisteswissenschaft.* In the event, Voegelin's effort was as futile as Plato's. It did, however, return us to the original theme of chapter 1, the centrality of meditation as a way to comprehend and perhaps to reconcile the inequalities and equalities of human beings—of which Plato's Phoenician tale is paradigmatic expression.

Today, however, one would not discuss the problem of governance in terms of a Phoenician tale or lie—nor, indeed, in terms of the progress or actualization of reason or the rational personality, as one might have done, for example, in Kant's time, or earlier in the eighteenth century. The reason, Voegelin said, was not because of any theoretical or philosophical limitations to (for example) Kant's argument, whatever faults can later be discovered in it, but because of a much more commonsensical and, indeed, empirical observation: "The differences between national types of mind [today] are so patently obvious" (*CW* 32:358). These differences, which had been expressed on the battlefields of the Great War, were apparent to Voegelin from his earliest writings and were confirmed emphatically by his experience in America.

As a consequence of the current historical configuration of "national types of mind," we must describe them "in terms of psyche, of character, and of spiritual content." Today what was common to both rulers and ruled was the "nation" that, because it was grounded in human beings, could be described in terms of "the physical and emotional features of the people who belong to it," which is to say the "spirit" of the people. Such an approach, Voegelin said, could tell us about the essence of a specific nation, but not what the "substance" of a nation might be beyond the specific phenomena because "only the phenomenal forms of the self-manifesting entity are given to our direct perception," and not the entity itself. Compared to the meditative openness to reality of Plato, to the rational universalism of Kant, or even to the attractions of Stefan George, the spirit of the nation was a "closed" source of meaning.

In the work of Carl Schmitt, particularly *The Concept of the Political,* Voegelin found a thorough account of the "phenomenal form" of the (closed) political, a "more consistent" theory of the source of power than "traditional accounts" that considered only one of the forms of power—spiritual content, type of personality, legal order, and so on—as essential. For Schmitt the essential unit was rulers-and-ruled. Thus the state could not explain the political but rather assumed its existence because, as Schmitt said, the "state is the political status of a people."[10] For Voegelin, however, this formula was "insufficiently radical," because it assumed a people could exist prior to the political when in fact it could not be understood without reference to the political, which is "the integral unity of the power substance," referred to in *The New Science of Politics* in terms of "articulation" (*CW* 5:116ff). With reference to the "power substance," Schmitt was, however, "very clear." His analysis was found in the famous category of "the antithesis of friend-enemy."

This category was to politics what "good-evil" was to ethics, "beautiful-ugly" was to aesthetics, or "profitable-unprofitable" was to economics. That is to say, *who* is friend and *who* is enemy "cannot be determined by external criteria" but was inherent in the process of political articulation. This category, moreover, explained the significance of war as an existential threat to one's way of life, one's national form of mind, and so on. That is, the political enemy was simply the other against whom the articulated community must fight. For Schmitt, therefore, the notion that the Great War was, as President Wilson announced, a "war to end war," was an "obvious fraud." As to the substance of a political entity, of a whole that bound individuals into a community, all one could say was that, in Schmitt's words, "it exists or does not exist." And Voegelin commented: "I truly do not know what more can be said about a substance we cannot define; we know nothing about it except that it inspires unity among men in the form of a community for which they are willing to die" (*CW* 32:366).

Voegelin did not know what more could be said but "there are others who do," notably Helmut Plessner, whose speculations might "for the last time, deepen our theme" (*CW* 32:367). In his review of Plessner's book (*CW* 13:38–41), Voegelin drew attention to Plessner's exceptionally dense language in *Power and Human Nature;* this observation applied as well to Voegelin's discussion of it. Plessner's objective was to bring politics and the spirit *(Geist)* into proximity by way of philosophy and, incidentally, situate Schmitt's argument in a larger context.

The question under consideration was the mode of existence of a whole that bound individuals into a community for which they were prepared to die, which was also a form of "service" in Wolters's sense. The most obvious difference between the existence of a community and the existence of the individual was that "we cannot meditatively arrive at the point where this existence, in its original structure, is given to us in experience" (*CW*

32:367). It nevertheless existed as a whole in virtue of the argument concerning governance. In his later work, Voegelin adopted a term coined by Adolf Stöhr in 1921, "cosmion" (*CW* 19:18), to refer to this "whole" composed of individuals open to the "objective spirit." In the *Herrschaftslehre* Voegelin formulated the problem in terms of Plessner's language, which referred to "vertical" and "horizontal" transcendence.

The difference between the two, again to simplify somewhat, was that with individuals, spiritual openness could be experienced personally and so had a direction toward the divine that was indicated by the term *vertical.* In contrast, the "beyond" of the community, including the one for which the individual was prepared to die, was a historical "super-personal existence" that was represented as a horizontal line. As with the notion of "objective spirit" discussed above, Plessner's distinction of vertical and horizontal modes of transcendence may not have been entirely satisfactory. It did, however, serve a provisionally useful purpose of distinguishing different aspects of superpersonal or sociohistorical reality.

The final section of Voegelin's *Herrschaftslehre,* identified by him as part II, was titled "Theory of Law." So far as our present problem is concerned, it amounted to a brief postscript inasmuch as the subject matter was confined to positive law. The intention of modern positive legal theory, Voegelin said, was "to analyze the a priori content of positive law in order to determine the form that every content must assume in order to become law." Accordingly, the actual content was irrelevant; what counted was the form of a specific social phenomenon called law. Likewise, therefore, the unity of any system of law did not depend on content but on organizational coherence. Thus every law-positing act must refer to a legitimizing legal principle, which referred to another until a fundamental positing principle, which Voegelin called (following Kelsen's usage) the basic norm, came into sight. The origin of the system of law, which the *Herrschaftslehre* intended to explore, necessarily transcended the law and was external to any particular system of law.

Historically, as we have seen, positive law and natural law or the "law of reason" were distinct and could come together only when legislatures had recourse to natural law, discovered by rational insight, as a "supplement" to positive law. This, Voegelin said, was the principle informing nineteenth-century law codes so that, if there were a conflict between positive and natural law, it was historical only, and not a conflict of principle. When the historical cause of the conflict was understood, it disappeared. The notion that positive law gradually approximated natural law presupposed a philosophy of history that tied the two together. There followed a lengthy and wide-ranging discussion of Kant, Hegel, Hobbes, Schelling, Schiller, Kierkegaard, Nietzsche, and Bergson, to name only the most important. Voegelin did not, however, come to a conclusion, and the manuscript ended abruptly.

Before we take up the question of philosophy of history, let me suggest the significance of this sprawling and roughly hewn manuscript. The most obvious comment is that for readers who have familiarized themselves with Voegelin's postwar style and with his concern with political ideas, then with later formulations of symbolization and experiences of reality, or even his late meditative philosophy of consciousness, understanding, let alone understanding the significance of these early writings, is a formidable problem. At one point Voegelin provided a summary of his argument that may be of assistance (*CW* 32:356ff).

Starting from the "state of affairs" of commanding and obeying, he analyzed the theories that accounted for such practices, and for the institution of the state, by means of which commanding and obeying concretely takes place. The question of governance raised the issue of what rulers and ruled had in common because, in the absence of commonality of some kind, which in his study of William James Voegelin discovered to be "likemindedness" or *homonoia,* governance would not be possible. To understand this problem from within the *Staatslehre* tradition, Voegelin analyzed several arguments concerned with law, power, the ruler's personality, openness of human existence, the objective spirit, and so on. One could explore these problems in one of two ways, either by starting from above, with the superpersonal, that is, the sphere transcending the person, and moving back to the immanent existence of the person. In plainer language, one could move from the objective spirit to the authoritative action of the ruler. In the alternative, the analysis could start from below, with the world-immanent personality of the leader opening to the world of the spirit, which the leader realized in his actions. A third mode of discourse followed the path from the ruler to the ruled and considered the problem of the instrumentality of rule over the ruled and of the ruler as protector of the ruled. In each case the analysis brought into focus the common spiritual substance shared by ruler and ruled.

The common ground, however, was disputed, which introduced the problem of the rabble who have, so to speak, no spiritual orientation at all. The problem of the rabble also brought a focus to the question of evil that, Voegelin said, clings to or accompanies all exercises of power, even that of a Platonic philosopher. Necessity seemed to require that the affirmation of a common spiritual basis for governance be followed by a means to deal with differences in spiritual proximity to the divine. These "means" included physical compulsion, which Voegelin understood as an index of human imperfection, which again accounted for the inevitable appearance of evil at the heart of governance.

Likemindedness, the common ground of ruler and ruled, was the starting point both for political science accounting for governance and for those sharing in the practice of governance. It was not, however, given directly to experience but was filtered, as it were, through the mediation of specific, concrete theoretical accounts. Moreover, those accounts change over time and place—hence the historical limitation of Plato's Phoenician tale or Kant's enlightened rationality. The reason for the inability of these older evocations to express the problems of governance, Voegelin said, was historical—namely the growth of differences among "national types of mind." We noted above that this problem had preoccupied Voegelin from the outset of his academic life. Given the recently concluded slaughter, this preoccupation was entirely understandable.

In a series of four lectures delivered in Geneva in December 1930, Voegelin brought together two topics mentioned in the *Herrschaftslehre:* philosophy of history and national types of mind (*CW* 43:430–82; see also *CW* 1:xxii–xxv). He began by drawing a contrast between Plato's analysis of the parts of the soul and the differing extent to which they were embodied in "national types" with modern philosophies of history of the Comtean or Hegelian variety. For Plato, acquisitiveness, courage, and reason, the three parts of the soul, were found in different proportions in Carthage, Scythia, and Hellas respectively. As noted above, this parallel between the soul and the "national types" was an early account of what nowadays would be called analysis of regimes. More to the point, for Plato, all types were similar in substance, although they may differ in detail, and this substantive similarity extended to the interpreter, Plato himself, otherwise the whole range of phenomena would be unintelligible.

In contrast, Comte's understanding of history as the growth of rationality or Hegel's as the growth of freedom, meant that the intelligibility and significance of the several "national types" depended on their place in the evolutionary sequence. Clearly this was unlike the Platonic scheme, where the types were intelligible "because of their substantial homogeneity with the interpreter's mind." That is, the Greek comparisons aimed to understand the Greeks themselves, and not, for example, the Scythians, whereas the modern ones sought to justify the speculators' historical context and actions taken within it. When the "law of the mind" was less grandiose than the growth of reason or of freedom, "the whole interpretation business becomes a farce" (*CW* 32:437). Here Voegelin referred to an anonymous text that divided American history into the dark ages before 1776, the glorious flowering between the time of the founding and 1900, and modern depravity. "Of course," wrote Voegelin, "the gentleman who wrote this book was able to give excellent examples of depravity before the American republic, and he could give equally excellent examples of greatness afterward—e.g., the glorious persons of Washington and Lincoln; and he could present a nice collection of corrupt practices after 1900—to demonstrate the correctness of his view. And, indeed, you could not say that he was wrong in his interpretations—the only argument against it is its utter stupidity, when we take into consideration the materials he selected and particularly those he neglected." The same argument, suitably modified, applied to Comte and Hegel, though Voegelin did not make it in detail until much later. In this lecture series, his criticisms were brief.

The significance of the Comte-Hegel scheme was that it culminated in the glorified present. The Marxist variant evoked a future perfection. All three, however, intended to help the formation of a collective consciousness, whether of the nation, the class, or something else. The difference was that the Comtean and Hegelian versions more or less assumed the current order of things and the "imperialism of the mind" was moderate enough that the nonscientific and not-yet-fully-free need only defer to their superiors rather than be exterminated because of their failures. It is safe to say that Voegelin's view of the "imperialism of the mind" in Comte and Hegel changed over the years (*CW* 5:194; *CW* 12:213ff). Not so with the Marxist variant. The "utter stupidity" of the nameless American historian, no less than the postulate discussed in the *Herrschaftslehre* that (somehow) positive law was gradually approximating natural law, likewise were intended to help the formation of a collective consciousness. These kinds of speculation, as is discussed in the following chapter, Voegelin called "political ideas."

During the nineteenth century, the growth of empirical materials, the sheer knowledge that Europeans gained about the rest of the world, made it no longer possible to organize them along Comtean, Hegelian, or Marxist lines. New methods were needed because it was self-evident that the history of humanity did not unfold along a single timeline of meaning. Instead, it was necessary to try "to work out a multitude of coordinate structural units" outside any evolutionary principle. Spengler's *Decline of the West,* for example, was an example of this kind of morphology of culture. Spengler assumed each "morphé" or structural unit was independent and developed through the same stages independent of every other one. There was no evolution among cultures, and, according to him, cultures were mutually unintelligible. Unfortunately, Voegelin said, Spengler's ignoring of the Platonic insight concerning substantive homogeneity between and among cultures rendered his own science of culture unintelligible.

By Voegelin's day, the "science of the types of mind" had solved the epistemological issue and acknowledged "the substantive homogeneity of all cultural units to be investigated as well as the fundamental differences between them according to the principle of mind that had become embodied in each one and that gives them their morphé, their unique style, from the innermost and essential phenomenon to the last and almost negligible detail." Voegelin had achieved just such an account in *On the Form of the American Mind.*

What remained to be considered was what Voegelin called the ethical activist element that was concerned not so much with national justification as with the place of the nation in a society of nations. With considerable irony, Voegelin noted that, interestingly enough, whenever a thinker, including the anonymous American, speculated on the question of the national mind, he was led to the conclusion that his particular national mind happened to be, in all modesty, the epitome of human achievement. This pattern also had existential consequences, not the least of which pertained to political science. "Political science is, therefore, rational discourse, directed objectively toward the phenomena of politics in an attempt to classify them, but always under the more or less control of national beliefs." Accordingly, it was a matter of course and to be expected that theories or accounts of politics showed the influence of the political motives that had gone into their formulation.

In other words, there could be no realm of politics in itself beyond which existed political science the way physics existed as a discourse beyond material reality. Rather, "political science itself is a part of political existence. The most important element in the existence of a state is the belief of the people in it." Thus did they accept the commands of the political leaders and ensure political unity, which in turn was a unit of analysis presupposed by political science and thereby legitimized by the discourse of political science. Voegelin's remarks amounted to a restatement of Aristotle's notion that political science was a practical science. Voegelin then provided a commonsensical example. The practical aspect of political science explained why modern Western *Staatslehre* was focused upon the theory of sovereignty whereas the political theory, or rather the *Staatslehre,* of empire tended to be an account and indeed a justification of "imperial peace," not sovereignty.

Indeed, discourse on sovereignty was inherently polemical. It was directed first against the imperial temporal and spiritual powers—the pope and the emperor—and then was deployed in favor of the position of the rulers against the ruled, the right of the prince to make laws, and the duty to suppress sedition. But even the assumptions of sovereignty may be abandoned in modern Western theories when, as we noted above in considering Voegelin's analysis of Schmitt and Laski, the importance of power eclipsed that of sovereignty. The theoretical problem, Voegelin said, was that even thinkers of the rank of Laski and Schmitt confused their own versions of politics, which were invariably also tinged with the attributes of their respective national minds, with scientific truth. This theoretical error had a pragmatic consequence because "well-considered national beliefs are but a limit to interstate relations; unreflected ones [such as confuse a particular understanding of democracy or politics with politics or democracy as such], as they are current today in Germany, England, France, the United States, Italy, and wherever you want, will put an end to them sooner or later, as they did in 1914." That is, Voegelin saw in the parochialism of national minds unaware of their parochialism both a danger to peaceful interstate relations—and he was, after all, delivering his lectures to a Geneva audience—and a defective science.

In his fourth and concluding lecture, Voegelin reminded his audience that he used the term "interstate relations" to refer to relations between national political existences, not the more normal "international relations." In this respect Voegelin said he followed Carl Schmitt, for whom states were closed political existences and "international" referred to a kind of likemindedness extending across the borders of national units, as with the Roman Catholic Church or the international Communist movement. Voegelin then translated Schmitt's distinction into his own terminology of political existences: "A political existence is conceived as a unit in terms of the type of mind found in its belief; the special sort of political existence we have to deal with is the nation-state with all its consequences for interstate relations." Voegelin's later formulation of the problem, as was noted above, borrowed the language of Adolf Stöhr and spoke of a "cosmion" or "little world of order."[11] Whatever the language used, his point was to emphasize that types of political existence other than the state were possible—and notably in the Western tradition, alternatives included the polis and the empire.

An international political existence, in the sense just indicated, was "a new phenomenon" and so far nothing more than "beliefs hanging in the air, not yet having come to constitute political existence." Were it to come into existence, present political existences with their national beliefs would have become sufficiently weakened as to be unable to resist the new reality. "As long as we have interstate relations, internationalism is a belief not yet in existence; when it comes into existence the states, and with them interstate relations, will be gone." Notwithstanding the insight afforded by Schmitt's argument, Voegelin thought Schmitt was not sufficiently reflective regarding the existence of states. That is, Schmitt's commitment to "decisionism" meant that the only reason a state existed was because it decided (somehow) to be a state. But, Voegelin asked, "who decides? Schmitt does not tell us; he says the state bears the decision within itself, thus avoiding naming the subject" (*CW* 32:477–78). The implication was clear: For Voegelin, there was no difference between decision and existence.

But what, then, of national types of mind? We have seen in Voegelin's earliest writings that he had a concern with understanding the expression of what he would by the 1930s call the British national mind as reflected in British sociology. In the third lecture, in his discussion of the account of sovereignty by Laski and by Schmitt briefly noted above, the same problem was raised. "That Laski still lives in the same sort of belief as [eighteenth-century common-sense philosopher Thomas] Reid did, just as the German writers with their problems of action and decision live in the traditional German belief, proves my point that national types of mind are rather stable and long-lived entities, and that their existence is a real factor to be reckoned with in interstate relations." Wherever national types of mind are at play, belief in the rightness of "our way," "our spirit," and the organization of such beliefs for action became paramount. "The essence of the nation-state, as of any other type of political existence, is belief, not morals and not decision" (*CW* 32:475, 478).

More to the immediate point, that Laski and Schmitt both clung to their respective beliefs without reflection as to its limit "is deeply regrettable, because mutual understanding between nations, their having a clear picture of each other's peculiar beliefs, is a first condition for relations free from distrust." Once again, the pragmatic implications of theoretical reflections within the horizon of the national mind were emphasized by Voegelin. No less than in 1924, Voegelin's recollection of the Great War was present to mind, if not top of mind.

There remained, then, the question of "internationalism," as conceptualized briefly above. The leading proponents of "internationalism" such as Lassa Oppenheim sought to combine the notion that the "Family of Nations" or "civilized nations" must establish international institutions to ensure lasting peace. Even though "progress will be slow," it was necessary and would occur only when "the international interests of all the Powers compel them to put aside their real or imaginary particular national interest."[12]

Given Voegelin's understanding of the limitations of seemingly universalist scientific accounts, whether British or German, it was not surprising that his first comment was "it is an almost hopeless task to disentangle a passage like this." The reason was almost self-evident. Nations, whether civilized or part of a "family," were interested first of all in their existence, in maintaining their belief in the justice of the national mind, or of their regime. The *ultima ratio* of any belief that has achieved political embodiment was war and the readiness of believers to die for it. That has not changed even though

> the average so-called internationalism wants to maintain national existence and at the same time abolish war, that is, to make existence and its maintenance a matter of historical accident. If history develops so as to let existence live, all right, if it turns out otherwise the respective existence will have to die without a word. National faith is to be replaced by a new faith in welfare, stable economics, security of life, abolition of violence. The antithesis of the two faiths is never put in all clarity; for no pacifist is so stupid as to say that life is a value in itself and to be maintained at all costs even if nothing remains that makes life worth living. On the contrary they are quite militant about their ideal of peace, and perfectly ready to make wars to end war, or wars to make peace. Oppenheim, too, admits the possibility of war in his international scheme, but, he says, it has to be "an exceptional phase and must be only for the purpose of reestablishing peace." I do not know of any wars that have been made for fun; all of them have been made to reestablish peace—[it] depends only what the peace will be like. And no better than a brutal nationalist, Oppenheim keeps military force at the back of the peaceful state of society as an "*ultima ratio.*" (*CW* 32:482)

One might usefully recall Voegelin's conclusion to chapter 2 of his *Herrschaftslehre,* that "the seed of evil . . . clings to all power." That was as emphatically true with notions such as Oppenheim's internationalism as it was with the attitude of the rabble. And the reason was, if not the same, at least comparable: the nonrecognition of sociohistorical reality.

By way of conclusion, let us summarize the argument of this lengthy chapter.

Voegelin's *Doktorvater* Othman Spann, his familiarity with the great works of German sociology, and especially his firsthand encounter with America all combined to indicate to him the limits of *Staatslehre* in general, and especially that of his other *Doktorvater* Hans Kelsen. From the *Herrschaftslehre* it was clear not only that Voegelin was critical of *Staatslehre* because it ignored the question of the form of the state or the regime as democratic, monarchic, and so on, but also because it ignored the question of spiritual rank with respect to the "core of the person." In short, the logic of the law was one thing, and social and political reality was another. On the basis of his analysis of *Staatslehre* as well as on the basis of his growing awareness of the empirical materials, Voegelin was increasingly drawn toward the position that the latter reality comprehended the articulation of it in the former. Voegelin's move "beyond *Staatslehre*" brought philosophical anthropology and political ideas into focus as the central elements in his scientific treatment of sociohistorical reality. The latter in particular provided content to the formality of legal analysis; the former provided criteria by which the latter might be understood and judged in light of their adequacy as an account of sociohistorical reality. In the next chapter we consider a central political idea of the late 1920s and 1930s, namely "race," as well as the adequacy of the philosophical anthropology, such as it was, that sustained the political idea of race. Moreover, as was evident in his Geneva lectures on national types of mind and the limits to interstate relations, the pragmatic implications of political ideas were always present in his analyses. Given the prominence of discussions of race during the late 1920s and early 1930s, it can be no great surprise that the discourse on race provided the subject matter for his next two books.

4

Race

In his *Autobiographical Reflections,* Voegelin recalled that the third part of his *Herrschaftslehre* was to deal with the question of political ideas. But, he said, "when I came to that third part I discovered that I knew nothing whatsoever about political ideas" (*CW* 34:66). In order to complete the project, therefore, he would have to study political ideas and so turned to "the concrete materials" at hand, namely the discussion of race or "race theory" and race ideas. "The National Socialist movement obviously was in political ascendancy; and though one could not yet foresee that it would come to power, the debate about races, the Jewish problem, etc., went on all the time" (*CW* 34:66). The appointment of Adolf Hitler as chancellor of the Reich on January 30, 1933, a few months prior to the publication of *Race and State,* added to the urgency of Voegelin's argument.[1] This event also displaced *Staatslehre,* and the project of a "system of *Staatslehre,*" from the center of Voegelin's intellectual life.

In previous chapters we argued that the long-standing goal of *Staatslehre* was to develop a legal logic independent of political contingencies. Voegelin was slowly coming to the realization that the primary reality of politics was precisely the contingent political ideas that were analytically independent of the law and thus of *Staatslehre.* That meant that political ideas were nonscientific (in the sense of *Staatslehre*) so that, notwithstanding their significance, they had to be discussed, analyzed, and judged on grounds other than those that governed *Staatslehre.* There were two elements to be justified. The first was to recast the methodological issues that arose in the course of writing the book on America in order to provide a rational and intelligible treatment of political ideas. The second, as we have on several occasions noted, was to provide a philosophical anthropology or a rationally defensible understanding of what was generally referred to as human nature. Voegelin made just such an argument in the introduction to *Race and State.*

A further introductory remark: David Levy has observed that Voegelin's two race books, *Race and State in Intellectual [or Spiritual] History* [*Geistesgeschichte*], and *The Race Idea,* which Voegelin said "supplement" one another (*CW* 3:1), are "exceptionally difficult texts to understand at all adequately" partly because of the "cold and objective" tone he employed instead of a more emotional and condemnatory one.[2] This was not the last time Voegelin was criticized for failing to engage in a polemic (see *CW* 5:1). There are two reasons why Voegelin approached this disagreeable material the way he did. The first reflects the legacy of Weberian science. As Voegelin put it a few years later, "our task here is not to moralize but to present a descriptive analysis" (*CW* 9:117). The second reason is that his style and content were largely conditioned by the more comprehensive scientific argument regarding the limitations of *Staatslehre.* For this second reason, incidentally, there are several internal references in this book to arguments that Voegelin reiterated at different times in these two books. Besides, when he did write in a more rhetorically accessible mode he was criticized for that as well.

Finally, there are some specific methodological issues associated with an analysis of political ideas that have to be considered. In this context, the most significant conclusion Voegelin reached in his effort to pull together a "system of *Staatslehre*" was that it had to be founded on a philosophical anthropology. The commonsensical reason, as Voegelin said, was "the incontestable fact that man is the creator of the state." Moreover, from the time of Plato's *Republic* it has been clear that different types of human beings would create different types of states—or, as we said above, different types of regimes. Indeed, Voegelin later called this famous passage where Plato said the polis was man written in large letters (*Republic* 368 c–d), to be an expression of Plato's "anthropological principle" (*CW* 5:136–38; 16:123–25). Using Voegelin's language of the 1930s, one would say that political ideas expressed contingent anthropological principles to members of a particular state. These ideas may be believed to be true—or not. Moreover, as was noted in the previous chapter, some of these ideas, such as ideas regarding equality, had a Christian provenance whereas others—Voegelin called them "Germanic ideas"—did not. The history of an idea, however, was to be distinguished from its truth. But how?

This was a crucial question. Putting it in other words: To say that ideas were expressions of various anthropological principles, ideas, or claims said nothing about the intelligibility or truth of them. Looking only to the *Republic,* one might say that the main issue over which the conversation ranged was the truth of the several anthropological principles articulated by the various characters. To put it bluntly, there are plenty of anthropologies or so-called "theories of man" at large, but some of them were more comprehensive, more adequate, or more true than others. As with other sorts of claims—over what is to be considered art, for example—the question of adequacy or truth of a claim can be decided only by analysis and argument. Following Plato's usage one may distinguish between a claim or opinion, *doxa,* and a genuine theory or a scientific account, *episteme.*

In the *New Science of Politics,* Voegelin related scientific or philosophic accounts to a specific class of experiences (*CW* 5:138ff). In the present context, it is perhaps sufficient to make the observation that theories aim to be coherent and refer to evidence. A philosophical anthropology, as distinct from an anthropological claim, opinion, or idea, aimed, accordingly, at a coherent account of commonly available evidence. Following Voegelin's usage in the early 1930s, one may call such an account a *theory,* as distinct from an *idea.*

In the previous chapter we noted that, invariably, "body ideas" are invoked in the constitution of a community as a "body politic." And, as just noted, the race idea was *the* manifestation in Germany in 1933 of a body idea. Obviously any study of the race idea would entail an account of its provenance. This would be a straightforward history of an idea in principle no different than a history of the American presidency or of whaling. In contrast, a *theory* of race claimed to be a scientific discourse and needed to be understood on scientific grounds.

This distinction between an idea and a theory, which corresponded approximately to the Platonic distinction between *doxa* and *episteme,* was emphasized for the first time in Voegelin's race books. He explained the difference as follows: Political ideas, he said, are not true or false but effective or ineffective in constituting the spiritual substance of the political community. Theories are true or false in terms of scientific criteria, such as evidence and coherence. The distinction is both important and necessary, Voegelin argued, because the race idea, as it was used contemporaneously, was made to shape the lives of those who were said to be part of a specific race (which thus excluded everybody else), *and* this exclusion was said to have been justified on the grounds of scientific reflection or theory. In this respect, the contemporary race idea was unlike other body ideas, which were obviously mythical constitutions of a community as a body politic and which made no claims to being scientific accounts. The race idea in contemporary German discourse also claimed to be scientific. Voegelin's first substantive task, therefore, was to find a way to discuss the question of race both as an idea and as theory (see *CW* 10:27ff).

Voegelin's two race books were published in 1933: *Race and State* in September and *The Race Idea* a month or so later. The latter, which Voegelin called "intellectual history," provided the context for the "systematic" treatment in *Race and State.* Thomas Heilke called *The Race Idea* a "genealogy" of the idea of race.[3] However one described the book, it makes more logical sense to discuss the historical subject matter of *The Race Idea* before the more contemporary treatment of German race discourse in *Race and State.*

Voegelin began *The Race Idea* with a commonsensical observation: "The knowledge of man is out of joint" (*CW* 3:3). Existing race theory was confused about what is essential and lacked the technical ability to know its own ignorance. Thus was it necessary to turn "to the history of a great idea" in order to analyze its creation "in happier moments of the world-spirit" (*CW* 3:3). This is not the kind of language that is used in political science today. A major reason, however, why no one speaks of race and politics today is because of the consequences of National Socialist race theories.[4] But that is itself a very good reason to undertake the archaeology of a once-great idea.

Hence, as noted above, there is the preliminary necessity of dealing with the question of methodology and formulating a conceptual vocabulary to discuss race. The race idea, Voegelin said, came into being at a specific time; its emergence marked the creation of a new "primal image" *(Urbild)* of man, which is to say there is no single primal way of seeing *(Urweise des Sehens)* and no final and perfect *Urbild,* though some may be more effective and adequate to experience than others. Historically considered, "the views and the images change with the times and nations" and even though we cannot understand the reason for the appearance of a new *Urbild,* we can understand the necessary conditions that accompany its appearance, its development, and its decline.

More specifically, the race idea emerged from the *Urbild* of Christianity along with a contrasting post-Christian, pagan image. The transformation was gradual and not always coherent. As a result, no one embodied the new *Urbild* with the decisiveness that Jesus embodied the Christian one. The Christian image raised human being above nature, by virtue of the soul and its ability to unite with the divine spirit *(pneuma).* In consequence, even though, according to the Christian image, human being exists in the flesh *(sarx),* as do other transitory animals, human being is essentially a supernatural and imperishable substance (*CW* 3:7).

The change in image was focused on the term *nature.* It consisted in a change in the Christian understanding that nature was a creature of God and was organized according to God's design from the outside. The new or chronologically post-Christian image was that of "a substance carrying the law of its construction within it." It was not animated externally but was a self-subsistent "primary force" that was sustained by "the wellsprings of its own aliveness." New forms of knowledge and new questions that could be raised on the basis of it "gradually led to a readiness to see the living world in a new way." Because the fading and eventual eclipse of a thousand-year-old tradition was not instantaneous, it was impossible to tell whether an eighteenth-century zoologist who studied "the anatomy of a louse" did so because he saw in it the hand of God, or not. All one could do was provide an account of the new circumstances—especially, as

Voegelin noted, the increase in biological knowledge in the seventeenth and eighteenth centuries.

Specifically, the idea of a "natural system" developed to classify nature according to a natural and not an artificial order, an order based on inherent or internal characteristics, not external ones such as God's design. Following the Renaissance, travelers' accounts introduced the question of classifying humans in terms of size, shape, color of skin, and so on. In turn, this knowledge raised the issue: Is human being to be classified along with animal being? And if so, how was this act to be reconciled with the Christian idea of the nature of human being (see *CW* 25:169–72)?

Corresponding to a change in primordial images was a change in "thought images" *(Denkbilder).* A methodological requirement to undertake the history of ideas, therefore, entailed the rejection of the traditional notion that philosophy was a rationally adequate account of reality. Instead, for the history of ideas, philosophical adequacy was henceforth to be judged in terms of (1) "intrasystemic consistency" and (2) the breadth and depth of the primal images. This meant that if there were changes in the primal images and in the primal ways of seeing, which sustained the entire system, then "the philosophical thought images must change with them." If consistency with the changing primal image was not possible, then doubts as to its validity would follow and revisions to the primal image would begin.

In other words, the constructions of thought images, including "philosophical" ones, were not understood to be true or false but were supported by primal ways of seeing. Their status as *primal* meant there was no third-party position by which two primal images might be judged: "They are all true, for they see what is real," rather like a Foucauldian *episteme.* Arguments surrounding a primal image did not therefore aim to demonstrate anything but were intended to defend a way of seeing. Primal images initially appeared because they were embodied in persons; then they became accepted by others as exemplary ways of living. Some were exemplary to the utmost degree—Jesus, Plato, Caesar—others less so. Human society, Voegelin said, had been structured according to the effects of these images and to the authenticity with which they have been emulated. "The connection between images and their function in establishing, forming, and structuring society are the basis that ultimately gives legitimacy to the philosophizing about man" (*CW* 3:17). It was not, therefore, the chronology of thought images that gave meaning to a history of ideas but the relation of them to the underlying primal images.

Readers familiar with Voegelin's later discussion of experience and symbolization and the problem of equivalence will see in this argument an early effort to deal with the question. It was not, therefore, so much a defense of relativism as it is a criticism of dogmatic finality. Voegelin was certainly capable of making a nonrelativistic judgment regarding the adequacy of theories and of providing a rational account of why such a judgment was sound, and he did so.

"Compared to its classical form," Voegelin observed, "the current condition of race theory is one of decay." The primal images have faded from sight and the technical ability to form concepts and images of thought has atrophied. For example, in the eighteenth century, the basic concepts of organism, species, and evolution were created as thought images connected to the primordial image of the phenomenon of life. They were understood to be three interconnected manifestations of the phenomenon of life, namely the individual life form, the order with a constant form, and the historical unfolding of the living substance in a context of related forms. In contrast, "today's biological and anthropological theory is characterized by complete ignorance of the classical state of the problem," especially as Kant formulated it in the *Critique of Judgement.* There Kant showed that the parts of the phenomenon of life cannot explain one another, which led to the obvious conclusion: "all attempts at explanation are fuelled by the desire to reduce the phenomenon of life to a law of inorganic nature" (*CW* 3:20). The unjustified ontological assumption of such a desire is that there is only one reality: matter. As a result, the history of biological *theory,* not biological practice or biological science, "is the history of a fiasco."[5]

The consequence of the reduction of the phenomenon of life to the laws of nonliving nature has been "a malevolent, deadly fatalism, hostile to life and spirit" that eventually radiated "into the higher levels of the world of organic forms and even into the higher one of the human body and spirit." That is, ignorance of theoretical biology on the part of contemporary race thinkers was not a matter internal to a specialized science: The people involved wanted to interfere in human affairs and "explicate the German nation to us and to the world—an undertaking with evil consequences" because not only were they ignorant of the phenomenon of life, but also they knew nothing of the image of man as an embodied spirit. "The great thinkers of the past would have been horrified at somebody finding in himself all the traits of the Nordic race with the help of a book on anthropology and then imagining himself to be somebody special who does not have to do anything else." This decline in the primal image was "disastrous" (*CW* 3:22).

What was needed to make a genuine history out of descent from another human was an account that made manifest a "human-spiritual primal content" in physically related bodies. In contemporary race theory, however, there was nothing but the material concept of laws that expressed nothing but "chance and necessity," to use a more recent thought image. Contemporary race theory, Voegelin concluded, along "with liberalism and Marxism," is "rooted" in the late nineteenth century by the "will to deprive the state of history, to hand it over to the masses, to destroy the historical substance and the primal image of man in its community-forming function." For both race theory and Marxism, reality determined consciousness, consciousness did not determine reality.

Drawing attention to the structural similarity of race theory to Marxism in the context of Germany in 1933 must have given Voegelin a certain amount of mischievous satisfaction. The major point, however, was that "man as a spiritual-bodily historical substance cannot be 'explained' through something that is less than man himself, through his *physis.* Only man himself can create his sphere of action, namely the historical community, which does not exist without men of strong imaginative force." If we substitute this genuinely historical and spiritual understanding of race for the notion "that the historical substance could be arbitrarily generated by diligent clubs for the breeding of racially pure bodies" we embrace a superstition, that organization can be a substitute for the natural attraction that noble human beings have for one another. "It is a nightmare to think that we should recognize the people whom we follow and whom we allow to come near to us not by their looks, their words, and their gestures, but by their cranial index and the proportional measure of their extremities" (*CW* 3:25).

Accordingly, Voegelin understood that his history of the race idea was not just an exercise in intellectual history—it was also intended to recall the primal images and thought images the understanding of which has been lost. Granted, Voegelin said, it was not always an easy task to understand Leibniz, Kant, or Schiller—especially for race theoreticians today. "We will not hold this against them; they may be excellent at performing the lesser services they are suited for—but then let them be silent regarding man and the state. Anyone who takes the easy way in matters of the spirit has no right to participate in this discussion" (*CW* 3:25).

With this emphatic criticism of contemporary race theorists, Voegelin began the analysis of the eighteenth-century account of the problem, starting with Carolus Linnaeus (1707–1778). The commonsensical reason for starting the analysis with "the father of modern taxonomy" is that, at first blush, "race" is simply a way of classifying human beings. In addition, as Voegelin said, the "pervasive simplicity" of Linnaeus's theory is especially useful for the question of race because it introduced all the relevant problems: By logic species must be invariable "ontic" units and procreation is a means to preserve them through generations; for Linnaeus, God is the source of both the units and the individuals.

Likewise, contemporary race theory retains the immutability of hereditary units in the doctrine of racial types, which is the necessary presupposition that sustains the notion that spiritual and cultural life is a consequence of race. Of course, modern race theorists overlook the little problem of origins—certainly God had nothing to do with it. So somehow things "evolved." But if so, the contemporary position is incompatible with the constancy of units. More to the point, the postulate of evolution says nothing about the speculative metaphysical problem of a real origin. Voegelin later drew attention to the problem in Marx's doctrine regarding "socialist man" as the type of person who does not ask such metaphysical questions regarding origins. On that occasion Voegelin characterized Marx as an "intellectual swindler" because he knew exactly what he was doing (*CW* 5:261–65). It is not clear that contemporary race theorists knew even that much.

Prior to Linnaeus, John Ray (1627–1705) developed a system of classification that was in some respects superior. His system of classification, unlike that of Linnaeus, referred not to a single trait to distinguish species but by "complexes of traits" that constituted "a real-ontological concept of species," a natural not a logical classification. That is, "nature . . . becomes the guideline for the method of typology" (*CW* 3:33). Voegelin's critical point was that "artificial systems" such as the one produced by Linnaeus cannot tell us anything about the real or "ontological" divisions in nature even though they assign a logical or "ontic" place to every specimen imaginable.

In other words, Ray was concerned not with specific differences *(differentia specifica),* which may be entirely arbitrary, but with *differentia essentialis,* essential differences. The distinction between the two, Voegelin said, was metaphysical: The latter entailed the manifestation of an essence behind an appearance, the former did not. This is what he meant by using the term "the real-ontological" (or, to use more graceful English, the "ontologically real") concept of a species. Ray was important as well because he (along with Buffon) supplied Kant with information for the philosopher's argument that differences within phyla are either hereditary, which are called races, or not, which are called variations. Race cannot, therefore, be the determinant of individuality; rather, individual traits must be the result of the direct unfolding of predispositions in the entire human phylum. "The possibilities of human nature are spread out before us in the infinite variety of human forms." This was why, for example, individual characteristics are not inheritable and why, for Kant, the physiognomical uniqueness of every human face was connected to the inner unity of the person, "thus transferring the problem of singularity from the merely physical sphere into that of spiritual expression," a formulation that was very close to the contemporary notion of a singular body-spirit unified person (*CW* 3:37–38).

The dominant idea Voegelin explored in chapter 1 of *The Race Idea* was the significance of the stability or fixity of classifications, which would include the category of race. This problem introduced the question of nature and ontologically real classifications, as distinct from ontic, logical-specific ones. The question of "natural" criteria was dealt with by Ray first by the thesis of unity of descent and the species-wide capacity to breed as the cause of species unity and second by reference to the essence of a species that is perceptible to humans. Finally, the genetic question remained open: It was not clear whether each individual was created by an act of God or by a one-time creation of the species.

On this issue Ray professed neutrality. Both versions, however, relied on a transcendent principle—either God or a mechanical device in nature. In contrast immanent explanations viewed life "as a unique ontic realm and assume an instructive agent along the lines of . . . an agent that determines the character of the life-form." For modern race theory, the body was neither an artifact from God nor a mechanism of nature but "a psychophysical union that carries the defining characteristics of its living existence within itself" (*CW* 3:98).

Voegelin called this process "the internalization of the body" because the image of external animation of matter was replaced by that of a "substance living as a unified and self-contained one out of its own inwardness" (*CW* 3:9). The second phase, which Voegelin called "the internalization of the person," followed from the first: If life is not animated from outside (by God, for example), neither is it lived toward a transcendent purpose or Heavenly City as Augustine said. Instead, as we shall see, all meaning had to be found in earthly existence, especially in the exemplary lives of "great men" or at least "demonic" ones who combine intensity of life with a well-formed body. The great prototype or new *Urbild*, for both Goethe and Hegel, was Napoléon. But then Goethe himself became the image of the person perfect in spirit and body, well-born, physically handsome, and filled with stamina according to the image drawn by his friend Carl Gustav Carus. "This completes the primary image on the basis of which man's physio-spiritual unity will be understood in the future, and the race questions can be posed in their full scope, irrefutable and unshaken by arguments, because they are backed by the certainty of an image and a direct experience," namely that of Goethe. Let there be no misunderstanding: For Carus, Goethe embodied a new *Urbild* similar in principle to that which Christ once did. Voegelin's methodological point was that both the internalization of the body and the internalization of the person were required for the development of the modern idea of race.[6]

The first step in that direction was taken by Georges Leclerc, Compte de Buffon (1707–1788). Using a "coarsened" Cartesian distinction between body and soul, Buffon simply eliminated the unity of the two by fiat. But then he had to introduce "strange conventionalist secondary constructions" to make sense of the artificial division between body and spirit for the obvious reason that any philosophical anthropology would have to consider the immediate experience of human being as a unit or as embodied spirit. When Buffon then applied this understanding of human being to the question of race, he did not differentiate between physical and spiritual traits but simply listed them together as if they belonged to the same order of being. He made no effort to bring consistency to his classification—by considering physical traits, for example, to be the "real" determinants of human being.

Instead, the principle, if that is what it was, that allowed him to juxtapose physical characteristics with morals and customs was that the attributes of civilized Europeans (such as Monsieur le Comte) were considered normal. According to Buffon, Laplanders, for example, "are just civilized enough to merit contempt" (*CW* 3:59). Deviation from the norm toward the exotic was a result of climate, diet, and customs, especially the first, which was responsible for skin color, and thus a major criterion of classification. Buffon was himself interested in the unusual and the exotic, not least of all because of the accumulation of geographic and ethnographic knowledge in European centers of learning as a result of military and scientific exploration as well as travelogues.

Buffon's ambiguity, indecisiveness, or simple lack of systematic concern regarding the relationship of body and soul could be resolved either by emphasizing one or the other as fundamental or by an argument that connected the two elements. The argument of Johann Gottfried von Herder (1744–1803) followed the last path. He began his reflections on race from the unity of body and spirit. "For Herder," wrote Voegelin, "man is not a composite of animal and spirit, but a fully rounded whole." Diversity among races, therefore, could not be biological but rather was a variation on the spiritually unified human being. As with Buffon, climate and region exercised an influence along with a superhuman destiny inherited from a kind of residual Christianity. In other words, for Herder, human being was a unity between the animals and a form of being higher than humanity.

Johann Friedrich Blumenbach (1752–1840) followed Kant's argument and considered human being to be a unity with outwardly different parts—body and soul—so that study of physical form was inherently meaningful by itself. "For both, the gift of reason distinguishes man from animal" and established the contrast between the inner human essence and the subhuman world. For both, but especially for Kant, the structure of reason was independent of scientific investigations of the human physical form. Indeed, Voegelin argued, Kant "offered the first systematic justification for the use of the word *race* in connection with the description of man." It appeared as a concept of natural history rather than as a part of nature and was confined to the physical attributes of the individual—along with a familiar climatic explanation of the origin of the differences. Kant was also the first to use the term *race* in a way that had no coarse and animalistic implications when applied to human being (*CW* 3:74, 86).

With Kant and Herder we are near to the beginning of the modern understanding of race thinking. As we shall indicate, modern race thinking has a multitude of problems associated with it, but at least initially the anthropological requirements were clear. Both Herder's notion of a being higher than human being and the radical division of body and spirit had to be replaced with "a basic reciprocal spiritualization of the body and embodiment of the spirit into the union of earthly-human existence" (*CW* 3:90). In short: no dualisms are allowed—neither of body and spirit nor of human and superhuman being. Hence the need for a shift "of the core of man's being from the transcendent realm into the inner being of this-worldly life," which, as noted, Voegelin called "internalization." The concepts of organism and of finite person combined to establish a "new this-worldly idea of man as a unity" (*CW* 3:90).

Caspar Friedrich Wolff (1733–1794) was the first to argue that the body was a living form, not a dead mechanism that was externally animated. Moreover, because the eighteenth-century usage of the word *organism* was synonymous with *mechanism*, he had to argue for a new meaning for the term, namely the contemporary one. There were several interesting philosophical problems to be dealt with before the concept of an inherently alive body could be made intelligible—and Voegelin provided a concise analysis, for example, of Leibniz's arguments (which he excused the ill-educated devotees of modern race theory from trying to comprehend). The argument regarding an immanent view of the living body led directly to a second point of great significance for the development of race thinking, namely "the species characteristics of a life-form and their constancy through the generations" (*CW* 3:115).

Fidelity of generations of a species to the species form was not a problem for Linnaeus, whose piety provided a transcendent explanation: namely, that God guaranteed that species would bring forth only their own kind. That is, God's creation of the world ensured fidelity in reproduction and fixity of species. But when God's creation of the world was doubted, so too was the account that ensured species reliability. What replaced the concept of creation at a specific time and place was speculation on the idea of infinity. But then the image of a finite succession somehow had to ensure that each individual was descended from a predecessor. "The result was a peculiar, undecided state." It resulted from the "error" of speculating on infinity, which is to say, of attempting to see a given whole in the succession of individuals as members of a species. Voegelin went on to discuss this "error" in detail in connection with both Buffon and Leibniz (*CW* 3:116–25). We will consider some of the political implications below.

Not until Kant's *Critique of Judgement* (1790) was there a balanced account of the concept of the organism that rejected both versions of creationist theory—whether the preformation version or the individual ensoulment version. Natural processes could be examined on their own, Kant showed, independent of any hypothetical external intervention. This argument, elegant though it may have been, left unanswered the problem of an absolute beginning of sequences of events. Moreover, because he was a first-rate philosopher, Kant understood clearly that the theory of evolution "merely shifts the real origin of the species back to the origin of evolution." His argument thus "not only takes the theory of evolution to its logical conclusion but also destroys it as meaningless as far as its explanatory purpose is concerned" (*CW* 3:143–44). The problem raised by Kant tends to be ignored by modern accounts of evolution.

The replacement of a theory of evolution designed to explain the origin of the species with Kant's account brought to light "the primary phenomenon of life." Because it is primary it can be seen or ignored, but not explained by something else, which would be "more primary." Because the primary phenomenon of life is present in the living individual, in the species, and in the interconnectedness of the living world as a whole, one element cannot be used to explain another. Accordingly, therefore, the life of the individual is not explained through the life of the species, the life of the species cannot be explained by the totality of life (as in the "theory" of evolution), and the totality of life cannot be explained by the laws of nonliving nature. The *Critique of Judgement* provided a fatal criticism to the possibility of an ontologically real theory of evolution even though a derivative and despiritualized evolutionary theory flourished a century later, as it does today.

As the arguments of Kant were forgotten, ignored, or simply not understood, "the idea of the living being" became an unproblematic term in the definition of social subjects. In this development of the metaphor of the living being, the direct experience of "a self-contained being that matures according to its inherent formative law combines strangely with the speculations on the problem of infinity" that, as Voegelin had already explained, arose as a consequence of the lack of credibility or intelligibility of the hypothesis of divine creation.

The direct experience of the living individual was then expanded to the whole living world. "Just as the finite created species is replaced by the speculation on the infinite succession and the resulting idea of a formative principle that constantly realizes itself, so the notion of rigidly defined species arranged side by side is replaced—first cautiously and then more explicitly—by the idea of a history of the organic world. The transcendent idea of the creation is replaced with the immanent idea of history" (*CW* 3:131). This process of reinterpretation with respect to species was more complex than the development of the idea of the organism "because the intellectual threads going from one idea to the other are more numerous and more intertwined" (*CW* 3:131). The direction of the interpretation, however, was clear and straightforward—from one of world-transcendent principles to world-immanent ones.

We noted above that the process just described, which Voegelin called the internalization of the body, was followed directly by the internalization of the person. In terms of "thought images," *Denkbilder,* the analysis of the "primary phenomenon" of the "spiritualized lived body" aimed to describe the concept of the human person "as a unified, unbroken being, who is neither spirit without body nor body without spirit." In short, the question of the organism recurred, only this time at a higher "ontic level" involving the entire human person. The same task of overcoming the duality of matter and spirit must be undertaken in order to clarify the notion of "the indivisible unit of the mode of being that is sought." With the internalization of the body, the problem involved the "vitalization" [*Verlebendigung*] of matter. With the internalization of the person, the problem involved the "sensorization" [*Versinnlichung*] of an immaterial spiritual principle. In both instances the objective was to attain the idea of the finite whole from the constituent elements of matter and psyche or of body and spirit. With the organism, the sensualization or sensorization of the idea required an abandonment of speculation regarding infinity. Likewise with the person: Instead of understanding the person as an immortal substance, as a result of internalization the person became "finite [and] this-worldly; it is to be understood on the basis of its own intrinsic laws" (*CW* 3:147).

Voegelin again drew attention to the fact that during the eighteenth century, whenever a rational account of the person was attempted, the doctrine of infinity made an appearance—either in the Christian form of an afterlife in a beyond or in the form of the transmigration of souls, which amounted to the repetition of finite existence an infinite number of times. The latter version was found in Lessing's *Education of the Human Race* (1780), which postulated a gradual progress of humanity, by way of finite, individual lives, toward love and virtue. "Thus, the perfection of the genus [the human race] coincides with the perfection of all individuals through the series of rebirths" (*CW* 3:149).

Once again Kant saw clearly the philosophical problem implicit in an infinite process of perfection: Every finite step toward perfection is infinitely small in relation to the whole. No finite distance moved on the path of education, no matter how big we take it to be, can show any change when measured by an infinitely long path. As a consequence, "the meaning of the finite life of the person in his earthly existence" was destroyed. Kant's criticism of the conceit of human progress was as devastating as his criticism of evolution. It too, of course, has been forgotten, ignored, or not understood by later progressives.

Kant went on to explore what Voegelin called "the mysteriousness of the situation." It was intelligible enough that the meaning of the life of an animal might be completed in its finite existence, because animals lacked faculties for any purpose other than what appeared to them between life and death. But humans, endowed with reason, had a faculty that could not be actualized in a single lifetime. Accordingly, "an infinite series of generations" was needed to actualize all human faculties. This conclusion led Kant to his well-known expression of astonishment or bewilderment [*Befremden*] that Voegelin several times quoted or alluded to:

> What remains disconcerting about all this is first, that the earlier generations seem to perform their laborious tasks only for the sake of the later ones, so as to prepare for them a further stage from which they can raise still higher the structure intended by nature; and secondly, that only the later generations will in fact have the good fortune to inhabit the building on which a whole series of their forefathers (admittedly, without any conscious intention) had worked without themselves being able to share in the happiness they were preparing. But no matter how puzzling this may be, it will appear as necessary as it is puzzling if we simply assume that one animal species was intended to have reason, and that, as a class of rational beings who are mortal as individuals but immortal as a species, it was still meant to develop its capacities completely.[7]

Kant understood this progressivist intersection of the individual and the species to be disconcerting because the individual and his accomplishments were merely the means to the end of perfected life in the final generation of human beings, which violated his categorical imperative and made the whole process unethical. Even if the idea of immortality took care of the perfectibility of the individual, it did not deal adequately with the problem of happiness here and now. And if we think of earthly life as perfectible, we are back with the problem of the disadvantage at which earlier generations find themselves compared to later ones. "There is no remedy in the Kantian system for these difficulties," Voegelin concluded, because even though reason had the same structure for the individual and the totality, there was no common image of the human totality that could be reconciled with "the singular totality of the person" (*CW* 3:154).

Kant's understanding of the theoretical problems of progress and of evolution had no impact on theoretical biology. Indeed, "a new phenomenal theory of evolution, operating with the conceptions of the struggle for life, the survival of the fittest, natural selection, etc., had a popular success and became a mass creed for the semieducated" (*CW* 25:184–85).

The story of the success of the theory of evolution may be "a source of bewilderment to the historian of ideas" (*CW* 25:184), but the same may be said of the success of the theory of progress.

In any event, the actual social changes that accompanied these theoretically incoherent doctrines still had to be endured and understood. Specifically, fragmentation, division of labor, specialization, particularization of human abilities, and a general diremption [*Zerissenheit*] of existence was reflected in the French *moralistes* as well as in Mandeville and Adam Smith, Schiller and Hölderlin. As a way to move beyond the loneliness of the masses, "the thought of an elite as the vehicle of humanity begins to emerge."

With Schiller, for example, dissatisfaction with the Kantian notion of infinite progress that was no progress prompted his desire for "a fully formed, noble humanity within a finite time period." Kant focused on the whole of humanity and its progress toward perfection; Schiller focused on the individual who, raised above the masses, might be able to develop the whole of his personality. Schiller's "astonishment," unlike Kant's, was that at least some individuals must be able to actualize a perfect life. "Kant had his eyes on the community of all men, who were all moving *together* toward their goal; Schiller articulated the idea of the beginning of the future perfection of *all* through the perfection of individual persons in the present" (*CW* 3:156–58).

Kant was also skeptical regarding the improvement of mankind because it required an already improved man to guide, lead, and encourage others on the path to perfection. As Voegelin quoted him in the previous chapter, humans "are cut from such crooked wood that it would be difficult to make something entirely straight from them." In contrast, Schiller was able to avoid Kant's pessimism by introducing the idea of the person of character of whom he found an exemplar in Goethe. Goethe, said Schiller, had overcome the diremption of the age and turned himself into a "demonic" man in whom both sensory nature and reason had been harmoniously united along with a "beautiful soul," a notion later demolished by Hegel.[8]

Schiller's concepts, wrote Voegelin, "present a characteristic stage in intellectual history for the development of a new thought" (*CW* 3:162). It would be insufficient simply to name the new attitude—as demonic or as a beautiful soul, for example—because Schiller's audience would not know how to connect the name with the reality intended by it. So it was clarified by reference to something concrete—in this instance by pointing to the person of Goethe—and by connecting him to specific historical concepts—in this instance the light, balance, beauty, and so on, of Classical Greece. Goethe was, in other words, seriously intended to exemplify the new, post-Christian *Urbild,* a new primordial image of human being.

Before connecting Goethe to the race idea, Voegelin summarized his argument. Just as the organisms internalized the image of the body, the internalization of the image of the person was envisioned as a new unity of the senses and of reason. The exemplary image of the person thus became a "representative" of humanity. Politically, the community was bound together "aesthetically," a community equal in its simplicity and innocence. Concretely, the image of Goethe served as the means to orient movement toward increased internalization of the person. Schiller realized that, in place of the conventional progressivist, step-by-step advancement toward an infinitely distant goal, meaningful human life could be actualized in the present "in select company modeled after the demonic man" who, drawing on deep sources of strength, breaks with the oppressive reality of the dirempted present (*CW* 3:164). Wilhelm von Humboldt continued Schiller's argument, only expanding it to include the internal development, *Bildung,* of the individual toward meaning (*CW* 12:18–32). Moreover, the body remained the foundation for the spiritual achievements of the individual and so must be favorably developed in order for the individual to achieve the highest things with his spiritual capacities.

Finally, Voegelin considered the arguments of Goethe's friend, Carus (1789–1869), who, he said, took the idea of human individuality as a self-contained total being to its conclusion: The body was the foundation for the full unfolding of the spirit. Again Goethe was an exemplar, a "well-born man" who inherited as well as developed his embodied spiritual characteristics. Carus realized, Voegelin said, "the full implications of the idea of the well-born person, in a way that is far removed from the barbaric natural-scientific dogmatizations of modern eugenics, which narrows the concept to apply only to particular physical conditions" (*CW* 3:170).

According to Carus, a healthy individual was capable of repelling spiritual as well as physical diseases. Moreover, along the lines later sketched by Nietzsche, Carus claimed that opposition of the diseased spirit to the wellborn one resulted from *Lebensneid*, "life-envy" or resentment. The internal and the external, spirit and body, were linked inseparably. On the one hand, the body was not simply the foundation of the soul. It was also the source of its "energy," which was both a spiritual and a vital force. On the other hand, therefore, works created on the basis of "inner sickliness" produced only a sense of unease or disturbance (*CW* 3:172).

Carus's essay on the unequal aptitudes of human races for higher spiritual development began by raising the question of how Goethe could be so superior to ordinary people. He answered with the observation that variety was part of human being because humanity was an organic whole, not a *partes extra partes* aggregation. As with all such organisms, the greater the variety of the parts, the more perfect the results. This requirement pointed to the need for inequalities of all kinds, which he said were initially understood in terms of tribe, class, status, temperament, and so on.

Carus rejected the external classifications of race—color, skull shape, and so on—and grouped races in terms of the relationship of the earth to the sun: day and night peoples, eastern and western twilight peoples. His focus was on the variety of human beings as a whole, which he said was governed by spirit, whatever their external differences. Thus, "the subdivision into races is not a bodily one to which is appended a typology of souls, as happens in modern race theory; instead, Carus tries to derive the possibilities of typological subdivision from the inherent lawfulness of mind and character" (*CW* 3:175). Just as the minds of some individuals were open and flexible and others were rigid and closed, so too with the inner dispositions of entire peoples. Thus some human groups were "active" in their spiritual life—especially the day peoples—and others were not (the eastern twilight peoples—the Chinese, for example). "What is disconcerting about a standstill and the shaping of forms in which no life moves any more," Carus argued, "is the alienation from the true nature of the spirit. Constant transformation, tireless growth, these are what distinguish the human from the animal soul. The style of rigidification lets man slide back into the twilight between the two realms" (*CW* 3:176–77).

In contrast to Buffon, who decided that the familiar European type was "normal," Carus argued that the nature of the human spirit provided the norm. Buffon looked upon deviation from the norm as an oddity; for

Carus inequality was part of the organic quality of humanity. Like Schiller, Carus saw one group (as well as individuals within it) as the flowering of humanity. But he added that that gave them special obligations to help the weaker.

For Voegelin, Carus marked the end of a major development in race thinking. He began with the figure of Goethe: This unique man was the starting point for a reflection on inequality. "The great individual was only possible when supported and surrounded by an outstanding race—namely, the day peoples." The superiority of that race enabled the superiority of Goethe to flourish. His reflections on the day peoples were echoed in twentieth-century race theory exalting the "Nordic" type, which association may account for the pall that has been cast over all race-thinking. Unlike most later race theorists, however, Carus developed a rationally defensible philosophical anthropology based on his understanding of human spirituality. As we will see in *Race and State,* only two twentieth-century successors, Ludwig Clauss and Othmar Spann, managed to approach Carus's level of clarity on this question.

Voegelin concluded: "these reflections on Carus lead us right into the center of the race idea as a political idea shaping the community" (*CW* 3:179). *The History of the Race Idea* described the systematic content and the historical construction of the idea of man presupposed by modern race theory. It became effective in the construction of a community in two senses: (1) as objectively basing the community on the idea of race, and (2) as subjectively convincing people within the community that race was essential to the constitution of the community. In this context race was not the subject matter of investigation but a "body-soul-spirit reality that included the scholar." Likewise the concept of race in that context was not a scientific concept but a means of interpreting the meaning of one's own life and the life of the community. It was not just a means to understand the community but an active instrument in the shaping of its future. It constituted the idea of the community "as a bodily context as it is projected into the future by its members" (*CW* 3:180). Thus did "race" become a political idea in an emphatic sense.

The fundamental distinction between race as a political idea and race as a scientific theory was continued in the argument of *Race and State* (see also *The Political Religions,* chapter 1, in *CW* 5). As we have seen at some length in the discussion of *The Race Idea,* the scientific or philosophical discussion of the problem of race dealt with classification, the question of body and soul, and so on. In the twentieth-century discourse on race, these kinds of issues, as indicated above, were hardly addressed.

One reason why there had been little reflection regarding the scientific status of race theory was that after Carus the prevailing discourse developed within a system of dogmas or "scientific superstitions" that operated independently both of philosophical anthropology and of biological science. The two chief dogmas, also familiar from *The New Science of Politics,* are: (1) the only real science follows the method of natural science; and (2) scientific progress is automatic, so that previous problems and ideas are assumed to have been overcome and so can be ignored. Adherence to these two dogmas or superstitions enables the so-called scholar or scientist who does so to remain an ignoramus with a good conscience. In biology, for example, nothing written prior to Darwin or Lamarck needed to be considered. Certainly Kant could be ignored. This situation determined the order of topics discussed in part I of *Race and State.* The first thing to be done was for Voegelin to provide his own account of the relations between body, soul, and spirit—that is, the constituent elements of human nature. Then it would be possible to account both for the biological and the anthropological significance of the concept of race and to show how biological accounts were necessarily limited to one aspect of human being.

Voegelin summarized his analysis in terms of six theses:

> 1. Human being is a unified totality that simultaneously belongs to all realms of being;
>
> 2. The scientific study of human being can thus proceed by several methods—an analysis of human chemistry, for example, or of human biology, or of human spirituality;
>
> 3. The problem with a race theory of human being is that it applies methods that study man as an animal (namely the methods of *naturwissenschaftsliche Anthropologie,* physical anthropology), but one can say nothing about the human spirit on this basis. Where physical anthropologists discussed racial types of souls, it was on the basis of the methods of

the *Geisteswissenschaften* (and usually very inferior ones). In any event, the methods of the *Geisteswissenschaften* are independent of those used by physical anthropology;

4. The application of biology directly to human collectivities has resulted in a number of methodological problems—because, in principle, or for philosophical reasons, biology cannot legitimately be so applied;

5. Among biologists the scope of biology and the methods appropriate to biology have not been clarified;

6. A natural science of race, or a science of body types, can, for reasons of epistemological principle and for reasons of philosophical anthropology, say *nothing* about the spiritual problem of race types—because the connection between body, soul, and spirit is not a matter of natural scientific judgment but rather, according to the first thesis, is an ontological given. This ontological given is not the subject matter of a single science but is the basis for the formation of *ideas* of the body, which Voegelin discussed in part II of *Race and State.*

Voegelin concluded this introduction by reiterating the importance of the distinction between scientific race theory and the race idea and raised a further question: Why are these two problems, and their conflation, so important in Germany? The answer, he said, lay in an analysis of German *political* history: The German nation does not exist as a body politic the way France, America, and England do because of the opposition in those countries—provided by the Christian doctrine of community, an opposition that was effectively absent from Germany (see *CW* 31:155ff).

Part I of *Race and State* discussed "the systematic content of race theory," and, for reasons just indicated, began with a consideration of the chief elements of philosophical anthropology—body, soul, and spirit—to use the title of the first chapter of his book.

The nature of man, Voegelin began, is constant, and the experiences that motivate speculation on human being are always the same. There is new information to be absorbed, but the scope of human being remains the same. "Our current study of man, anthropology, has no other materials to take as a starting point than those already available to Aristotle when he embarked on his investigations, and Aristotle had no materials but those the myth-forming imagination of earlier times concretized into mythical figures" (*CW* 2:19). Accordingly, the same type of problems and solutions to them recurred historically because the available options were so few. Moreover, the basic experiences available to interpret human being, whatever the speculative form—whether myth or philosophy, for instance—cannot be definitively described, and a final interpretation can never be concluded.

The fundamental experiences belong to the condition of human being as inorganic, vegetable, animal, and human nature; within human existence, the fundamental experiences are of death, sleep, illness, anxiety, skill or power, control over action, depersonalized ecstasy, mystical submission to God, and the "spiritual self-involvement of meditation." All of them can serve as departure points for reflecting on human being and the internal articulation of it.

Voegelin then provided a number of illustrative examples. Considered externally, for instance, death was a change in the mode of existence where the body could remain the same for a while but the soul was absent or at least was not observable. This experience has motivated several kinds of speculation about what has taken place in the change between a living human being and a dead human body. Likewise changes exist between sleep and being awake, dreaming and being awake and under the control of reason or character, being healthy or ill, and so on. These observable differences then motivate the speculative construction of a hierarchy whereby human being can be differentiated according to whether any particular "level" is controlled by another. Thus, for example, a dead human body was subject only to life (and its absence) whereas sleeping and dreaming were controlled by intelligence or the soul when the human being was awake.

Likewise success and defeat and the act of thinking and taking action seem to be the result not of antecedent conditions but are experienced as spontaneous. In language that could have come from the pen of Hannah Arendt, Voegelin wrote: "We experience ourselves then as starting points *(Anfangspunkte)*, not merely transitional points *(Durchgangspunkte)*, of an event of initiating something new and thus affecting the course of the world." And, of course, we could fail at an action, as our bodies could fail in illness and death. Accordingly, we are both centers of power and initiative and we are powerless before greater forces.

Description of these fundamental experiences can be expanded by comparison with other great classes of being—inorganic, vegetable, and animal. Human being thus appears composed of different modes of being, and these can be seen as being unrelated to human being. Thus, he said, animated matter without any psychic form—of instinct, memory, or purpose—characterized plants. Animals had, in addition, instinct and perhaps memory and intelligence but not spirit *(Geist)*. "Only in human beings does the spirit join the other functions of the soul as a formative principle" (*CW* 2:22). As Voegelin had put it in his article "*Staatslehre* as *Geisteswissenschaft*": "Spirit is what frees itself from life's organic bonds and, without ceasing to be life, confronts life as an autonomous entity." Or again: life is "the substance that transcends itself in spirit" (*CW* 32:421, 426). None of the lower forms anticipated the higher, because each form was complete in itself. The higher forms differed from the lower only by the addition of one more element that distinguished it from the lower one. These experiences of hierarchy served as the point of departure for speculation on the meaning of the whole and on how the unity of being can be combined with a multiplicity of constituent elements.

Voegelin then discussed several examples of "constructions" of a priori systems that took a single unique human element as privileged. But, rather as Merleau-Ponty later argued in the *Phenomenology of Perception* (1945), Voegelin rejected any argument that destroyed the whole on the basis of a postulated autonomy of one or another part. The idea of the somatic existence of the spirit, for example, was legitimate "in the sphere of the spirit [*Geist*] itself" but not in the sphere of the body. Likewise, the intellectual penetration of the mysteries of physical existence was legitimate, but that activity did not justify a natural science of the body that also elucidated the phenomena of the spirit. Physical anthropology legitimately existed on other grounds, namely the study of racial types according to various classificatory schemes dealing with physical traits that are transmitted through heredity, as in other animals. But this science could not deal with spiritual phenomena. In other words, the relationship of spirit to body is not a scientific question but a metaphysical one and can be discussed only on those grounds.

Having established the ground rules, so to speak, Voegelin then discussed race as a biological unit. There is a difference, he argued, between race as understood by contemporary theoretical biology and the way it was understood by so-called race theorists. For the latter, as for Linnaeus, race was understood to be a subunit of the species *Homo sapiens.* It was reasonable enough to classify humans according to physical traits because of certain constants that followed Mendelian rules of heredity. However, when this theory of the constants of racial traits was turned into the basis for the "historical philosophical thesis," namely that spiritual qualities connected to specific groups were the permanently effective causes of history, there were no grounds for doing so on the basis of current theoretical biology. Instead such assertions have been advanced on Darwinian grounds, the success of which, as has been indicated, resulted less from his abilities as a naturalist than from its appeal to liberal notions of competition and survival.

On the basis of his own understanding of contemporary theoretical biology, which he learned in the lab of Thomas Hunt Morgan at Columbia in 1924–1925, Voegelin argued that, because hereditary mutations and nonhereditary variations were distinct, it was simply impossible to establish a "pure line" of descent. As a consequence, he reported that "a unified principle of the origin of the species can never be found; rather, in each case special conditions of genesis prevailed" so that the notion of subspecies was equally problematic and "cannot be the one on which the race theories of man are based" (*CW* 2:54). In short, the biological basis for race was highly questionable *on biological grounds.*

Anthropology or ethnology was no better off. Because it was impossible to establish biologically pure lineages to serve as the basis for classifying human beings, anthropologists have had to be circumspect "in responding to the demand that only hereditary traits be included in the description of races." As a result, the groups of traits used to distinguish "races" have only "empirical significance" because it was impossible to tell, with a given individual, which "attention-attracting" attributes were a result of heredity and which were a result of the environment (*CW* 2:57). In fact, the ethnographic discussion of race was not simply concerned with classification of people, but was intimately linked to the interests of the state.

So far as the state is concerned, it was self-evident that it required a physical human basis for its actualization. On the other hand, not just any collection of human beings would do, because, the argument went, the "nation," which was to supply the specimens for the physical basis of the state, has resulted from "orienting propagation according to a norm" that nevertheless need not be always met. Thus, disturbances and mixtures arising from the physical realm could have an effect on the harmony of the overall "spiritual formation" that constituted the state. But in that case, the physical realm was not simply part of nature but also belonged to the spiritual realm. Race thus turns into "a norm for the physical and mental development of the nation in its state." Hence advocates of this position, whom we may call German nationalists, stressed national or German stock above "racial" or "Nordic" stock (*CW* 2:62).

On the surface, the argument regarding the nation and the state had a commonsense plausibility. However, it posed some major problems for anthropology as a natural science because the state, which was a spiritual formation, was taken to be the guide for the idea of the nation. But these principles regarding the state and the nation were higher than those developed by biologists for the animal and plant world, so it was difficult to see how the lower could be the cause of the higher. Ants, for example, may be "social" beings, but they were not internally organized as nations.

Before considering a central doctrine, the "soul-characteristics of races" and their transmission—which also influenced such classic African American books as Du Bois's *The Souls of Black Folk* (1903)—it is necessary, Voegelin said, to recollect the premises of the problem. On the one hand human beings were physically procreated and the totality of human being was an entirety or a whole, from the spiritual to the physical. The genesis of human being was "an essential source" of the "experience of fatality or inevitability," but fatality could not be the subject of scientific judgment, which would entail the dependence of the phenomenon of the spirit on bodily processes. That would be an ontological claim that was not supported by experience. Specifically, "there are experiences of the activity of the spirit, from which, equally compellingly, we know our existence to be freely creative" (*CW* 2:5–6). Hence the remark quoted above that spirit freed itself from the organic bonds of life in such a way that it both remained alive and confronted life. Here Voegelin's arguments resembled those made decades later by Hans Jonas, particularly in *The Phenomenon of Life* (1966).

Consider a negative example: If we assume that spiritual traits were closely paralleled by physical ones, one would have to assume that for "musicality" or "sensitivity" there was a corresponding physical condition. Most race theorists, Voegelin said, did not follow the implications to their logical conclusion. Most took some traits as inheritable and consigned others to tradition or education or some such variable connected to freedom. In fact, however, the body was both a constraint and a locus of freedom, as was the spirit. The body was not just passive but could initiate changes in the world; the spirit was not just free but was also passive and receptive. In short, the problem was far more complex than these "race theorists" imagined.

Voegelin then proceeded to demolish the detailed arguments of a couple of these individuals. The first was Fritz Lenz. Lenz began by noting the existence of "spiritual differences" among people. The cultural world was shaped by the human spirit, but human beings had very different aptitudes and intellectual talents. Lenz wondered what the cause of these differences might be and, "thinking in biological terms," concluded without hesitation "that a person's spiritual characteristics, just as the physical ones, have their roots in hereditary predispositions" so that "external influences" are only secondary (*CW* 2:71).

Voegelin then dissected Lenz's position. Lenz argued, on the one hand, that culture and what shaped it, the human spirit, were facts of experience. Acknowledging the significance of the human spirit and its creation, culture must therefore be based on some kind of philosophy or, to use a term favored by National Socialists, a "worldview" that considered spirit and culture to be the defining attributes of human reality. But this position was inconsistent with the notion of heredity, for which the spirit was an illusory or abbreviating expression of more basic and real material processes. In short, Lenz argued for two antithetical propositions: (1) that spirit was a defining attribute of human reality, which made possible the existence of those who were spiritually superior, and (2) that spiritual characteristics were determined by hereditary predisposition, race, which was completely external to the human spirit. But if hereditary disposition were part of nature, so therefore must be spirit.

Notwithstanding this basic inconsistency, Lenz went on to dismiss those who insisted on the independent importance of the spirit as mere *Geisteswissenschaftler* of no significance for true and genuine natural science—despite the "grand words and magical style" of people such as

Hegel and Schelling (and Voegelin added Pascal, Augustine, St. Paul, and Plato). At the same time, Lenz was compelled to concede that his theory of psychological heredity was difficult to understand and even more difficult to measure. And yet, somehow, he also believed that the spirit was of higher value than the body. In what followed, despite its apparent scholarly seriousness, Voegelin in fact poked fun at Lenz's treatment of artists and writers and philosophers. Voegelin undertook a similar analysis of several other writers who also sought to discover spiritual traits by using a theory that denied the reality of spirit. If they would consider why a sonnet by Shakespeare was poem whereas "formally quite perfect verses" by Wilhelm von Humboldt was a nonpoem, then the problem of spiritual faculties might look quite different, and "the barbaric notion that Dante and Beethoven were pretty talented dudes [*Kerle*]" surely would disappear. So much for "the standard work of recent scholarship in race theory" (*CW* 2:76).

The ultimate achievement of a good race theory was the listing of the psychical [*seelischen*] types of the major races. The problem was to relate "soul characteristics" to genetic structure. In this respect "we know absolutely nothing about soul characteristics," which raised the obvious question: "What takes the place of scientific inquiry in the theory of psychological types within race theory?" The answer: "Joining bits and pieces from a smattering of knowledge into a pseudoscientific edifice" (*CW* 2:86).

One of the critics whom Voegelin quoted favorably on the efforts of "standard" race theorists to indicate "the connection between genetics and soul-characteristics" was Ludwig Clauss. Voegelin examined Clauss's theory and concluded that, despite its defects, it had the virtue of treating race as a "stylistic type" that referred to human being as "the unity of the human form permeated by the spirit." Accordingly, the "phenomenon of races" must refer to "varieties of body-soul types within humanity." That is, as a simple, empirical reality of the variation in human beings (*CW* 2:10).

Finally, Voegelin considered "the only major philosophical attempt to get to the heart of the race problem," which was undertaken by his *Doktorvater* Othmar Spann. He began, however, by distinguishing his approach to the problem from that of Spann. Instead of several fundamental experiences, Spann was concerned only with two—spirit and matter—and how they may be "paired." Voegelin, in contrast, was less concerned with "constructions" of this sort. The fundamental experiences and the "thought problems" they engendered did not lead to any conclusions or constructions other than "simply, that the classes of being have each their own proper lawfulness and that they are able to enter into connections with each other whose inner nature remains a mystery to us." Spann, in contrast, sought "to bring this variety of phenomena under one roof" by way of his theory of "pairing." For Voegelin, however, the notion of "pairing" was not based on experience. Instead it was an image that signified an enigma or mystery rather than explained it (*CW* 2:105–11).

Spann's great contribution to race theory was to emphasize the problem of the relationship of matter and spirit. Spirit (or mind; *Geist*) did not create matter, which would have meant there could be no race problem, but rather spirit manifested itself in matter. Spann did not begin from biology and then try to figure out how biology could become ethnology or anthropology. Rather, he began with the direct or commonsensical observation of the world of spirit and its articulation in society. Because the order of society was spiritual, every person not only descended from the parents who begat him "but is also a member of humanity as a self-articulating idea." Now, if the individual were a "self-articulating idea," this must mean that the individual spirit could develop characteristics that were novel or unique and that could not be explained by biological heredity.

For Spann, as for Clauss, "purity" could not refer to genetic purity because, as Voegelin argued on the basis of contemporary (not Darwinian) biology, biologically pure races "do not exist among humans." Instead, also as in Clauss's work, purity referred to "style" or a general likeness of image, which referred necessarily to "the unity of spiritual expression." That is, the formation of a race was chiefly the work of the spirit—not that "an individual's spirit could change his race by an effort of will," but that race belonged to the social nature of spirit. New socially constitutive ideas emerged from preexisting ones "and acquire the physical image appropriate to them in the organic genotype." Accordingly, race history was not about biology but about those religious and philosophical sources of insight—what in *The History of the Race Idea* Voegelin called the incarnation of primal images—who were able to change the image of society.

That is, race history was spiritual history; it referred to the social character of the spirit, "within which the physical basis for the manifestation of the spirit is a subsidiary problem" (*CW* 2:113).

The conclusion reached at the end of his analyses of natural-scientific race theory, that such theories were in reality spiritual formations, brings us back to the class of problems discussed in Voegelin's book on America. Accordingly, part II of *Race and State* dealt with the spiritual formation of race—or as Voegelin increasingly used the term—the contemporary idea of race.

"By idea," Voegelin began, "we mean not a concept but the real substance that appears as the *one* in the *many*," which is to say it has a "twofold meaning" (*CW* 2:117–18). Community ideas, of which the race idea was one, existed somewhere between the idea of humanity and the idea of the individual person, with innumerable steps along the way—tribes, movements, schools, and so on—all of which were hierarchically ordered. "Each idea is related to every other idea through their shared connection in the idea of humanity, of which they all are individual articulations. But each one is also isolated from all the others by virtue of being a particular individual and historical step of articulation." Any particular individual could lead his or her conscious life on any given level of ideas, from humanity, to nation, to any level at all that could be invested with the meaning of "destiny." In any event, for Voegelin, the term *idea* did not indicate the independent existence of a substance unconnected to the historical developments of any given time; it did not refer to anything akin to a Platonic "idea" because "the idea of a community cannot be found anywhere except in the spirit of the people belonging to the community and in their spiritual creations." In this sense, ideas were experienced directly in terms of a common structure to the spiritual world of the community—as, for example, in the notion of a national spirit or mind, which was real both for the observer, as Voegelin showed in his first book, and especially for those living within the community constituted by it.

Accordingly, as noted above, the idea of a community was both objective and subjective. It was objectively real insofar as the community *is* the realization of the idea; it was subjective insofar as the reality of the idea *comes to be* in the minds of people who built the community. That is, the individual mind was the locus where the objective and subjective meaning of "idea" came together and contributed to the building of the community (*CW* 2:120). The effort at making a community idea objective was plausible only because, like cows and cats, human individuals were part of a chain of ancestors and descendants. But this objective position was not reflected in the order of the spirit, which created the notion of (matrilineal or patrilineal) family or of clan, dynasty, nation, or race.

Voegelin then provided a detailed analysis of two body ideas, the tribal polis of antiquity and the realm of Christ *(das Reich Christi)*. His intention was to remove "the character of the extraordinary" that the race idea "takes on in the eyes of people who have come to consider the political ideas since the seventeenth century with their anti-body rationalism" as being the "only conceivable kind of political theory." This was not true in Classical antiquity, as nineteenth- and twentieth-century scholarship has shown. If one extended the notion of the West to Classical antiquity, it was evident that the race idea was just one of several body ideas within Western political history. In all examples, however, the body idea existed within a complex structure of ideas that in turn existed in the mind, which was what made it a body *idea*. More important, all post-Classical body ideas, including race, were in one way or another variations on the explicitly Christian idea of the *corpus mysticum*.

Voegelin then undertook a detailed analysis of the Christian symbolism surrounding the body and soul *(pneuma)*, the flesh and the glorious body of the resurrected, and of the expansion of the symbolism from the individual Jesus to the community who shared in Christ. "Thus we must distinguish among three concepts of the body of Christ: the *soma* [human body] of the crucified one, the *doxa* [glorified body] of the resurrected one, and the mystical *soma*, the community in which the resurrected one has earthly, historical reality" (*CW* 2:135). The spiritualized Christian mystical body was thus unconnected to biological and organic notions. This spiritualization however made it vulnerable to the possibility of being replaced by other body ideas, such as monarchic bloodlines, nationality, and race. "The possibility," Voegelin wrote, "opens up for the new body ideas to take the place of the old one of the *corpus mysticum* in the life of the community" (*CW* 2:141). Whether such a replacement took place in any particular community depended chiefly on the internal political spirit of that community.

We noted above a distinction Voegelin made between German and Western political ideas. With respect to the dissolution of the Christian ideas of *pneuma* and *soma,* the replacement, which centered on the people, the *Volk,* was more complete in Germany than, for instance, in Western countries—France, the United Kingdom, or America.

Voegelin began an analysis of how this came about by considering Fichte's version, which endowed the partial human community of the Germans with "the imperial claim of the Kingdom of God," and then Schelling's "mythology" as the ground of being of a people, as distinct from humanity. But with both Fichte and Schelling, this sense of particularity was accompanied by an awareness that, precisely, the part was not the whole community of mankind, from which arose the anxiety that this particular *Volk* might someday lose its standing in the world and become extinct. The possibility of extinction, in turn, reinforced both the chosenness of one's *Volk* and the diabolical nature of the other—for Fichte, the French. "The particularist community overcomes its anxiety of forlornness by claiming for itself the status of 'world' and regarding all others as 'non-world' [*Nicht-Welt*], as forlorn" (*CW* 2:152). The animating experience of *Volk* as body idea is thus anxiety, *Angst,* and from anxiety arose the hatred of the counterworlds [*Gegen-Welten*], the mere existence of which could return the individual to a state of anxiety. From anxiety also arose the radical distinction between us and them; for Fichte between the Kingdom of God and the Kingdom of Evil, or for Othmar Spann, the *evil* demon, the monstrous. In short, the replacement of the Christian ideas of *pneuma* and *soma,* which were structured by the experiences of faith and hope, with post-Christian *volkisch* derivatives was accompanied by the experience of panic at being abandoned by God.

The collapse of the Christian community had other consequences as well for the growth of particularist communities. Each particular community endowed itself with the status of being a unit of history, which in turn changed the structure of history because pre- and non-Christian history became equal to Christian history. As a result there emerged a series of fragments, which may be flourishing or decaying, but in either instance were not ordered by "the ultimate aim of the redemption of mankind." Accordingly, the experience of an increased range of historical and pragmatic knowledge was "accompanied by an equally powerful loss of meaning in history." The implications of the process of increased knowledge of distinct and particular communities—beginning with the history of Classical antiquity and expanding to the history of the ancient Near East and to non-Western history—gradually became clear: "As the historical horizon expands, the observer's readiness to regard peoples and cultures as autonomous and to study them in terms of their uniqueness comes together with the experience, continuously nourished by more research, of lack of meaningful connection among the individual historical figures" (*CW* 2:155). Hence the readiness with which Fichte's divine and diabolical communities were accepted in Germany. Today, Voegelin said, the collapse of the Christian *pneuma* and *soma* has been formulated by Carl Schmitt in terms of "the existential friend-enemy opposition" (*CW* 2:160).

Comparative historical knowledge, which informed the eighteenth-century classifications of races discussed in *The History of the Race Idea,* later enabled people such as Gobineau, and after him, Spengler, to make comparisons regarding the rise and decline of cultures, to parallel structures or "stages" and cycles of recurrence, "all of which rendered any idea of infinite progress naive and scientifically unjustifiable." In this way, the cycle of cultures replaced by analogy the belief in divine or at least providential guidance toward a goal. "The systematic ordering of world events by an otherworldly power disappears, and man finds himself abandoned to an inner-worldly ordering of being, a destiny that oppresses and paralyzes, a destruction of traditional values that spares no goal hitherto considered worthwhile" (*CW* 2:166). The question of meaningful units of history was a problem that Voegelin revisited several times in his later work.[9]

Voegelin made two implicit points here that need to be emphasized directly. First, the dissolution of Christian ideas—or, as he would later say, Christian symbols—provided an opportunity to substitute other body symbols of the community, including race. Second, a growing knowledge of ethnography and of non-Western history introduced a genuine problem: How were "primitive peoples" who deviate significantly from European conventions to be understood? Even without making facile judgments about savages, awareness of the other drew attention to the problem of humanity as a unified being. Moreover, it is exacerbated when Europeans entered into social relationships with "primitives." Accordingly, "explaining the different manifestations of the human being as caused by physical differences is always very tempting," especially where social relationships consisted "of rule and obedience," the chief theme of the *Herrschaftslehre* (*CW* 2:173).

Postulating the existence of active and passive races with the former engaged in migration into the homelands of the latter did not solve the problem so much as intensify it because the passive races had also, once upon a time, to have migrated as well. So why did they, who now may be passive, once migrate? "Their motives are shrouded in silence." Beyond the limitations (or incoherence) of the migration theory, "the difficulty comes from the fact that, beyond the 'migrations,' the mystery of the origins of humanity arises." This issue, as with the ontologically real origin of species, was necessarily ignored when the focus was upon the differences among races. At the same time, of course, so too was ignored the unity of humanity from which arose the characteristic moods and anxieties noted above. So far as the actual mood of any particular race theorist was concerned, Voegelin indicated that it tended to reflect his own position in European society. Thus Gustav Klemm, for example, showed the optimism of the "rising" middle class and Arthur Gobineau expressed the pessimism of an aristocracy being eclipsed. It almost goes without saying that such contingencies and idiosyncrasies do not lend coherence to the idea.

The early development of the new particularist community to be realized through body ideas retained some of the previous universal human ideas as a final goal of history. Kantian rationality, Fichtean statelessness, or the optimistic and pessimistic outcomes of Klemm and Gobineau were all examples of how "the scope of the material that furnishes the proof" for the particular destiny of a community, including race, "coincides with world history" (*CW* 2:173). So too was the final blessed state of the Third Reich in Nazi theory. In this latter, the field of redemption was confined to the nation and the agent of community within the nation was a specific elite engaged in a struggle for power with an enemy. The division between divine and diabolic was already present, as was noted, in Fichte's account of Germany and France. For the National Socialists the counter-race or antirace was the Jew; in the United States there were two: Africans and southern and eastern Europeans.

The point of the counteridea was not primarily to know the Jewish character (or, in America, African or southern and eastern European character) as to contrast it to one's own. With Fichte, the diabolical French at least lived on their own territory; because Jews live in the midst of non-Jews, additional and highly emotional experiences were attached to the existence of the anticommunity. Voegelin then provided an analysis of the formulations of the "Jewish problem" by competent scholars such as Treitschke along with a host of second- or third-rate reflections such as that of Houston Stewart Chamberlain and his notion of the "inner Jew."

This disagreeable task provided Voegelin with an opportunity to state the obvious: "In order to preclude even the slightest possibility of a misunderstanding, let us again point out emphatically that the contrasting descriptions of the Semitic and the Aryan, the Jewish and the German character, even in the best work . . . contain little that is true about the nature of Jewishness." The reason was that the various works were motivated not by a desire to understand anything "but by the desire to elaborate one's own idea of community and personality; the juxtaposition to the Jews is here only a means to an end." Hence all the negative qualities attributed to Jews. Indeed, the discussion of Jewish rootlessness among Germans was important "because there is no natural and immediately sure political rootedness in actuality for the German ideas of community as there is for the world of ideas of France, England, and America." This condition resulted in an "inner uncertainty" (*CW* 2:206). In short, the only connection of the race idea, whether in its Nazi form or any other, with science, was that it furnished subject matter for analysis by political science.

Voegelin concluded *Race and State* with reflections on the significance of the "Nordic idea." He began by connecting the two parts of the book, on race theory and the race idea. "The formulation of ideas," he said, "makes use of the scientific form; that is, though it relies on politically real oppositions and ethical convictions for its impact, it does so not directly but by way of theories about social structure, social hygiene, race, and the like, that claim to be scientific" (*CW* 2:207). Thus did the polemicists of race pick and choose among the several elements of race theory, which in turn engendered disputes of little theoretical interest, whatever their political significance. As a result, in the existing German political situation, "the race idea appears in everyday politics only in a form that eschews any clear-cut elaboration of the details that would lead to political difficulties." Thus a communist "is a red subhuman creature only as long as he follows international socialism; when he converts to national socialism, he becomes a nation-building element." Because of the numerical size of a "pure" Nordic race in Germany, "the practical-political race idea" was defined negatively, "through opposition to the Jews," which was its sole and entire significance.

In contrast, in America the Nordic ideal was important chiefly because of the closing of the frontier—though it was still vigorous even there—that had been settled by English, Germans, and Scandinavians, not those who later in the nineteenth century settled in cities. Even so, English and American democracy, with or without the Nordic ideal, was conservative, whereas in Germany it was revolutionary because it was not based on a political human type—such as the British aristocrat or the American frontiersman. Thus in Germany the purpose of the Nordic ideal was to shape and form the German *Volk.* This purpose meant that it was not in any sense a "national idea," because the Nordic elite that was said to be endangered "is viewed as the elite of *all* the great cultures of Europe." Hence the Great War was, from the point of view of race, a civil war. Accordingly, the Nordic idea in Germany tended to be "international" rather than national, an analytical insight elaborated after the war by Hannah Arendt in *The Origins of Totalitarianism.*

Academic and political reviews of Voegelin's two books began to appear intermittently over the next few months and years.[10] Early in 1934, Voegelin published an article in the newspaper *Kölnische Zeitung* (*CW* 9:13–16). This was the first time he wrote for a newspaper, even a highbrow one. It presented a simplified and preemptive attempt to make his argument accessible to a wide audience. There was no attempt at persuading Nazi supporters, but he did wish to instruct intelligent readers and scholars as to what was involved in the Nazi revolution.

"The National Socialist revolution," Voegelin began, "has made the race idea the principle idea in the construction of the German *Volk.*" This was a political and a scientific issue, and perhaps a legal one as well. In any event, it was necessary, if one was to be clear about the significance of events, to distinguish the distinct aspects of the problem. The issue was important precisely because the race idea and language of race science had become fused. Voegelin then provided a concise account of the methodological observations he made in the introductions to the two books.

Ideas are "propositions that we must deem to be an immediate expression of experience per se that cannot be scientifically either proved or disproved." The race idea in particular was "rooted" in the fundamental experience of human "corporeal-psychic unity." Human being was "fused" or "integral" being. This applied to individuals and to races equally. Racial solidarity was possible because racial uniformity did not destroy the individuality of the persons who identified themselves with any particular race. Empirically, some people experienced racial solidarity at some times and others did not. But either way "in no case does it fall within the confines of intellectual scrutiny; it cannot be rationally substantiated; its importance cannot be impressed on those who do not possess it. It belongs entirely to the sphere of the psyche, and not to a superficial layer of excitement at that, but to a depth that is decisive for one's comprehensive attitude toward human existence." This attitude Voegelin earlier referred to as the primordial way of seeing *(Urweise des Sehens).*

Once a person experienced himself or herself as a member of a race, the experience then enabled individuals to fashion a primordial image of community and of history (the *Urbild* of *The Race Idea*) that reinforced the original attitude and thus could serve as a norm for action. "In the process of shaping a world view that corresponds to the personal encounter with race, fusions creep in that are contestable." Because history was the product of innumerable causes, "it is quite impossible *rationally* to ascertain which of them is the determining factor." Race may be *one* factor in the unfolding of history; no more than economics could it be the sole one. As a result, in any scholarly enterprise it was important to distinguish the experiences that guided interpretation from the principles of science.

One of the problems in keeping the two issues distinct was the superstition, a legacy from the nineteenth century, that everything could be proven "scientifically." Thus emerged the distrust of the personal encounter and a flight from spiritual reality. "Everyone must bear *responsibility* before community and history for his personal encounters and the convictions and attitudes that spring from them. Pretending that these convictions are scientific propositions is an abrogation of responsibility; this leads to the invention of a kind of anonymous legality that can be burdened with the responsibility for one's beliefs and actions." For those who nevertheless adopted the worldview of the race doctrine, their position was very close to that of historical materialism and "scientific" socialism. Both positions shared two defects: "(1) a shift of responsibility to a system of 'scientific' propositions, and (2) bringing historical processes under a law, and thereby making room for a feeling of a paralyzing, action-blocking fatality," an artificial escape from both freedom and responsibility. What was needed, therefore, was more realism, precision, and responsibility with less yearning to escape responsibility. "These demands are aimed less at the politician who wishes to implement the race idea through legislation, than at *the scholar.*"

Shortly after *Race and State* appeared, it was the subject of a hostile review by Norbert Gurke in the *Reichswaltungsblatt und Preussisches Verwaltungsblatt.* Gurke was the assistant to, and son-in-law of, a leading Nazi lawyer, Otto Kollreutter, and after 1939 he ended up teaching at the University of Vienna. In his response in the same journal early in 1934, Voegelin proposed to correct Gurke's misrepresentations of his argument. He did so in considerable detail (*CW* 9:17–20) and concluded by reiterating his major point in simple language: "The race experience comes first, science comes second. If the reverse order is followed, we expose ourselves to the danger of the intellectualist absurdity of 'scientific' Socialism to be followed by the similar absurdity of 'scientific' National Socialism; the fundamental requisites of politics do not spring from either, but from fundamental experiences." Voegelin could not have been unaware of the consequences of showing that a leading Nazi intellectual was a bit of a *Dummkopf.* Any thought, however naive, of an academic career in the Reich was over.

5

Austria

Voegelin's book on Austria, *The Authoritarian State* (*CW* 4), was first published in 1936. As with the two race books, it earned him further disapprobation from official sources and deepened the divide between him and his former teacher Hans Kelsen. The fate of the books as physical objects was even more dismal. With the Anschluss between the Third Reich and Austria two years after publication, all further distribution of the book was ended, and the remaining copies were stored away in the basement of the publisher, Springer. During the Soviet assault on Vienna in 1945, the Springer building was bombed, which incinerated the remaining copies. The text was reissued in 1997 and an English edition was published in 1999. For these reasons, as well as because of seemingly endless pages of minute and highly technical legal analysis, this is not one of Voegelin's best-known works. It is however an important publication, particularly in light of the subject matter of the present book.

There is one additional preliminary circumstance that needs to be noted. In her "Historical Commentary on the Period," Erika Weinzierl (*CW* 4:10–38) observed that Voegelin's Rockefeller years in America and France coincided with "the relatively calmest and economically best years of the [Austrian] First Republic. . . . When he returned to Austria in 1927 he came back to a tense situation . . . in domestic politics, one already characterized in part by violence." This novel political situation conditioned Voegelin's "more lively interest" in politics (*CW* 4:24).

Voegelin's position in Vienna was still economically precarious. He became a *Privatdozent* at the university in 1929 and an associate professor seven years later, but as he later remarked, "neither of these dignities was connected with any material support" (*CW* 34:67). Since he had married Lissy Onken in 1932, "material support" was no longer a matter of relative indifference. Voegelin earned a modest income as an assistant to Kelsen, who soon left for the University of Cologne, and then as an assistant to Adolf Merkel. The modest income he received as an assistant was supplemented by a few newspaper articles, discussed below, and by teaching political science at the Ottakring Volkschochschule in Vienna (for an account of this experience, see *CW* 9:79–90).

In his 1927 article "Kelsen's Pure Theory of Law" (*CW* 7:182–91), Voegelin drew attention to the fact that Kelsen "had the singular opportunity of drafting the Austrian constitution in accordance with his principles" of jurisprudence (*CW* 7:188). The result was a "legal document" that, technically speaking, "may fairly be called the best of its kind now in existence. In contrast to the American constitution, the Austrian is a model of consistency."[1] In 1927, Voegelin was particularly impressed by the "restriction of the content" of the constitution to "statements of operative facts for enforcing actions" and "statements of the enforcing behaviors." More specifically, Voegelin admired the *absence* of a preamble and other declarations "of merely political importance." The only defects, he said, were the result of political demands; the only incomplete specifications were the result of accidental oversight. Where political declarations were present, as in Article 1.1, which declared "Austria is a democratic republic," no legal consequences followed. Moreover, when one added Kelsen's commentary on the constitution, which explained the "deficiencies introduced for political reasons," the combined text was both a technical masterpiece and "a remarkable contribution to the development of democracy."

There were two reasons for Voegelin's high praise. First, in the German context, Kelsen had eliminated the residua of "natural law ideas" from "the theory of positive law." That is, when positive law was understood as somehow expressing the insights of natural law, the results were necessarily dogmatic and arbitrary. In addition Voegelin interpreted Kelsen's pure theory of law, as embodied in the Austrian constitution, as akin to the American "due process" doctrine, which had also been proven effective (at least in the 1920s) in blocking popular demands for changes in labor legislation that had been advanced on grounds surviving "from the 'natural law' period."

As a consequence of Kelsen's arguments, law was understood to be "an apparatus or a machinery capable of protecting any set of social relations according to the current code of social ethics. Laws are technical means for the performance of certain social ends." This understanding had the effect of indicating that the law was not some eternal order "but a compromise of battling social forces." Accordingly, there was nothing sacred, for instance, about the German or Austrian monarch. The theory of the Austrian constitution, in Kelsen's formulation, therefore had important implications for the German republic as well: It marked "not only an important progress in legal analysis and technique, but also a development from the half-absolutistic philosophy of the German empire toward the spirit of the new democracy." The historical, as distinct from the jurisprudential significance of the Austrian constitution (including its applicability to Germany) was that "no state entity" could hide behind the legal rules and manipulate them, as the Hapsburg monarch had been able to do by dissolving parliament and enjoying absolute rule for a time. In contemporary language, the rules of Kelsen's Austrian constitution were models of transparency.

That was how things looked on paper, from America, during the mid-1920s. In 1930, Voegelin published the first of several analyses of Austrian politics that were both more realistic and much less sanguine. "The Austrian Constitutional Reforms of 1929" (*CW* 8:148–79) began with an observation that Voegelin reiterated several times: "The Austrians are not a nation and the Austrian republic is not a national state" (*CW* 8:148). One must begin, he said, with this "basic fact" in order to understand "the peculiar character of the Austrian constitution." In other publications he reiterated in different ways what sort of collectivity the Austrians were and what kind of state they had created. Indeed, one might say that nearly all of Voegelin's analysis of Austrian political realities, including its constitutional documents, were an elaboration of the implications of a politically nonexistent Austrian people.

Before considering the details of his argument, we would draw attention first of all to the emphasis Voegelin made: The basic or fundamental reality was to be found not in the formalities of the Austrian constitution and certainly not in the legal theory that informed it but in the political character of Austria as a nonnational state. As with his focus on political ideas in the race books, the emphasis on the political foundations of the law of the constitution marked a new dimension in Voegelin's analysis.

In Western democracies, he explained, the nation-state has been organized in terms of citizens. The citizen provided the image to organize the state, and the state, in turn, conditioned the sentiments and rationality that influenced the conduct of citizens. "A single ideal of the citizen's form of political life pervades the whole nation." In its internal organization the nation-state fit the ideal of a citizen in a national community; in turn, the national citizens were of the opinion that this form was superior to all others and was even sanctioned by divine favor so that they could fulfill a special mission. In short, "the ideal of the citizen life-form and the citizen's faith in the chosen status of his people are the principle motives in the life of a nation." More to the point, Voegelin argued, it was from this complex of sentiments, emotions, and motives—"these primary expressions of national vigor"—that the constitution received its meaning. Precisely this layer of meaning was what Austria lacked: There was no "political ideal of the Austrian" akin to the political ideal of the Frenchman, the Englishman, or even the American; there was no "chosen status," no *mission civilatrice,* of the Austrian nation.

If the constitution did not reflect these profound national purposes, then its meaning must be provided by secondary constituent elements—the "diversity of legal forms" and the "structural principles" of this diversity, which is to say the "application" of the legal form on behalf of a particular interest. In short, if the constitution could not draw upon the resources of national sentiments, it must draw upon legal ones based on current political principles—in 1930, those would be "either the principle of parliamentary democracy or that of dictatorship." The interjection of concrete political interests into a legal form, then, could give it a specific direction, which was usually partisan and necessarily degraded or corrupted the political principles and their purely juristic formulation.

In 1930, Voegelin found a "more or less pure case" of a federal constitution in the 1920 document drafted by Kelsen. The amendments of 1929 opened some additional breaches in the rational construction of the original argument, which required further historical (not juristic) analysis to be understood properly. The abolition of the monarchy after the war was attended by several unpropitious events. To begin with, there was an atmosphere of resentment, which was hardly unexpected after losing a war, accompanied by vague hopes regarding either an *Anschluss* with Germany or the formation of a Danubian federation. "One thing the Austrian revolution did not have was ideas" (*CW* 8:152), especially political ideas about the Austrian state. Their presence might have provided a sense of direction and purpose. Instead there were mere political "gestures," which included such trivial matters as the expropriation of castles or the creation of empty but "sonorous titles" such as state councillor or state notary.

The original 1918 resolutions proposed a unitary state, not the federal one that Kelsen eventually put together two years later. Voegelin detected three reasons for the change. The first was another "gesture," this one by the chancellor to the *Länder* to send to the capital their declarations of agreement; the second was an absence of political energy in Vienna, which allowed the *Länder* to develop their own organizations; the third was the strength of the parties and the division between agrarian, Catholic provinces and socialist, judaized Vienna. This particular equilibrium, along with an absence of political experience, allowed the constitutional forms to take on an independence of their own. Hence the federal constitution, which in this context may by considered a political accomplishment directed by Kelsen. It contained special provisions for Vienna and additional centralizing clauses as well as a "fictitious federal content," namely that the *Länder* took part in governing. The reality was that federalism meant little more than the division of patronage between the parties—the socialists in Vienna and the Catholic parties in the provinces.

The amendments or reforms of 1929 aimed to consolidate partisan advantages so that "an observer consulting the text of the bill alone might well conclude that Austrian constitutional life consists in no more than a struggle of party machines, and that the Austrian people, unless they belong to the class of career politicians, have nothing to do with the matter" (*CW* 8:166–67). In other words, the 1929 amendments strongly undermined both federalism and parliamentary democracy. In reality, Voegelin said, "the basic situation of the population and the territory remains the opposition between Vienna and the provinces," with Vienna on the decline and the agrarian forces on the rise. As a consequence, "the Austrian people continue to be torn between the two great state-transcending world-views of Marxist internationalism and Catholicism," neither of which supported the state so much as sought to use it "to achieve the ends of a world-view that transcends it." These two "spiritual powers" were likely to remain the driving force of Austrian politics. "Constitutional reforms cannot change anything about this unfortunate situation." At best they can create a dictatorship of one of the two parties, which has nothing to do with a "will to statehood." The only real alternative "would be annexation to Germany. This step would take the German nation into the meaning of Austrian politics as well" (*CW* 8:178–79), which even in 1930 was not an attractive proposition. The two options, dictatorship or *Anschluss,* defined the Austrian political alternatives until the country ceased to exist. As a consequence, Voegelin's account of Austrian politics grew increasingly grim.

Between April and November 1934, following "the most turbulent year of Austrian domestic politics" of the interwar period, as Erika Weinzierl said (*CW* 4:19), Voegelin wrote four articles for the newspaper *Wiener Zeitung,* three of which dealt with additional changes to the Austrian constitution (*CW* 9:23–36). The fourth, "Danse Macabre" (*CW* 9:37–39), dealt with several celebrated deaths and was written in what might be termed a slightly hysterical Viennese gossip style, an amusing *feuilleton* rather than more-or-less highbrow political journalism.

"Austria's constitutional history," Voegelin said in the first piece, "proceeds in a series of paroxysms that set in every time the chronic internal affliction passes into an acute stage as a result of an external cataclysm." This was why the best guide for understanding Austrian constitutional history was to grasp the significance of external impulses, the last two of which were the Home Defense Force *(Heimwehr)* movement of 1929, which in fact contained some elements of genuine citizenship, and the German revolution of 1933, which did not.

Considered internally, owing to the peculiar constitutional structure of the Hapsburg *Reich,* which was discussed in detail in *The Authoritarian State,* the Austrian populace remained a kind of fossilized *Reichsvolk,* an imperial people, even after the collapse of 1918, and so never became a *Staatsnation,* "a nation of common spirit intent upon the formation of a state."[2] Instead, the Austrians as a populace learned what Voegelin had earlier noted, that "there was no such thing as an Austrian nation" and that the constitution, which was built upon democratic and parliamentary axioms, "had no foundation in political reality." Instead, the political reality, as noted above, was simply a field of partisan conflict. And finally, Voegelin concluded, "the predominant political theory identified the state with the legal order," which simply reduced "the substance of the state to a system of norms" or, more accurately, to rules.

Voegelin's concluding remarks were an allusion to Kelsen's pure theory of law. The implication was that, as a political theory, it added to the misconceptions that beset Austrian political life. That is, Kelsen's notion that the state was a legal order and that its substance consisted of rules was not just a questionable argument, as Voegelin had suggested on previous occasions, but that it had regrettable political consequences as well, because it augmented both popular and scholarly confusion.

In the last of his political articles in the *Wiener Zeitung,* Voegelin made an argument that provided a great contrast to his 1927 comparison of the Austrian constitution informed by Kelsen's pure theory of law with the "due process" clause of the Fifth and Fourteenth Amendments to the U.S. Constitution. In the earlier article, he praised the absence of political declarations, including a preamble. In 1934, the absence of such nonjusticiable guidelines was understood in a rather different light.

The political and constitutional problem following the collapse of the *Reich* in 1918 was that the legitimacy of the monarchy had disappeared, but the apparatus of the state remained, but without the legitimacy of a national state that on the surface succeeded the monarchy. Nor was the state willing to gain legitimacy by creating a national political people. This situation presented a problem a few years later, when it came to providing a source of legitimacy to the 1934 or "authoritarian" constitution. Indeed there was a problem accounting for where the 1934 constitution came from, which was the task conventionally performed by a preamble (*CW* 4:252). The problem was that the source of the 1934 constitution, which was "received" by the Austrian populace, was simply not specified. In fact it was the authoritarian state, "a tradition-bound and authentic heritage of the authoritarian conduct of the affairs of the empire by the Austrian monarchy." That is, the Austrian executive, which was in fact the source of the authoritarian constitution, amounted to an imperial state apparatus without an emperor. Accordingly "it is proof of an admirable wisdom and of a realistic assessment of the situation that the executive has given up the right to set itself up as the source of the constitution's legitimacy, withdrawing anonymously behind the invocation of a divine author of all law, and making use, within the bounds of possibility, of the form of the old constitution in order to lay hold of those fragments of legitimacy that fit the democratic mold" (*CW* 9:32). In *The Authoritarian State,* to which we now turn, Voegelin elaborated in considerable detail the several dimensions of the crisis in Austrian political life and how the 1934 constitution both expressed that crisis and was intended to be a means of coping with it.

As on previous occasions, Voegelin began his book on Austria with a methodological reflection. The scientific account of historical materials, he said, "uses sharply outlined concepts, which confer on it a definitiveness that reality never holds." As a result, "the uncritical reader will turn the author's evaluations into dogma" and "the critical reader" already "believes them to be dogmatic." Either way, the problem was one of dogma. Or rather, the problem was how to avoid dogma.

So far as a study of the Austrian authoritarian state was concerned, Voegelin said, avoiding dogmatic formulations and analyses meant distinguishing the constituent elements of the concept of the authoritarian state from the richly textured historical evidence. If the account was successful, the temptation would be enhanced to mistake the self-enclosed typology for the reality. Accordingly, it was important to emphasize two points at the outset. First, in the context of European politics, Austria was relatively insignificant and therefore was strongly influenced by factors in the history of European ideas and power politics. This observation referred both to the "external cataclysms" mentioned above and to the postwar geostrategic position of Austria situated between Germany and Italy. Second, considered domestically, the authoritarian state must be examined with a view to the options of enhancing its organization in the direction of totalitarianism or weakening it in the context of the liberal tradition, which was also strongly expressed in the 1934 constitution, and which is discussed below.

Voegelin anticipated three kinds of readers: first, scholars interested in a theoretical discussion of a political subject; second, persons interested in obtaining information about the subject. "And then there is a third class of readers, those who take neither a dramatic nor an objective interest in a work of political science but expect from the author a confirmation of their political sympathies and antipathies. As on earlier occasions, I will disappoint this group of readers on the present occasion as well. The intention of a theoretical work is diametrically opposed to the desire for political enthusiasm" (*CW* 4:48). His intention, in other words, was to write a scientific analysis of a novel political phenomenon.

The introduction to the book outlined Voegelin's understanding of the problem and how he was prepared to approach it. The existence of the postwar Austrian state and the authoritarian regulation of its internal affairs "are subsidiary problems within an all-encompassing process that we can call Austria's growth to statehood" (*CW* 4:49). Such was the subject matter Voegelin proposed to deal with. The concept of the state, which may first have been employed by Machiavelli, was essentially developed by the French, from whom subsequent usage has been derived. By this account the state is a postmedieval creation of a centralized governing organization accompanied by the spiritual shaping of the territorially defined population into a nation. The state was not, therefore, "the essential human form of existence in a political alliance" but a historically and geographically limited contingent spiritual formation.

Voegelin reiterated that, in Austria, the formation of the state took place later than in the West, and the creation of a nation "was never accomplished at all." As a result, "institutionalized power" never gained the legitimacy of a national state—the people never saw in the state a national representative. To the end of its existence in 1918, the Austrian monarchy retained the essential traits of an empire, a *Reich,* along with an internal administrative rather than political organization. This legacy was transmitted to the Austrian republic. Because there existed no Austrian body politic in the sense that Austrians were not a political people, the power organization "lacks the authority it can acquire only when it is the representative organization of a people." As a consequence, the actions of political leaders were not representative of the national state and did not reveal a will to national existence. Instead, "the national power apparatus" was an "autonomous non-representative instrument available for use by anyone entitled by the stipulations of the constitution to employ it." Not surprisingly, "the national power apparatus" was employed first of all to ensure its own self-preservation, namely maintaining the rules.

It is also not surprising, therefore, that the dominant constitutional theory, Kelsen's pure theory of law, exhibited the attributes of this administrative style. Thus when emergency political action was called for, as happened following the German revolution of 1933 and as continued during the subsequent prolonged period of civil unrest and violence, political events appeared first of all to be violations of a given administrative order rather than realities that had to be dealt with through innovative political action. In Voegelin's words, "the national leadership had to leave behind its position as administrator of the constitution and proceed to laying down a constitution" (*CW* 4:52). That is, they were called upon to act rather than simply to preserve the "administrative style" inherited from the Hapsburg *Reich.* The creation of the new authoritarian state was not therefore just changing the rules within an uninterrupted constitutional regime. The response to the emergency of 1933–1934 changed Austrian politics from an administrative to a political style because the new state was legitimated by the beginning of a national will to exist as Austrians.

One of Voegelin's tasks, therefore, was "an attempt to overcome Austria's 'administrative' constitutional theory," namely Kelsen's pure theory of law, "and design a 'political' one." This meant dealing with four sets of problems: (1) analyzing the political idea of the authoritarian state in the context of the European idea of the "total" state (this was covered in part I of the book); (2) connecting the current problems of the Austrian state with the legacy of the Austrian *Reich* (this was covered in part II); (3) dealing with the relationship of constitutional theory and constitutional reality (dealt with in the introductory chapters in part II and part III); and (4) providing an analysis of the new Austrian constitutional law, which constituted most of part III of the book.

Voegelin added that critics can find plenty to object to: There may be too much legal detail in places and not enough in others. But the problem lay in the diffuse reality he wished to consider and the absence of theoretical instruments by which it might be organized. Critics "will be sure to cite good reasons for their opinion—let them consider that our reasons for choices are likely just as good" (*CW* 4:54). The structure of the book, which was designed to deal with the four sets of problems connected to the growth of the Austrian state, may be specified in terms of an increasingly focused and concrete analysis—from the European context, to the analysis of the mixed legacy of Austria, to the analysis of the current constitutional structure.

Part I, on "'Total' and 'Authoritarian' as Symbols," continued the argument initially established in the race books regarding the distinction between a political idea or political symbol and a scientific concept. In *The Authoritarian State* the distinction was almost taken for granted, and Voegelin's rhetoric changed from the kind of enthusiastic argument that accompanied his initial discovery or insight to a more considered and reflective attitude.

Political changes, he began, engender new verbal formulations regarding the significance of what has happened. This presented problems for scientific knowledge because "the political form of language is valuable for the struggle and as symbol, while the value of scientific language has knowledge value." Accordingly, the same verbal expression can have quite different meanings in the political or the scientific context, a point he made again in *The New Science of Politics* (*CW* 5:110ff). In the scientific analysis presented in *The Authoritarian State*, it was therefore necessary to acknowledge that the terms "total" and "authoritarian" were first of all political, not scientific. Thus "we cannot 'define' a total state and an authoritarian state." This did not mean abandoning scientific precision but acknowledging that political language was one of the component elements of political reality. "Refusing to misunderstand the creation of a political symbol as an act of perception, renouncing the assumption that the political symbol has to *mean* something and not just *be* something, allows us to understand it as a symbol in the full richness and force of its expression" (*CW* 4:58).

As an illustrative example, Voegelin took Carl Schmitt's term "total state," which Schmitt had adapted from Ernst Jünger's notion of "total mobilization," which in turn was based on his intense experience as a storm trooper on the western front during the Great War. The notion of a total state received its contextual meaning from Enlightenment and post-Enlightenment accounts of the relationship of the state to civil society and the growth of the state from a "neutral" state, which acknowledged the autonomy of civil society, to the "total" state, which organized it entirely, thus putting an end to the state-society distinction. "Instead, all spheres of human life in society acquire immediate political relevance" (*CW* 4:61).

However insightful, Schmitt's usage omitted several connotations found in Jünger's term "total." For instance, the arguments of Marx and Engels regarding the interdependence of public and private enterprises "creates the 'total' social structure within which the antithesis of public and private, of state and society, of political and unpolitical, daily loses ground." Likewise the papal encyclical *Quadragesimo anno* raised similar concerns. The more interesting question—apart from the agreement of Marx and Engels with the Catholic Church—was "the prerequisite for this entire cluster of problems," namely "the existence of a social context experienced as obligatory, within which the phenomena of differentiation of power and domination occur." Here the issues of economic power turned into questions of "political totality" (*CW* 4:72).

Central to any notion of political totality "is the permeation of people in a shared context with a common idea, a common spiritual and intellectual outlook—the totality of ideology." The purpose of ideology was simply to connect the substance of the individual with the substance of the community. Voegelin described the solution hit upon by the National Socialists and by the Fascists, namely the evocation of the *Volk* and the *Italita* respectively, as being essentially "Averroist."

Readers of Voegelin's *History of Political Ideas* will be familiar with his concept of Averroism (*CW* 20:153–54, 178ff). The essential feature of Averroism was that the human personality was absorbed into a collective spirit. With Averroës (also known as Ibn-Rushd, 1126–1198), the emphasis was on a specific interpretation of Aristotle's theory of the soul so that the human intellect was considered to be simply an instance of a single, collective, and therefore individual-transcendent intellect. This Averroistic "solution" to the problem of linking the individual and collective substance could in principle be applied to any community. Thus for Mussolini or for

Hitler the human personality was absorbed into the *Italita* or into the *Volk*, not Averroës's postulated collective intellect.

Voegelin undertook an analysis of the Nazi and Fascist symbols of the collectivity and again emphasized that, even though they had no scientific or theoretical status, they nevertheless were useful in political struggle—a point he had already made with respect to the so-called "race theories" discussed in the previous chapter. Now, however, the methodological point was made more emphatically and more explicitly: "Only if we insist on this differentiation will we, as originally noted, be able adequately to grasp the significance of the situation; it must remain concealed from us if we accept political symbols into the scientific context without translating them into the language of science. There's no help for it: science and politics are simply not identical" (*CW* 4:79). Thus the scientific account was concerned with the Averroistic question of the substantial relationship between the individual and the community, whereas the political issue was the relationship of the state to the people—with the Nazis according priority to the *Volk* and the Fascists to the *Italita.*

In addition to the by now familiar problem of political symbol and scientific theory, Voegelin also reminded his readers of the significance of history. In European history, for example, the state may be a general political form, but its actual meaning will vary according to the period at which the state was established. "Surely," Voegelin wrote, "it is clear that the proportions of the political realities are different when a state makes the transition from dynastic state authority to one that takes its legitimacy from other sources in the eighteenth century than when that transition occurs in the twentieth century." Obviously there is a difference in the authority of a dynasty over a *Volk* that has existed for five hundred years (as in the example of France) compared to a territorial principality that has only recently been consolidated (such as Prussia). "The idea of *Volk* is different when the *Volk* arrives at consciousness of its political unity and ability to act under the impact of the eighteenth-century idea of personality rather than achieving that condition under the influence of the collectivist and race ideas of the nineteenth and twentieth centuries." Accordingly, it was necessary to consider the historical significance of the constituent elements of the state, which is to say there is no pure "state type" (*CW* 4:82–83).

Nevertheless, when one looks to the "theory" of the Austrian authoritarian state, it bears a family resemblance to the accounts of Hauriou and Renan regarding the origin of the French state. The resemblance, however, was neither deliberate nor coincidental. "It is conditioned by a situation that compelled the head of government to consider the basic questions of a state's existence and the sovereign authority, and such considerations, if they are logical, lead precisely to the classical European theories of the state as they were developed in France, the model European state, beginning in the sixteenth century" (*CW* 4:102–3). That is, similar conditions are apt to result in similar accounts of historically distinct political crises and lead to similar resolutions of them.

Voegelin concluded part I with a summary. "Today the expressions *total* and *authoritarian* are political symbols that can be understood only in a specific situation of conflict in which it is a matter of liquidating a condition of political fragmentation and establishing new authorities" (*CW* 4:105). The task of science was to clarify the structure of this situation and to describe the symbolic value of specific expressions that both illustrated the problems of the state and tried to deal with them. In part II, Voegelin applied this understanding of science to the development of Austrian constitutional theory and Austrian politics after 1848.

The foundation of Austrian constitutional theory was laid down by aristocratic statesmen in the aftermath of the political upheaval of 1848. Apart from Prince Metternich, a central role was played by the Hungarian man of letters József, Baron Eötvös. It was not easy for them, or anyone else, to resolve the principle of a dynastic and multinational regime ruled by aristocrats, who were also a kind of ethnic group, with the principle of the nation—to which liberal and democratic principles were later added. Eventually the notion of an ethnic-based sovereignty proved to be revolutionary and even "religious." Voegelin summarized Eötvös: "New gods have arisen in the struggle with old ones, new sources of religious ecstasy have appeared, new emotional forces have become active, still untempered by reflection and reason, with the relentlessness of intellectual blindness" (*CW* 4:119).

That the growth of national consciousness within a multinational *Reich* could bring only disorder was self-evident to Eötvös and was formulated in terms of Montesquieu's notion that every state must be based on a "principle" that permeates every individual as well as the entire regime. This "theory of principles," as Voegelin called it for short, was "the backbone for interpreting political phenomena" just as the existence of a "principle" was the essential precondition for the continued existence of the state. To reiterate a previous observation by Voegelin, the constitution *cannot* perform the task of providing a "principle" for the regime, because the meaning of the constitution is effectively derived from the regime. In contemporary terms, there can be no *Verfassungspatriotisimus*, "constitutional patriotism," contrary to what some Germans believe today.

For the Austrian statesmen, the national movements unleashed by the French Revolution and the wars of liberation, these new "religious mass movements," could not be extinguished and so had to be controlled. If left alone, the national idea or the national principle would destroy the Hapsburg *Reich.* Thus the sole question was to find "a constitutional construction that reconciles the central state organization with the vital needs of nations." The inner logic of the French Revolution could lead to a constitutional monarchy or a republic because there existed a French *Volk*, but this was not so in the Austrian *Reich* because, as has already been indicated, there was no Austrian *Volk* (*CW* 4:122).

During the period 1848–1849, the absolute monarch issued an authoritarian decree or *octroi* that "granted" a constitutional provision in order to establish a new relationship with his subjects "because he is the sole legally empowered, functional authority" (*CW* 4:131–32). In this way, an authoritarian gesture by a monarch appointed by God "captures the revolutionary element of the movement for a constitution and transforms it into an act by the monarch." Likewise, *octrois* were issued to try to transform the *Reich* from a collection of provinces overshadowed by an imperial title into an Austrian imperial state. But an imperial state would have been "based on entirely different political foundations." As a result of the contradictory ideas embodied in the acts of the emperor, namely the "gesture" of granting a constitution by decree, "it is impossible to determine unequivocally what the constitution of Austria was during this period." Only with the constitution of March 1849, which was both an imposition by *octroi* and the foundation of a new state created by the king-emperor, did there emerge "an order of power and also . . . a legal system" (*CW* 4:135).

The great problem of the Hapsburg *Reich* throughout the nineteenth century was that, on the one hand, the multinational character of the *Reich* meant that the monarch could enter into relations with the constituent peoples of his realms only on different terms. The possibility might exist, for example, to create a constitutional monarchy in the province of Austria because the monarch was Austrian. Unfortunately, in law the monarch could not treat the Austrian people any differently than any other people, so there could be no move toward a constitutional government either in Austria (the Austrian province), in any other province, or in the *Reich* as a whole.

Such changes as have taken place in the Hapsburg lands have usually been responses to foreign events, Voegelin's aforementioned "external cataclysms," starting with the Paris revolution of 1848 and proceeding to the Crimean War, the Russian Revolution of 1905, the collapse of 1918, and the German revolution of 1933, which "initiates the period of reform in which we find ourselves at present" (*CW* 4:140). In each instance, situations of uncertainty were temporarily stabilized by and within an authoritarian structure, which soon enough had to be suspended, internally altered, or in other ways changed. What was missing "is the authority of the state in itself" that in the West European states was the heritage of national monarchies. "Austria entered the period of political peoples as a '*Reich.*' Its domestic political problems are almost entirely the result of the delayed transformation into a 'state'" (*CW* 4:143).

A recurrence of the problematic nature of the "power apparatus" after the postwar collapse made Voegelin's use of the image of a cycle persuasive. This time the effort was directed at establishing a regime based on "democratic ideas of legitimation," but once again, the one necessary constituent was missing: "There was no *demos* with the will to statehood." Instead, the executive committee of a provisional assembly passed a resolution. "There seems to have been no awareness that political existence can be founded only on the basis of will, not by having a representative 'organize' it" (*CW* 4:149). This Schmittian insight had the consequence, as noted, that there was great uncertainty whether the "German Austrian" state would be independent, part of the German national state, or part of a post-*Reich* league of "Danubian" states. This uncertainty was also a symptom of the problem "Austria," however understood, faced.

Once again, therefore, the outcome was conditioned by external circumstances that "forced the government of Vienna to organize the state, but since there was no will to found a state, the subjective feeling of authorship, of authority, was not strong enough, the legitimation perforce had to be supplemented by something of more convincing reality," namely the "tradition of realism" that was found in the provinces. Hence Austria became a federation, but as we have seen, a federation where the parties were more important than the *Länder.* Indeed, the parties "play a similar role in the history of the republic to that of the nationalities in the monarchy." The parties, however, were not mentioned in the constitution but were "concealed behind the idea of democracy" (*CW* 4:155–57). Unfortunately, the parties also ensured that the creation of an Austrian *demos* would prove impossible: The Social Democrats did so by using the internationalist rhetoric of class war, and the nationalists did so by advocating union with Germany. In this context of violence, crisis, and confusion, Voegelin sought to understand the effective implications of Kelsen's jurisprudence.

Voegelin began this part of his argument by reminding readers that the situation in 1918–1920 provided an opportunity to actualize "the idea that the definition of the state lies in its identification with a legal system, understood as an embodiment of norms" or, as we prefer to say, an embodiment of rules. This was, of course, Kelsen's great achievement, but it was also "representative of the Austrian political complex of problems." For the first time Voegelin connected his reservations concerning Kelsen's legal theory to political realities.

In another new direction, Voegelin situated Kelsen's argument in a more comprehensive spiritual context, namely the metaphysics of positivism. Positivism was derived from a great range of historical and theoretical sources,[3] but its importance for the pure theory of law was that it united several epistemological, methodological, ontological, and other problems into one whole (*CW* 4:163–64). In Voegelin's words, he "supplemented" his earlier arguments by relating Kelsen's various theoretical theses to the "dogmatism of a positivist metaphysics" (*CW* 4:164n1).

As we have seen in previous chapters, the mediation between positivism and the pure theory of law was supplied by neo-Kantianism, specifically by the application of Kant's method, which was developed to study inorganic nature, "uncritically and essentially unchanged to all other scientific subject matters." Voegelin rejected the argument that this application was faithful to Kant's philosophy on the entirely sensible grounds that Kant "developed a metaphysics of reason" that deviated considerably from the methodological requirements needed to study inorganic nature. The neo-Kantian consequences were thus bound to be defective. "Even without knowing more about the content of the legal object as defined by the pure theory of law, we can state that generalizing the methodology derived from the model of mathematical physics must result in very significant limitations for the object of a theory of the state" and a "serious impoverishment" of the subject matter previously indicated by the term *state* (*CW* 4:166, 171).

In this introductory chapter to part III of *The Authoritarian State,* called "Kelsen's Pure Theory of Law and the Problem of an Austrian Theory of the State," Voegelin brought into sharp focus the criticisms developed over the preceding decade and, not without a certain degree of ironic detachment, placed Kelsen's achievement, notwithstanding his admiration for its perfection, into the decidedly limited category of the "dogmatics of law" *(Rechtsdogmatik).* Moreover, Voegelin took a certain degree of glee in showing how Kelsen's system was sufficiently closed, indeed airtight, so that external criticism could be dismissed on grounds of being an ideology, of introducing pseudo-problems, or simply of being nonscience. Necessarily, as any positivist, Kelsen had to defend the metaphysical claim "that man is a natural phenomenon." Kelsen was obviously not alone in his positivism, but it did make for some surprising metaphysical bedfellows. "We find," said Voegelin, "very similar claims in particular movements of race theory, insofar as it is rooted in the same positivist thinking of the end of the nineteenth century as are certain traits in Kelsen's view of the world" (*CW* 4:181).

A further metaphysical doctrine that, for Kelsen, made his jurisprudential system even more impregnable was his understanding of historical progress. It was simply a given that humanity advanced from a phase of "primitivism" to the organizational forms of the present, which were nevertheless still in need of improvement but would eventually "progress to a perfect final state." As for those who dare to doubt the theoretical consistency of such an argument, or the empirical existence of the "linear development from primitivism to the order of universal law," or to think that law could be a substitute for politics, by so doing they invite attack as ideologues, as professors of pseudo-problems, or perhaps as defenders of imperialism (*CW* 4:189).

Having "attacked" the "fundamentals" of Kelsen's system, namely its positivist metaphysics (*CW* 4:182), Voegelin proceeded to situate it in the equally limited context of Austrian reflection on the theory of the state, thus indicating how the pure theory of law was also an expression of parochial Austrian political problems. It fit the Austrian tradition because the restriction of science to "pure theory" meant that there could be no scientific consideration of the highly "impure" legal structure of the Austrian *Reich,* which as Voegelin had shown earlier in the book was a multinational regime unified only by the Hapsburg dynasty.

Voegelin's summary of nineteenth-century Austrian jurisprudence emphasized the claim that it followed methods that were akin to natural science—and for that reason was, in fact, remote from the reality of the Austrian *Reich.* In contrast to the growing abstraction of legal thinking, which reached an apogee in Kelsen's theory, Voegelin argued that it was necessary to discover what the contents of the legal rules actually meant. Norms and rules relating to "voting," for example, depended for their meaning on what was meant by the term "people." And that question could be answered only by examining the actual contents of the term "based on the judgments of a political science oriented towards reality," which was just what Kelsen wished to exclude from his "pure" jurisprudence. But, Voegelin added, "we cannot interpret norms if we do not know what the words in them mean, and we can know this systematically and completely only if the field of the subject-matter to which the expressions relate is made the content of a science" (*CW* 4:207–8).

For example, the act of voting does not consist in a member of the animal species *Homo sapiens* putting a mark on a piece of paper and transporting the paper to various parts of the planet called voting booths or ballot boxes. Rather, such behavior constituted "meaningful acts by spiritual persons" so that the meaning must be included in the description in any adequate interpretation of the norm *voting,* even though such a meaning would in principle be excluded from Kelsen's science if he in fact followed his own metaphysics. Fortunately no one, and certainly not

Hans Kelsen, actually proceeded on the basis of their professed metaphysical dogma. They proceed on a commonsense understanding of what the act of voting entails just as everyone else.[4]

Likewise, "we cannot tell whether a constitution is, for example, democratic from the content of the legal text." Rather, we first must be aware of what a democracy is, which awareness can be derived only from sources other than the legal text. The 1920 Austrian constitution was in form a democracy but in fact was something else. Thus, Voegelin concluded, it was always an error to take the formal language of the constitution to be a description of the actual and meaningful constitution of a state. The formal constitutional rules took their meaning from the concrete, historically significant character of the state, not the other way around. Voegelin illustrated the importance of the actual, empirical political situation in his detailed analysis of the Austrian constitutional transformation between March 1933 and May 1934 (*CW* 4:213–48). As has been noted, this was a year of unparalleled turbulence, violence, and civil disorder amounting to civil war.

It may seem self-evident that the formal language of a constitution necessarily relied on a context of common sense for its intelligibility. That it is not self-evident was indicated again by Kelsen's pure theory of law. For instance, constitutional continuity was said to be preserved so long as changes followed the rules established in the constitution itself. The substance of the constitution—the issue of democracy or dictatorship, for example—was excluded on principle. If changes were made by means of the formally correct procedures, there was continuity, period. But this argument also meant that discontinuity was impossible. Discontinuity, which is to say, so-called discontinuity, would, *per impossible,* have meant constitutional change that did not follow the prescribed rules. But following that procedure, according to the pure theory of law, would have resulted in an external, *partes extra partes,* juxtaposition of two distinct and unconnected constitutional orders. That is, a "violation" of the constitution would necessarily entail the founding of a new "state," because the state was understood to be identical with the legal order (*CW* 4:213–14). Not to put too fine a shading on the implication Voegelin was suggesting, the real discontinuities, which were accompanied by serious political disorder, simply could not be intelligibly accounted for by Kelsen's system.

These rather surprising considerations raised another issue: *Why* did people "in full possession of their mental faculties" comply with a norm or a rule in the first place? This question could not be answered without introducing the question of ethical substance, which was not permitted by Kelsen's theory. In reaching this insight, it was clear beyond any shadow of a doubt that Voegelin had concluded that the theory of the author of the Austrian constitution was of no use in understanding either the actual work he produced or the political regime to which it gave formal shape.

From the dead end created by the pure theory of law, Voegelin turned to Maurice Hauriou as a means of "clarifying the particular Austrian problems." Specifically, he elaborated the argument of Hauriou that constitutional laws had no meaning outside political institutions. By this understanding, constitutional norms were legitimated as the ruling order of the institution, and over time the institution came to legitimize the constitution. "The meaning of 'legitimation' is thus reversed: the ruler, who was legitimated as the representative of the institution by dint of his work on its behalf, is not legitimated by the norms, which are compulsory because he normalizes the situation and thus has prepared it to be regulated by norms" (*CW* 4:223). That is, rulership entailed the creation, preservation, and extension of an institution. The ruler was legitimated not by the rules but because he ruled the situation, represented the institution, and gave it its ruling order. In short, the ruler's position was never legitimated by the rule of law, but the other way around.

Having endorsed the approach of Hauriou, Voegelin proceeded to undertake an exceedingly detailed commentary on the substantive or institutional (and in any event not merely formal) changes in regulatory and constitutional provisions enacted or promulgated during 1933 and 1934 leading to a further, equally detailed examination of the "1934 Constitution." The purpose of this commentary was to demonstrate that changes made by the Austrian federal government were both real and substantive, and they were legitimate "because it [the government] had prevailed as such and was sufficiently supported by its practical means of power and the *consentement coutumier* of the population." Thus, despite the violation of certain legal formalities, it was still entirely legal. The only complicating factor was the desire of the federal government to establish "legal continuity," which was both unnecessary and impossible but not because of the logical inconsistencies of Kelsen's legal formalism discussed above. Rather, the real issue of continuity or discontinuity could not arise because "the lack of a politically united people imbued with the will to existence—that is, a *demos*—is precisely *the* problem of the Austrian constitution," not any derivative or subsidiary legal provisions, and even less so when those legal provisions were interpreted by (and as) legal dogmatics (*CW* 4:235, 243).

For reasons already noted—the cyclical pattern of Austrian constitutional developments since 1848, the rhetoric of democracy, the weight of administrative tradition regarding the *Reich*, and so on—the actual characteristics of the Austrian constitution were difficult to see. Nevertheless, "Austria has an authoritarian constitution," which in this context first of all meant that "authoritarian" did not simply function as a political symbol or idea. Indeed, Voegelin provided a certain amount of conceptual precision to the term. First of all, it meant no "representation of the people," however dubious that phrase may be, "participates in the formation of the state will in general and the creation of the general norms in particular." The state was legitimated by the fact that it maintained itself as an institution. "There is no other significant source of legitimation." Nothing could be said of any sovereign monarch because there was none, nor, in the absence of a political people, did the notion of Thomas Paine apply—that "the constitution of a country is not an act of its government, but of the people constituting its government."

Instead, one found "the unique phenomenon of anonymous exercise of power." The institutions of the authoritarian state were erected "as it were, behind a veil consisting of the forms of the administrative state." Thus as Voegelin noted in his journalism, the Austrian people received the constitution, but no mention was made of the source of the constitution in the sense of an actor who provided what the Austrian people nevertheless received. Nor, interestingly enough, was there anything said of its most important characteristic—its authoritarian nature. The most obvious expression of authoritarianism was the promise that it would be relaxed, but the mechanism for so doing was surrounded "with so many provisos that the real power at the core is hardly affected" (*CW* 4:252–56).

Austrian political leaders also declared that the country was a "corporative" society and a "corporative" state, or "status" state, a *Ständesstaat.*

Voegelin argued that, in contrast to the term "authoritarian," which could be refined in such a way that it could serve as a scientific concept, the term "corporative" was simply a political symbol or idea. It was used to combat the notion of class struggle, "one of the most dangerous" of political ideas because it was "destructive to the state." Corporative language was also used to combat the danger of mass democracy and the idea of the totalitarian state. Its effectiveness in that regard obviously did not turn it into a scientific concept: hence the statement that Austria was an authoritarian and not a corporative state exemplified the difference between the scientific and the political use of language.

Voegelin's broader argument was intended to show that the Austrian state in many respects "corresponds" to the "classical English parliamentarianism," which is to say, "a far-reaching actual control by the government over the parliament." The actual institutional arrangements by means of which Austria was ordered, and which Voegelin described in great detail, were quite different than those used in the United Kingdom. Specifically, the great difference between the 1934 Austrian constitution and British parliamentarianism was that, in the latter, "in spite of the authoritarian structure" of the executive, parliament "remained a source of the formation of the political will," whereas in Austria whatever political will existed also came from the executive (*CW* 4:303, 309).

The final "peculiarity" that characterized the Austrian constitution was that, in addition to the "ordinary constitution," there existed an emergency powers provision that established "a kind of extraordinary constitution" that amounted to "the expression of political experiences made since the founding of the republic." The purpose of the emergency powers, as in other regimes, was to transfer (authoritarian) legislative authority to the (authoritarian) executive. At the same time, these emergency powers, unlike the ordinary legislative powers, were subject to supervision and oversight, which raised "a fundamental problem" with respect to the coherence of the constitutional theory of the authoritarian state (*CW* 4:332, 338). On the one hand, "by *authoritarian state* we mean an institution whose highest organ, state leadership, is legitimated by its authorial endeavors in establishing, preserving, and developing the state." Under the "ordinary constitution" there were subordinate authorities that contributed to the overall state organization, but they were auxiliary, not central, despite the democratic language that camouflaged their subordinate status. In contrast, the emergency powers were balanced by oversight and review provisions. These provisions must, therefore, constitute a threat to "the fundamental features of the authoritarian state institution" (*CW* 4:339). Consequently, or paradoxically, it would have been more consistent for an authoritarian state construction not to have emergency regulations if such regulations were to be subject to judicial oversight and review. Failing that, the emergency provisions could have been given a legal status equal to that of ordinary laws, which, of course, were not subject to routine judicial oversight and review.

Voegelin then characterized this incongruity as "stylistic" and attributed it to "the continuation of the constitutional ideology of 1920," namely the attempt to create a constitutional court with an oversight of the "highest political authority" without, however, seeing or dealing with the political problem that this supervision of supremacy entailed (*CW* 4:346–49). In other words, in the "1934 Constitution" political realities "were largely neglected, and the interpretation of the legal formulation as the manifestation of a power position was deliberately ideologically repressed in constitutional theory" (*CW* 4:346). So as to ensure there was no ambiguity regarding the source of this "constitutional ideology," in the next sentence Voegelin quoted Kelsen's commentary and reiterated his observation that the author of the 1920 constitution sought to replace political with legal principles. That particular attempt was the source of the "constitutional ideology of 1920," and it was traceable, ultimately, to Kelsen's neo-Kantianism and to his fidelity to a "natural-scientific" approach to political reality.

Following some 360 pages of analysis, Voegelin provided a summary description of the concept of the authoritarian state. "In the authoritarian state," he said,

> the only politically legitimated authority is the "executive" representing the institutionalized state. The government issues the constitution and the laws, or initiates the legislative process, utilizing for the purpose an auxiliary agency, the authoritarian chamber; the highest political agency is also the head of the administration. Administrative control cannot be exercised politically over the state leadership, nor can a representative

> of the sovereign, placed outside the administration, exert it by technical means. True to form, in the authoritarian state even the constitutional mechanisms become instruments of the state leadership as it asserts its will, which is realized on the highest level in the form of laws. (*CW* 4:360–61)

These remarks near the end of the book are significant for Voegelin's later political science as well as for their function as a summary.

First, in part I of the book, Voegelin noted, as was quoted above, that terms such as *authoritarian* and *totalitarian* were first of all political ideas, not scientific concepts (*CW* 4:105). As with the term *corporativist, authoritarian* was useful in mobilizing the Austrian population to resist the totalitarian political movements. The "authoritarian state" in this respect, was a means of sheltering the Austrian populace against the revolutionary regimes of Germany and Italy until such a time as the Austrians constituted themselves as a people and a nation with a will to exist as a state.

In addition, "the authoritarian state" was also a phrase that was capable of "critical clarification," to use an expression from *The New Science of Politics,* so that it might serve as a cognitive instrument (see *CW* 5:111–12). That is, the long quote from pages 360–61 just given was, in effect, a conceptual definition useful within the discourse of science. In *The Nature of the Law* (1957), Voegelin observed that "definitions come at the end of an analysis, not at its beginning" (*CW* 27:11). Hence the position of this "definition."

Voegelin then concluded his "study of the particular problems of the Austrian state" by noting what he did not consider, namely the "liberal element" in the political arrangements that had just been described. "By 'liberal' we mean a metaphysics of the human being and the state according to which the individual, as a metaphysical substance, must also be a power in the state structure, a power that sets absolute limits to the authority of the state." Such issues as liberty and fundamental rights "affect the organization of the authoritarian state just as they affect every organization." Discussing them, however, "would open up basic questions of philosophy of the state" that went beyond the issue Voegelin set for himself to discuss (*CW* 4:362). Mentioning them, however, underlined the non- and indeed antitotalitarian political purpose of the authoritarian state in

Austria. Voegelin completed *The Authoritarian State* in December 1935. Austria existed for another twenty-six months.

The Authoritarian State was not Voegelin's final word on Austria. During late June and early July 1937, Voegelin took part in the tenth meeting of the International Studies Conference in Paris as secretary of the Austrian Coordinating Committee for International Relations. The International Studies Conference was sponsored by the League of Nations, and the 1937 meetings were devoted to "Peaceful Change" (*CW* 9:96–98). Voegelin's contribution was called "Changes in the Ideas of Government and Constitution in Austria since 1918" (*CW* 4:367ff, 9:99ff).

Most European countries were centers of unrest and so were threats to peaceful change—either because after the war they had got what they wanted and were trying to keep it against the wishes of others, or, if they were the "others," they had not got what they wanted and were trying to get it. In contrast, "Austria has been during the greater part of the last two decades a danger-spot of Europe because of its strong inclination towards non-existence." The source of this peculiarity, as was clear from the foregoing analysis, was that the population currently resident on the territory of Austria "has never formed in history a political unit." There was, of course, the glorious history of the Austrian or Hapsburg *Reich,* but postwar Austria "had a population, but it did not have a people in the political sense of the word" (*CW* 4:369).

Voegelin provided the by now familiar account of the legacy of the multinational Hapsburg *Reich* and of the great flaw in the 1920 constitution: It presupposed a democracy when there was no *demos.* Instead, as Voegelin had said in *The Authoritarian State,* the parties pursued their own interests, including the creation of "private armies, which in the case of the Socialist army was bigger and in some respects better equipped than the state army." As a result Austria was split into "several state-like personal organizations" sharing the same territory and held in place by external pressure and a common "constitution" to which they professed allegiance until they were in a position to change it (*CW* 4:371).

The German revolution of 1933–1934 brought an additional crisis to bear on the Austrian state and a fundamental change in its structure. On the one hand, the existence of the state had to be secured against the Nazi agitation in favor of an *Anschluss,* and on the other, the internal organization of the state had to be stabilized against the ideology of class war. "The two exigencies were met by the authoritarian and corporative reorganization of the State." In 1918, the Socialist and Catholic parties were amenable to an *Anschluss* because their German counterparts had considerable influence. After 1933 this was no longer the case, and they discovered a "very real interest in the independent existence of Austria" (*CW* 4:372, 375). Only the Austrian Nazis favored union with Germany. The Socialists, with their class-war ideology, extinguished themselves in the brief civil war of February 1934, which left the Catholic parties alone and with new responsibilities. Prior to 1933, that is, Austrian independence was more or less imposed by the Treaty of St. Germain. After 1933, independence was necessary in order not to be absorbed by the Nazi *Reich.* As a result, new discoveries were made, which is to say, were made up, of an Austrian-German Mediterranean heritage, a Germanic *Romanitas,* and so forth.

Voegelin's account of these rather desperate measures reads more like the libretto of a Viennese comic opera than a serious political program—the first two volumes of Musil's *Man without Qualities* had appeared a few years earlier. Voegelin was not, however, writing satire and tried to put the post-1934 changes in a favorable light. "It would be an exaggeration," he said, "to say that now an Austrian people exist in a most satisfactory way—but certainly it is now in the making." And in consequence "the consolidation of a political unit" is also under way (*CW* 4:379). Austria had nine months to exist.

6
Political Religions

Looking back on the circumstances surrounding the publication of *The Authoritarian State,* Voegelin remarked that this "somewhat heterogeneous" book, this "piece of forced labor, written to show that he was a competent political scientist," was also his "first major attempt to penetrate the role of ideologies, left and right, in the contemporary situation and to understand that an authoritarian state that would keep radical ideologists in check was the best possible defense of democracy." He was struck, he said, by "the stupidity of ideologists as represented by the leaders of the Social Democratic party. While I agreed with them regarding economic and social politics, this silliness of their apocalyptic dream in face of the impending Hitlerian apocalypse was simply too much to stomach" (*CW* 34:79, 69).

Political events may have supplied the "stimuli" to probe deeper into the question of ideology, but, after having understood the limitations of a legal analysis of political reality, the problem of finding or forging the appropriate scientific analytical tools remained (*CW* 34:68–69, 52). In the race books he had distinguished between scientific concepts and political ideas; in *The Authoritarian State,* he noted in passing that the "totality of ideology" as found in Italian Fascism was described by Mussolini as a "religious idea" that related individuals in the Fascist state to a "super-personal being, to a *volontá objettiva.*" The Fascist state was "a spiritual force, which pervades all of human moral and intellectual life" (*CW* 4:73). The problem was not simply that the Fascist (and National Socialist) conglomerate of political ideas was unscientific or even that they might be considered, as Mussolini observed, as "religious ideas." Rather, it was to discover a scientific language to account for the *perversion* of genuine religious ideas into ideologies or "political religions."

Voegelin did not appropriate the term "political religion" one fine day in 1936 after he published *The Authoritarian State* but seemed to have come to the concept gradually. Indeed, for reasons of economic necessity, his writings immediately following the publication of his book on Austria were written for the "quality" but still popular press. They dealt with questions seemingly peripheral to ideological politics. Beginning in late May 1937, he wrote a series of articles for the Viennese newspaper *Neue Freie Presse.* The first, on public opinion and its influence on politics, began from the distinction between mere expression of opinion *(Meinungsäusserung)* and formed or cultivated opinion *(Meinungsbildung).*

The notion that public opinion was a source of legitimacy in modern political regimes was based on an eighteenth-century understanding of rationality that ignored emotional, traditional, and religious influences on the formation or cultivation of character and opinion. The notion that opinion could be influenced by propaganda and half- or unconscious influences was hardly noted. As a consequence, "this image [of Enlightenment rationality] is empirically false," though not a complete illusion. The image could be made effective in practice as a political idea and was, in fact, modeled on a Rousseauian "middle bourgeois" whose station was not so high that he would make exorbitant demands nor so low that he had nothing to lose (*CW* 9:11).

Such an individual depended for his existence on readily available information and an ability to turn it into an opinion. However, when "opinion groups," including parties, came into existence, the ability of the individual to form and assert his own opinion evaporated, leaving nothing but a collection of aggregated private opinions. That is, public opinion, as the moderate arithmetic mean of several private opinions, no longer existed when information became filtered and nonbourgeois social strata rose in prominence.

In addition to this change in the conditions for articulating private into public opinion, the content of the notion of "formed opinion" *(Meinungsbildung)* changed as well. The assumption that the community consisted of middle-class bourgeois individuals more or less sharing the same basic attitudes, namely that their views were guided by reason, no longer obtained when people or parties "champion incompatible worldviews." These new conditions make the establishment of "formed opinion impossible" (*CW* 9:112).

Matters were particularly grave among German-speaking people, Voegelin added, because the German language did not easily distinguish between conviction and competence so that "any *Dummkopf* may have an opinion" even though what was meant by "opinion" was that it was well-founded and could be defended by rational argument—or in other words, that the opinion was "formed" or even "elevated" and "refined," as Publius put it in *The Federalist.* As a consequence (and the observation need not be confined only to German speakers), convictions and inclinations, vehemently held, are disconnected from the source of their worth, namely its content and the grounds for holding the opinion. "Today," he wrote,

> the idea of opinion has been formalized and includes every utterance that claims to be an opinion—ranging from an utterance that is paid for to one that is hammered in by propaganda, from opinions formed in good faith to those shot through with bad faith, from a rationally founded opinion as one of the steps in a discussion to an unfounded assertion intended to stir up emotions and pursue social "integration." Under these circumstances the institution of the right to voice opinions freely can become a tool for the annihilation of the person whose community-creating achievement this institution was intended to protect. (*CW* 9:113)

Contemporary states have developed two distinct ways of dealing with the occasionally antithetical demands of free speech and public order. On the one hand, democratic states have enacted legislation in order to protect the individual person, typically by banning paramilitary organizations, emotion-stirring uniforms, provocative speech, and so on. On the other, the totalitarian ones have enhanced the emotional impact of speech under a state monopoly on propaganda in order to shape the opinions of individuals. Here the notion of the individual person is simply dropped in favor of the political ideal of the *Volk.* "Today we cannot as yet pass judgment on these solutions," in the sense that it is not clear whether the "enduring tradition" that stems from the era of the classical, middle-class bourgeois can continue to "resist emotionalization" of language and of politics or whether the proponents of emotionalization, which "runs the risk of leading to the rule of depersonalized masses," will in fact be triumphant (*CW* 9:114).

A few months later Voegelin revisited the question of free speech, again in the pages of the *Neue Freie Press* (*CW* 9:115–19). Freedom of speech, Voegelin began, did not mean that all opinions are to be aired; censorship did not mean that none can see the light of day. Both positions favored certain opinions over others, and both seemed to ignore the listeners, who in turn may wish to hear some things and not others, to say nothing of the great number of people who were indifferent.

So the real question was: Could the people be allowed to know everything? And if not, what could the people not be permitted to know, and on what grounds? Most importantly, who was to do the prohibiting? We certainly know from experience that no one wanted to know everything and that denial and repression were psychologically as important as receptivity and an open mind. Advertisers knew this as a matter of operational necessity. And brand loyalty had a political analogue of even greater significance, because a "community consciousness" helped preserve the community by keeping it intact "in the face of its great mass of members." In this context Voegelin selected "from the profusion of questions one theme: loyalty to a political community."

The best-known formula expressing these sentiments was "my country right or wrong." It articulated an enduring conviction and devotion to a political community. In order for it to be maintained, there must exist "a permanent restraint on thought and speech lest faith in the idea be jeopardized." That is, knowledge of the good qualities of the community, not its bad ones, was required. This meant that, one way or another, the bad qualities were rendered unbelievable and worthy only of being forgotten or trivialized. "This is why ethicists came to the conclusion that unconditional loyalty is a questionable virtue—but our task here is not to moralize but to present a descriptive analysis."

The most obvious method of promoting loyalty amounted to a version of "Whig" history—improving the historical record, for example, regarding military victories or the contribution "we" have made to civilization and culture. More aggressively, there was mass propaganda. "It fills the souls of the community members with the appropriate images in a grand style and excludes all inappropriate ones. In addition, its effectiveness is extraordinarily intensified by the current religious situation and the ability to project evil outward." That is, an externalized "other" as the source of evil intensified the internal sense of loyalty to the virtuous "us." Thus party members might reinforce their loyalty by knowing what was needed to ensure loyalty and not knowing what might question it.

Whatever the problems with an unfettered defense of free speech—the *Dummkopf* problem noted earlier, for example, where intensity of conviction was mistaken for intelligibility of opinion—there were even greater ones associated with propaganda. The philosophical anthropological observation that human beings were not just political beings has a social corollary: "People who have made it their business to recognize reality without regard for social and political taboos," which is to say, people such as Voegelin, "are seen as a nuisance." Hence there arose a conflict between what people's loyalties allowed them to acknowledge and what they nevertheless knew from other sources. This was a major issue within societies that developed a scientific culture: how to protect the organization of loyalties from knowledge. For physics and mathematics the problem could be managed easily enough, but the historical, social, and political sciences "always find themselves in a tricky situation." Moreover, during periods where intense loyalty was demanded, the number of things that we must not be permitted to know increased. This was why "wise men" have concluded that there were many things that could be said only in a small circle and some things were not to be said at all.

Voegelin concluded with a quotation from Plato's Second Letter (314b–c), that the most important of his teachings had never been written down so much as expressed in the conversations of Socrates, who had become beautiful and young. Given that Socrates was in fact old and ugly, Plato's point was an indirect hint at how to interpret his dialogues (see also *CW* 16:74). Voegelin's point in quoting Plato was less hermeneutical than political: The demands of "intense loyalty" make even philosophical conversation among "wise men" impossible. When he wrote these lines he had just completed his last prewar book, *The Political Religions.* Voegelin's world was about to become as unhinged as the world around him that attracted his analytical attention.

In the introduction to the English translation, Manfred Henningsen noted that *The Political Religions* continued "the search for the body politic in Germany" that began with the race books and was continued in his book on Austria, which discovered "the nonexistence of a political people," as was discussed in the previous chapter. This book, as his previous ones, began with the self-interpretation of the political actors. Indeed, we have already quoted Mussolini's view that Italian Fascism was a religious movement. Prior to Mussolini, the term *political religion* was used by Mazzini to refer to his "Young Italy" movement and, as with so many new political notions, such as liberalism, conservatism, and terrorism, the term "political religion" was used during the French Revolution as well (see *CW* 11:83–99).[1]

Used conceptually or scientifically, rather than as a political idea or a means of self-interpretation by a political movement, "political religion" and associated terms were introduced into scientific discourse because political scientists needed a concept to describe certain characteristics of phenomena that existing terms such as "despotism" or "tyranny" ignored.[2] As Klaus Vondung noted, the concept of a political religion highlights one essential element of totalitarian domination, "namely the claim of these regimes to dominate and control not only the political and social sphere, but all aspects of human existence, and secondly to explain the outrageous and unprecedented use of violence against foreign enemies as well as against members of their own societies."[3] That is, political scientists interested in understanding totalitarian domination noticed that the organization resembled a religious order with dedicated ceremonies, holidays, rituals, and so on. There was propaganda used in the service of faith. For example, at the center of the National Socialist symbolism was *Blut,* blood; then came the *Volk,* the people as the substantive bearer of the blood; then the soil, *Boden,* the land that nourishes the *Volk;* then the *Reich,* in which the *Volk* finds political actualization, and the *Führer* as the representative of both the *Volk* and the *Reich.* Not surprisingly, the most holy symbol was the flag at the center of which was the swastika.

The trappings of religiosity that were central to the National Socialist regime rendered the conceptual language of law and more broadly of *Staatslehre* as a suitable approach to political phenomena nearly completely irrelevant. A state-centered approach to politics made no sense when the actions of the state, including the exercise of rule by means of legal instruments, served what were essentially pseudo-religious purposes rather than political ones. As we shall see, Voegelin henceforth preferred to speak of the political community. In a sense he had recovered an insight from antiquity, that politics and religion were intimately linked.[4]

In his *Autobiographical Reflections,* Voegelin emphasized more the limitations of the concept than its usefulness at the time. Political religion, he said, "conformed to the usage of a literature that interpreted ideological movements as a variety of religions." Such an approach "is not all wrong, but I would no longer use the term *religions* because it is too vague and already deforms the real problem of experiences by mixing them with the further problem of dogma or doctrine" (*CW* 34:78). He mentioned Louis Rougier's *Les mystiques politiques* as an effort similar to his own analysis, and, in the sources used in writing the book, references Etienne de Greeff's notion of *mystiques humaines.*[5] In commonsensical terms, Voegelin discovered, in trying to make sense of the Nazi revolution, that all particular political orders, including the totalitarian ones, justified and legitimated themselves by means of a narrative that linked the actual social movement to a larger, transcendent, more "real" order of things. Secularization, widely viewed as the great achievement of modernity, did not end the desire to find a meaning beyond it (*CW* 5:60). *The Political Religions* can be understood in this narrow sense as an exploration of several alternatives to secularization.

The book was published in April 1938, a month after Austria had been extinguished and absorbed into the German *Reich.* In late March, Voegelin was given the friendly advice that he had better make tracks for America because he had no future at the University of Vienna. On April 22, his license to teach, the *venia legendi,* was cancelled, and on May 17 he was told that, as of the 31st of the month, he was fired. He escaped by the skin of his teeth to Switzerland, from where he and Lissy Voegelin eventually reached the United States.[6] In Cambridge, Massachusetts, Voegelin wrote the preface to the second edition of the book, the first edition having immediately been confiscated by the Gestapo.[7]

The original preface to the second edition answered in public a letter Voegelin had received from Thomas Mann (HI 24:11). "I was reproached for presenting a case so objective that it seemed to advertise for the very worldview and movements—for National Socialism in particular—that I had set out to combat. It was said to lack firmness of judgment and the decisiveness of condemnation that would put my own attitude beyond all doubt." As was noted above, this criticism had been raised earlier in connection with Voegelin's race books. His answer was to discuss the attitude of the individual toward "the contemporary world situation."

There was, Voegelin began, one "type of politicizing individual" who was pleased to indicate his strong distaste for National Socialism by making ethical pronouncements about it. That was easily enough accomplished, and the epigraph from Dante made plain Voegelin's aversion to every kind of "political collectivism."[8] There were, however, good reasons for not engaging in political outbursts, and chief among them was the insight, which Voegelin developed in the remainder of the book, that political collectivism was not just a moral phenomenon but a "religious" one—and that this second feature was much the more significant.

Literary polemics were useful enough, but only insofar as they did not obscure the more important problem. Enthusiasm in opposition, Voegelin said, could have the consequence of impeding one's spiritual and intellectual understanding. To illustrate what he meant, he referred to the "specific case" of Herschel Grynszpan, a stateless German Jew of Polish ethnicity, who on November 7, 1938, entered the German embassy in Paris, asked to see an embassy official, and, after being admitted to the office of Ernst von Rath, shot him. Von Rath died two days later, on the fifteenth anniversary of the 1923 Beer Hall *Putsch,* an important Nazi festival. The Nazi propaganda minister, Goebbels, delivered an inflammatory speech at the Munich beer hall where the attempted *Putsch* had been organized and declared he would not be surprised if the German *Volk* took matters into their own hands to avenge the death of the German diplomat. Over ninety people were killed during the ensuing riot, *Kristallnacht,* and thirty thousand Jews were arrested.

The assassination of the third secretary, Voegelin said, might have been an occasion to discuss the legal and moral relationship between Jews and Nazis. Such an analysis would have to deal with two major points. First, within the *Reich*, Jews were members of a community outside the law. Such exclusion, by definition, was reciprocal: "The individual who stands outside the community of law has no legal obligations to the individual who excludes him." Thus Grynszpan could not legally be condemned (*CW* 33:20). The moral argument, that killing was in principle wrong, depended on the axioms of the ethical system being invoked. If we assumed the validity of the ethics of "personalism," there was a problem because the Nazis treated Jews "not as persons, but as things." The evidence for such treatment was overwhelming. According to the ethics of personalism, "in which the value of the personality stands higher than the value of life," the implications were obvious. "A person who is robbed, spat upon, and sold is morally obliged to put an end to such actions—if necessary by murder. In terms of the fundamental principles of ethical personalism, a murder committed by a Jew upon a National Socialist who treats him as a thing would not only be excusable, it would be a duty" (*CW* 33:21). And as for the related objection that, as Socrates taught in the *Gorgias*, it is better to suffer than to commit injustice, or that, according to the Gospel of Matthew (26:52), he who takes the sword shall perish by the sword, to this "gentle soul" Voegelin answered first that "the evildoer who reaches for his sword does not die by the same sword but by another one, and the other sword must be wielded by somebody." And second, the context made clear that Jesus was discussing the "mystery of divine sacrifice." Accordingly, the invocation of Jesus' words to justify the submission to violence in the area of mundane affairs "would be blasphemous, were it not so naively stupid" (*CW* 33:21).

In fact, however, the moral and political opponents of the Nazis had undertaken no such analysis, Voegelin said, so "skepticism towards the morally and sentimentally motivated aggression of literary intellectuals" is "understandable."[9] Voegelin offered two reasons for the absence of any serious analysis: first, the "abysmal mindlessness" of his contemporaries who lacked the "spiritual strength" to pursue the problem to its roots; and second, a fear of the unpleasant consequences of such reflection.

Specifically, one would have to consider National Socialism "from the standpoint of religion," beginning with the assumption that there was evil in the world. And by evil was meant not merely the absence or the lack of good, but "a genuine substance that must be combatted" (*CW* 33:22).

This is not to embrace Manichaeism, though the fear of so doing provided a convenient and dogmatic excuse to do nothing. On the grounds of this phony defense of an anti-Manichean dogma, "a representative of the organized church will prefer to let his church and the entire world be destroyed by evil than to scorch his finger on a problem of dogma"—unless, of course, his own organization or its revenue were to be threatened.[10]

Once the insight was gained that a "religiously evil and satanic" (and not merely a morally distasteful) substance did indeed exist in the world, a second insight would follow: "It can only be resisted by an equally strong religious force for good." That is, satanic evil could not be resisted by humanistic moralism alone. Moreover, "no major thinker in the Western world is unaware" of a spiritual crisis the origin of which lay in secularization, from which it followed that only a religious renewal could proceed against it and that such a renewal would require "great religious personalities." Unfortunately such personalities could not be summoned at will—although everyone could "prepare himself" and "do what he can to prepare the ground in which resistance to evil may grow" (*CW* 33:23).

It is precisely in this area that politically moralizing intellectuals failed so completely. They complained about Nazi barbarism and a return to the "dark ages" without suspecting "that the secularization of life, which the humanitarian ideal entails, in fact created the soil out of which anti-Christian religious movements like National Socialism spring up in the first place." For secularized spirits, any talk of religion would disrupt "their humanitarian, tolerant, and ethical peace of mind," so it was understandable why such "unpleasant consequences," as Voegelin called them above, were avoided.

Voegelin's position was not meant to suggest that an ethical fight against the Nazis or moral condemnation of them along the lines offered by Thomas Mann was entirely a waste of time.[11] It was, however, a "rootless and hence questionable ethical fight" because it ignored the genuine and religious source of the problem. If Voegelin seemed too objective, that was a sign that his argument was accurate because "the Luciferian aspect is not simply morally negative or abominable, but is a force, and a very seductive one at that. If my description were to create the impression that National Socialism involves only a morally inferior, stupid, barbaric, and contemptible matter, it would be a poor one. That I do not regard the force of evil to be a force of good will be evident to all readers of this treatise who are open to religious questions" (*CW* 33:23). One may conclude, therefore, that for Voegelin the notion of political religion was not simply a handy enough concept in political science during the 1930s that, as all scientific concepts, could be refined and improved. It was also a term that demanded an existential response, namely resistance to the attractions of evil.[12]

It was not yet customary, Voegelin began, to use the term "political religions" in connection with contemporary social movements, "even though the factual situation would force the attentive observer to take this position." The reason for this resistance to a perfectly sensible usage was historical. Religion, following the dissolution of the medieval *sacrum imperium,* became associated with the church and politics with the state. Following the lengthy struggle between pope and emperor (see *CW* 23 and 24), the state emerged victorious over the church. Along with the accompanying secular spirituality, the opinion that politics involved only the state has hardened into an unquestioned and self-evident doctrine. Accordingly, the concepts—the political and the religious—are understood to be derived from the institutions of state and church, and the polemical context in which they were forged has all but been forgotten. Thus *religion* referred to Christianity and other redemptive religions and *state* referred to political organizations along the lines of the nation-state. For an adequate understanding of the concept "political religion," it was therefore necessary to expand the concept of the "religious" beyond the great redemptive religions to include other phenomena that accompanied the historical development of European states and at the same time to examine the state critically and with a view to whether it was simply a secular organization with no connection to the religious.

Voegelin provided a "textbook" definition of the state without indicating what particular textbook he was thinking of. For reasons discussed below, he probably had Hegel's *Philosophy of Right* in mind. In any event, the textbook definition of the state, he said, emphasized the organizational unity of a sedentary people that endowed itself with an original or primordial power to rule *(ursprünglicher Herrschermacht).* The empirical observation of a sedentary people was one thing, but the notion of primordial or original power to rule required clarification. The adjective, Voegelin said, must refer to the claim that power to rule had no source but the state itself, that it was not derived from, or was not subordinate to, anything else. But this claim to absoluteness, he said, "is false" (*CW* 5:28). The reason was obvious: All rulers were limited internally in the sense that there were certain things no ruler could do without being deposed, and externally in the sense that external ruling powers also imposed limits.

That is, a plurality of ruling powers compelled us to consider their origin and legitimacy in light of a general power that transcended any particular power in order to convey legitimacy. Unless we were willing to believe that the world was inhabited by demonic powers of equal primacy, and that, therefore, the question of unity and legitimacy was pointless, we will have to refer to a unity or a "higher power" that, since the time of Dante's *De Monarchia,* has been described in one way or another as divine. However, the textbook definition omits any reference to supremacy beyond the assertion of empirical ruling powers. "The order of creation, which is excluded completely, is, as it were, decapitated by it [the claim of empirically ruling power to be supreme], i.e., the divine head is cut off, and the state takes the place of the world-transcendent God as the ultimate condition and origin of its own existence" (*CW* 5:28–29).

To clarify the genesis of the problem, Voegelin first discussed the meaning of the term *state,* and then *religion.* If the textbook definition was inadequate, the next step would be to examine its experiential origin as expressed in Hegel's political science. Here one finds the argument that the *Volk,* having achieved the form of the state, became the unmediated reality of the spirit *(Geist),* which made it absolute on earth. This absolute character, for Hegel, required obedience and the renunciation of personal opinion and reason, which is to say the spirit of the individual personality, in exchange for the more intensive and collective spirit that animated the state. Personal courage, for example, was transformed into "mechanical" or "impersonal" obedience, and the individual was turned into a killing machine obedient to the will of the state. "Now," Voegelin added, "we feel more distinctly what is at stake: The issue is not the correctness of a definition; the issue is a matter of life and death" (*CW* 5:29). Even beyond the admittedly important question of life and death, there was the issue "as to whether man may exist personally or has to dissolve into a superpersonal *realissimum,*" which is to say an entity of greater, more intense, or higher reality.[13] That is, the supremacy of the state was not an empirical fact of submission to rule but "the dogma of a believer." When the state is the sole reality, the personality of the individual is dissolved and then is restored by the state in such a way that the individual has become transfigured into a constituent element of the superhuman *realissimum* of the state. "We have become caught in the center of a religious experience and our words describe a mystical process" (*CW* 5:30).

Still keeping with the Hegelian idiom, the several *Volksgeister,* which were externally related to each other as states, were also related internally in terms of the *Weltgeist.* Much as the individual personality was dissolved in the state, so the rise and fall of states reflected the "world court-of-judgment of the spirit" *(das Weltgericht des Geistes).*[14] For Hegel, the external conflict of states was guided by the internal development of the *Weltgeist,* which used the *Volksgeister* to actualize the reason of the world. Accordingly, the fate of individual *Volksgeister* was as insignificant as the fate of the individual personality within the state. Both were mere instruments of a higher power—in Hegel's language, the higher power was called the "world spirit."

Voegelin then noted that he was uncertain which of the implications of this Hegelian speculation was more surprising: the imperative of a world-ordering understanding that transfigured historical materials into the revelation of the spirit, or Hegel's indifference to the problem of theodicy—that the world spirit had nothing more at its disposal than history as a "slaughter bench" and a tale of misery. "The gigantic structure of the system and its strict order is woven together over an abyss of human nihilism, using itself up in a search for the fulfillment of reality by means of a collectivity" (*CW* 5:30). In his later discussions of Hegel and of the genesis of the Hegelian state, Voegelin resolved his surprise and astonishment, not least of all because of the insights of Kojève's interpretation.[15]

Turning next to an analysis of the subject matter of religion, Voegelin began with the common human experience of creatureliness, which made the very integrity of human existence highly questionable. "Somewhere in the depths, at the navel of his soul, at the place where it touches the cosmos, the question keeps tugging at him" (*CW* 5:30). Religiously inclined individuals spoke of primordial feelings *(Urgefühl)* to indicate experiences deeper than ordinary emotions. When people mentioned the "infinitude" of such feelings, they were seeking to indicate that it was not oriented toward any specific object but was a sense of "absolute dependence," of being "bound to a superpersonal, all-powerful something." This experience was also described in terms of a return to the point of their origin in the divine. The emotions that accompany the primordial feeling ranged from anxiety, despair, restlessness, agitation, and rebellion to hope, tranquillity, bliss, humility, and renunciation.

Moreover, the range of responses that followed from the experience of creatureliness were multiplied by the different modes by which human existence was open to the world and to the beyond: in the body and in the spirit, in man and in community, in nature and in God. These possibilities, in turn, were linked to attempts at self-interpretation—including mistakes and rationalizations. For some, the gates of existence were open and granted a view of the whole of being, from inanimate nature to God; for some, the world was transparent for the rational relations among its contents. For some, in turn, these relations formed a hierarchical order of being and, in response to the question of a reason for being, they formed an order of creation. That is, for some, God was once again recovered as the condition and origin of human existence (see *CW* 5:28–29), which Voegelin described as the maximum of openness to reality combined with a maximum of rationality in the understanding of the order of reality.[16]

Such openness and rationality were not, however, the experience of all human beings. Others may have only scant glimpses of reality and perhaps only one single glimpse: "of nature, of a great person, his *Volk*, mankind." What was glimpsed by that person nevertheless becomes his *realissimum* (see *CW* 5:29). The glimpse of these worldly realities then "takes the place of God and, thus, hides everything else from him, above all, [it hides] God" (*CW* 5:32).

Voegelin's analysis of the two kinds of experiences and of the adequacy of the experiences to the full range of reality was intended to illustrate certain problems of cognition, not to indulge in moralizing judgment. His formulation of the problem between the maximum of openness to the full amplitude of reality including a sense of its world-transcendent dimension, on the one hand, and the single glimpses of a world-immanent reality on the other, amounted to an early formulation of the problem of experience and symbolization of reality that was central to his later work (see, for example, *CW* 12:52–94).

The argument Voegelin made on this occasion, however, aimed to make the point that the two kinds of experience—of reality including its world-transcendent dimension and of reality as world-immanent only—were equivalent *as religious experiences:* "Wherever a reality is disclosed in religious experience, it becomes the *realissimum,* the most real thing there is." The transformation of the natural to the divine resulted in a sacred reconfiguration of the whole of reality around that aspect of reality, namely a specific world-immanent reality that had been acknowledged as divine. In turn, the acknowledgment of a world-immanent reality as divine was typically followed by the creation of entire worlds of symbols, linguistic signs, and concepts that coalesced into systems that then could be filled with religious emotions and fanatically defended on the grounds that they expressed "the 'right' order of being." Our time, Voegelin said, was filled with such religious political fervor. Moreover, much of it was mutually unintelligible because the experiences of the various speakers were incommensurate.

The mutual unintelligibility of religious political fanatics was most obvious in the fragmentation of language. "We do not have self-evident words that could be used to name spiritual facts." Thus followers of movements that resolutely wish to be atheistic and antireligious stoutly deny there is anything religious at the root of their fanaticism. Voegelin therefore proposed to make a distinction that, for reasons of clarity, we have already employed, namely between spiritual religions that find the *realissimum* in the ground of the world *(Weltgrund),* which were to be designated world-transcendent religions *(überweltliche Religionen),* and those that discovered the divine in the things of the world, which were to be called world-immanent religions *(innerweltliche Religionen)* (*CW* 5:32–33).

In the final paragraph of this preliminary account of the "problem" of political religions, Voegelin returned to the issue of the range of human beings who sought and found those different kinds of religions—namely the world-transcendent and the world-immanent. If the heart was sensitive and the intellect keen, a glance at the world was sufficient to grasp the misery of creatures and to sense the path to redemption; when they were insensitive and dull, massive and intense impressions would be needed to stimulate even weak feelings. It was enough for Siddartha to see a beggar, an invalid, and a corpse to become the Buddha. "A modern writer sees piles of corpses and witnesses the gruesome destruction of thousands of people in postwar Russia, and it occurs to him that something is wrong in the world and writes a series of mediocre novels." One responded to suffering in the world by seeking deliverance in the *Weltgrund,* another saw it as a grievance that was to be remedied. Some experience a beyond only if it appeared in a powerful person surrounded by an organization accompanied by glamor, noise, force, and terror; for others the gestures of every person were transparent for his connection to God. "And wide is the realm for places of the soul from which ecstasies arise." Voegelin then listed a hierarchy of experiences by which human beings transcended their existence: "from the *unio mystica* of the individual personality with the spirit to exaltation that accompanies the celebration of the community; to the devotion to a brotherhood; to the loving extension of oneself into the landscape, the plants and the animals, and on to the animalistic convulsions of the sexual act and to the bloodlust" (*CW* 5:33).

Having described the problem, Voegelin then provided examples of how historical communities ordered religious along with political experiences. He began with the ancient Egyptian worship of the sun, which came to a climax in the cult of Akhenaton, who ascended to the throne as Pharoah Amenhotep IV (*CW* 5:34–41; see also *CW* 14:141–50). Voegelin's presentation of the rather recondite aspects of Egyptian mythology, cosmology, and history was less important than his development of a number of principles that were expressed by means of his analysis of events and texts. The growth and catastrophic end of "the oldest political religion of a highly civilized people" illustrated the problem he wished to analyze better than did later Mediterranean civilizational examples such as the Greeks or Romans. Compared to Voegelin's later analyses in *Order and History,* his conceptual vocabulary seemed primitive—he wrote of a "state religion," for example, or of pharaoh as a "state God." Likewise, he simply began "at the beginning of historical time" with the Egyptians without so much as a nod in the direction of their predecessors. Many of these lacunae would be overcome following the publication of additional historical materials after 1945, but by then the purpose of his scholarship had changed as well.

In this earlier formulation, the earliest kings were described as understanding themselves as successors to the sun god Horus, who ruled over the pantheon of Egyptian gods. From "the beginning of historical time," he said, "the state form of religion" existed. The king, who embodied the "state" in Voegelin's usage, was the mediator between human and divine beings. He was supposed to be the sole person able to worship the gods, but in fact he was assisted by priests and collegia of priests. Gods, kings, and priests thus constituted the chief protagonists of "the internal political and religious power struggle." Voegelin's concern was with the power struggle far more than with the finer points of Egyptian theology. The analysis accordingly focused on the king as the son of Horus (or of Re, also manifest in the sun).[17] The political struggles took place between the priests of Horus-Re, the priests of the other major gods, and the cities where Horus-Re and the other gods were supreme. Changes in mythology kept pace with the changes in power: "Old myths were transformed and new ones were added" so that "the state theology very closely followed political developments." Thus when political power shifted south from Memphis to Thebes, Amon, a local Theban deity, became Amon-Re, and "another step toward monotheistic myth-formation was accomplished."

The creative political and military expansion in response to the challenge of the Toynbeean "time of troubles," the Hyksos invasions, created a new political unit extending beyond the old boundaries of Upper and Lower Egypt. Voegelin called this new power organization a "world empire." Economic and territorial expansion led to changes in the "state religion" as priests pushed their speculations beyond the old structure of gods-king-people in order to integrate the new experiences that came with military and political expansion into the existing myths. For the most part, these speculations confined the effectiveness of the various gods to the Nile valley. "Only in connection with the sun god did the speculations go farther." Pharaoh Amenhotep IV built a new temple to the sun god, Aton, now conceived as "the life-giving principle as such," and proceeded to suppress the old priesthoods along with the old gods whom they served. At the same time, he changed his name to Akhenaton ("It pleases Aton") and built a new capital at what is now Tel el Amarna.

The new "state theology" claimed that the conquests were undertaken on behalf of God, namely Aton, but also that Akhenaton was himself God. Accordingly, the two realms, the divine and the human, merged, and the expansion of Egyptian military power was understood as the creation of the (new) world. The "Hymns to Aton" expressed the new "state theology." Aton became a "world God" or a "universal God" whose power extended to the ends of the earth, which is to say, from Syria to Nubia, with Egypt in the center, and with Akhenaton at the center of Egypt. The relationship between Akhenaton and the world of the Egyptian empire was reciprocal. On the one hand, the son of God was a divine king who both sustained the world by means of the life-giving sun and ordered the world by means of his divine commands. On the other, creation served God and his empire by paying taxes and worshipping Him.

In volume 4 of *Order and History*, Voegelin discussed the inherent spiritual limitations of what he later called ecumenic empires. In this early example his analysis remained close to the actual events. Following the death of Akhenaton, the individual, the priests whose gods had been absorbed by Aton reasserted their position along with the generals whose military expansion had been curtailed by diverting funds from the army to the cult of Aton. Adding to the problem of this "conservative reaction," Voegelin said, was a decline in religious support among the people. The reason for the latter was not difficult to find: The new state religion of Akhenaton had little to say about "the morality of earthly existence, the judgment of the dead, life after death, and the punishment and rewards for the individual soul in the other world." All of these concerns were central to the lower classes, whose experiences were remote from the high politics of an imperial religion. The sun cult may have dealt with the order of a world empire, but the popular "cult of Osiris touched the fate of the individual soul." No wonder it made a resurgence.

The balance between the sun cult of the rulers and the Osiris cult of the ruled, which together constituted the traditional polytheistic religion of Egypt, enabled the entire society to exist more or less in harmony "without any rational construction forcing them into a system." The abolition of both the cult of Osiris and the traditional sun cult by Akhenaton destroyed a finely balanced polytheism without replacing it with anything but "the monotheistic cult of empire," which proved unsatisfactory both to the ruled and to the rulers. The former found no solace for the mysteries of life and death; the latter were unsatisfied when imperial expansion ended. The main problem, so far as Voegelin was concerned, was that the political religion of Akhenaton made no provision for "the other characteristics of man" to be able "to develop their own religion." The other problem, which Voegelin did not on this occasion emphasize, concerned the inherently unsatisfactory nature of the cult of empire: Even if expansion kept the armies and the priests busy in the short term by administering the new conquests and developing accounts about what it all meant, eventually the empire would reach a limit, suffer military defeat or stalemate, and then decline. Somehow, those events would also have to be integrated into the myth of imperial monotheism.[18]

An answer to the problem of a spiritual substance concentrated in a divine ruler that somehow ignored the spiritual problems of the ruled was to legitimize "the radiation of power" in a hierarchy of rulers and offices, from God at the top to the subjects at the bottom. Accordingly, hierarchy and its symbolization was the next topic Voegelin discussed (*CW* 5:42–52).

Voegelin singled out Bodin, whose works he had studied during the 1934 academic year, which he spent in Paris, for having "brought the symbol of the sacral hierarchy into a rational order that covered in detail all the stages of state and law."[19] At the top, of course, was God, who was bound by no one; the king was bound by divine will; the magistrates were bound by divine will and the will of the king; and the subjects were bound by divine will, royal will, and the will of the magistrates. The great change from the hierarchy of Akhenaton was the immediacy of the human person to God, whatever his or her place in the political hierarchy.

Bodin's resolution of Akhenaton's "Osiris problem"—that is, the existence of a cult outside the official hierarchy, where only the king mediated the empire to God—entailed a change in the spiritual substance that had its own significance. Voegelin's concern, however, was with the persistence of a hierarchical structure whatever the spiritual contents. "The hierarchy of offices and standards immanent to the state," Voegelin said, became independent of any particular spiritual substance, "and following the decapitation of God was able to combine itself with any kind of legitimizing symbolization" (*CW* 5:44). Voegelin then outlined the historical preconditions for the deification of the world-immanent political order and the simultaneous decapitation of the world-transcendent God. The story was elaborated in much greater detail in his *History of Political Ideas;* even *The New Science of Politics* provided more information than Voegelin provided on this occasion, so a degree of textual interpolation is required to make sense of his terse formulas.

"In principle," he wrote, "the symbol of a community constituted through the *pneuma* [spirit] of Christ can be transformed into intramundane bodies whenever the spiritual entity that was once a reality"—that is, the spiritual body of Christ, which included a world-transcendent element—"is reconstituted by means of natural [and not supernatural] contents." Whether it is constituted by the mystical body of Christ or by some other world-immanent spiritual substance, Voegelin identified the resulting community as an ecclesia—an assembly or more precisely a sacred assembly or a church. "The ecclesia constituted by Christ has changed in many ways. Throughout all its transformations, however, the basic structure, which is what concerns us, remains recognizable." Moreover, even where a world-immanent ecclesia conflicted with the Christian one "as in German National Socialism," the basic form of the mystical body bound together by the spirit continued to exist. Spiritual conformity was simply a requirement for corporeal unity.

The first conclusion to be drawn from Voegelin's analysis of the continuity of the structure of a spiritual community was commonsensical enough: You cannot have a world-immanent spiritual community in the absence of a spiritual community as such. But his primary concern was with the formation of *world-immanent* spiritual communities. Logically such communities could not come into being until the world-transcendent and world-immanent dimensions had been distinguished. In *The Political Religions* Voegelin discussed this problem in terms of a "schism" within the Christian ecclesia between the spiritual and temporal (*CW* 5:47–50).

The first important interpretation of this question was provided by St. Augustine in *The City of God.* Citizenship in the *civitas terrena* or the *civitas Dei* depended on one's love—the love of self to contempt of God; the love of God to contempt of self. The symbols were developed in response to the pagan criticism that the new state religion of the empire, Christianity, had not preserved the empire from disaster at the hands of the Visigoths, much as Scipio Aemilianus had feared. As Voegelin said, Augustine had to argue that "Christianity was not a form of life and accident insurance." In so doing Augustine developed a complex argument about what a genuine Christian attitude entailed.

Augustine's text, *De Civitate Dei contra paganos*, reflected a number of unresolved problems. To begin with, it was written within the context of apocalyptic experiences of a new age and eschatological expectations of the coming of the final kingdom of Christ. He was accordingly able to express in an unsurpassed way the tensions between the requirements of the church as an institution and so subject to the vicissitudes of all human things and the church as the representative of the heavenly city. But third, he could no more resolve the opposition between spiritual and worldly power than he could resolve the contradiction between the this-worldly and the other-worldly loves of the personal life. True, in his later work Voegelin developed a precise vocabulary to analyze the contradictions and ambiguities of existence—tension, in-between, reflective distance, and so on—but it is important to emphasize that intellectual clarity concerning the nature of ambiguity, contradiction, and tension did not, by itself, resolve or diminish the existentially real problems indicated by those terms. On the contrary, by describing them with analytic precision they were made more acutely present to consciousness. Certainly the compromises of life and of politics examined by Augustine were not dissolved by the understanding he imparted to them. Likewise the institutional compromises of church and empire remained compromises even when their status had been clarified.

According to Voegelin, this problem came into sharp focus again when the institutional compromises of the *sacrum imperium* began to dissolve during the twelfth and thirteenth centuries. The offices of the ecclesia of Christendom had no sooner become independently established than they began to change. The empire began to disintegrate into the great feudal organizations that later became states, and the church began transforming itself into the first "state within the empire." Moreover, the reception of Aristotle's *Politics* endowed the problem of political institutions, which Augustine had pretty much ignored, with a new importance. It was only a matter of time until the "state institutions" rid themselves of their subordination to the feudal church and absorbed the sacred meaning of the church within their own political structures. The conquest of Jerusalem by Frederick II, for example, was soon followed by his self-elevation to the status of messiah-king and God-man. Roman *justitia* became a state virtue and the cult of *justitia* the state religion. "The pope declared the emperor to be the Anti-Christ. The first world-immanent political religion has sprouted from the soil of the Christian ecclesia" (*CW* 5:50). In *The History of Political Ideas,* Voegelin told this same story, though of course in much greater detail (*CW* 21–23).

The transformation of the external structures of the ecclesia was accompanied by an internal awareness that not just institutions were changing but the structure of history as well. Again, the problem was dealt with in more detail in his later works, but Voegelin was aware in 1938 of the significance of changes in historical consciousness associated with Joachim of Flora, the Franciscan spirituals, and the other late medieval apocalyptics. The Third *Reich* of Joachim introduced not a revolutionary institution to replace the church but a new impetus for world-immanent spiritualization and perfection of the ecclesia. In this respect it constituted "the historical basis for the apocalyptic dynamism found in modern political religions" (*CW* 5:31), including Nazism.

As in *The New Science of Politics,* discussion of Joachim and the new apocalyptics was followed by an analysis of Hobbes's argument in *Leviathan.* The establishment of territorial states during the "age of Absolutism" created not merely particular political communities but closed spiritual ones. These new ecclesia enjoyed such intimate "worldly political and sacral interpenetration, with state and church in such a close unity that the opposition between temporal and spiritual becomes meaningless" (*CW* 5:53). With the symbol of the Leviathan, Hobbes evoked "the omnipotent state [existing] immediately under God and acting upon divine orders." Accordingly, any opposition to the state-church could only be the work of the archfiend, Satan. During the course of the politico-religious history of Europe, the phenomenon of the particular world-immanent ecclesia "brought forth the corresponding empires of Satan" (*CW* 5:58). That is, once the spiritually closed particularist community was established, its chief task was the evocation of diabolic enemies, which in turn were used to justify the continued existence of the first community. Even when the characterization of other political communities did not achieve the intensity of religious anathema, they typically found "standard amenities by which members of the principal European nations express their disgust for each other's national peculiarities" (*CW* 24:73).

The last chapter before the epilogue dealt with the creation of a world-immanent community. The final step in breaking the tie to the world-transcendent peak of the hierarchy, God, was to perform the act of decapitation. Voegelin made no reference here to Hegel or Marx or Nietzsche, nor did he reflect on the feasibility of the project as an act of the imagination. Instead he pointed to "the symptoms of the new meanings, which are widely known as facts but rarely interpreted as expressions of political religiosity" (*CW* 5:59).

First came the foundation for the new world-immanent religious sense, namely the interpretation of the world as a storehouse of facts. Everything from plants and animals to peoples and their history, the life of the soul and of its desires, filled the encyclopedias of humanity and excluded knowledge of divine order. The question first raised by Leibniz (Voegelin quoted a later version from Schelling, but see *CW* 12:43–44, 17:123–24), "Why is there something and not nothing?" meant nothing to "the religious attitude of the masses. The world as content has displaced the world as existence." That is, one could ask any number of questions about the contents of the world, but raising metaphysical questions of the Leibnizian or Schellingian variety—such as why there is a world at all—was indecent and must be prohibited. Indeed the term *metaphysics* was considered a term of abuse, much as religion was either an opium (Marx) or an illusion (Freud). As a consequence, "science" was charged with taking an inventory of the world and solving its mysteries, and nothing else.

As noted above, Voegelin had not yet developed the conceptual tools to analyze the origin and significance of the shift implied by the term *decapitation,* but he was clear about the symptoms—which nevertheless he expressed in a somewhat terse and dogmatic way. "Man," he wrote, "can let the contents of the world grow to such an extent that the world and God disappear behind them, but they cannot overcome [*aufheben*] the problematics of their own existence." These "problematics" continued to exist in the individual soul so that "when God is invisible behind the world then the things of the world become new gods; when the symbols of transcendent religiosity are banned, new symbols develop from the world-immanent language of science to take their place" (*CW* 5:60). The structure of this "problematic" was imported from Christian apocalyptic to the apocalypse of a world-immanent community. It was a relatively simple matter to purge Joachim's language of its Christian echoes to create a historical structure leading to, for example, a Kantian perpetual peace ensured by a cosmopolitan community of suitably enlightened republican leaders. Voegelin again emphasized the collectivist implications of Kant's vision and Kant's "astonishment" at the implications—that only the last generations would enter into a world-immanent paradise. Voegelin considered Kant's response to this surprising outcome, namely a reassertion of the Christian doctrine of personal immortality, to be expedient rather than rationally connected to the rest of his argument.

The carrier of the Kantian apocalypse was the whole of humanity, but less inclusive communities could also be nominated to do the job—the Germans (Fichte), the French (Comte), the proletariat (Marx), the Nordic race (Gobineau). Along with the salvific community a satanic one was also evoked—the Catholic Church, human desires, Napoleon, the religious and metaphysical remnants, the bourgeoisie, and above all, the Jews.[20] The claim to be "science" remained the common attribute of all these world-immanent apocalyptic movements, from Comte's scientific history to Marx's scientific socialism or the race science of the twentieth century.

In the initial stage of this development, the belief in science was naive in the sense that the scientific claims were more or less advanced in good faith. When the scientific character was then challenged on the grounds of evidence or intelligibility, instead of revising the account, "the concept of truth is transformed instead" (*CW* 5:62).[21] What counted was not the adequacy of an argument in terms of logic or evidence, but, as Machiavelli would have said, its "effective truth," namely the capacity "to bind the masses emotionally and to arouse in them the politically effective expectation of salvation." Truth—scientific truth—became what promoted the existence of the world-immanent community. The preeminent examples were those constituted by the National Socialists and by the Bolsheviks. For the former, art, knowledge, myth, and customs were true if they served the Aryan race; for the latter, if they served the proletariat. In this way any rational discussion of the formation of the world-immanent apocalyptic community was prohibited.

The consequence of a change from naive belief in a myth to conscious acceptance of effectiveness as the criterion of truth was to reinforce the importance of hatred and aggression—because they were highly effective in mobilizing mass emotions—not to destroy the charm of the world-immanent revelation on the grounds of reasonable analysis.[22] Voegelin then compared the self-manipulation involved with belief in "effective truth" to the reflections of Ignatius Loyola on the selection of the right means for the goal of salvation. For Loyola, the conduct of life gained its significance from its world-transcendent and holy purpose. When the world-immanent collectivity was substituted for God, the individual still retained his place as the servant of a larger purpose, only now it was not salvation by divine grace in death but some sort of imaginary but also worldly salvation. Knowledge of the world and the accompanying techniques of propaganda were no longer temporary compromises undertaken in the hopes of attaining world-transcendent salvation, as Loyola argued, but rather "the life-blood of the world—immanent God himself." They were a means of binding together the collective mystical body; they were deliberately and uncompromisingly promoted as a way of achieving "religious-ecstatic ties between man and his [world-immanent] God. . . . The engendering of the myth and its propaganda by means of newspapers and radio, by speeches and communal celebrations, by assemblies and parades, the planning for and achievement of death in battle, constitute the world-immanent forms of the *unio mystica*" (*CW* 5:64).

In principle the symbolism of a world-immanent ecclesia was achieved by Hobbes's decapitation of God as the head of the commonwealth. In place of God, the community itself became the legitimation of the collective person. Political organization transformed the people from a plurality of individuals to a unity, to a spiritual incarnation. The *Volksgeist*, the spirit of the people, was most fully present in the *Führer*, the *Duce* or, indeed, the First Secretary. "The *Führer* is the point at which the spirit of the people breaks into historical reality; the world-immanent God speaks to the *Führer* in the same way that the world-transcendent God speaks to Abraham, and the *Führer* transforms God's words into commands for his immediate followers and for the people" (*CW* 5:65).[23] The oft-noted difference between the Italian and German variants was, for Voegelin, that the Italian leader incarnated a more spiritual personality whereas the German symbolism emphasized the importance of blood. In both instances the leader was the true carrier of the people's will. Accordingly, elections and plebiscites were not expressions of the people's will but declarations of subjection and loyalty to the leader.

Notwithstanding the closure and completeness of the symbols associated with the leader, Voegelin added that "we want to descend to the original sources, to the [spiritual] forces that created the symbolic forms" (*CW* 5:67). Specifically, Voegelin proposed to analyze Gerhard Schumann's *Lieder vom Reich* as an expression (or symbolization) of (the experience of) politico-religious fervor.[24] Schumann's songs, he said, "allow us to trace the movements of the soul" that engendered the "symbols and historical reality of the world-immanent community." The basic experience was one of "creatureliness," but redemption was found not in God but in the *Volk* and the brotherhood of comrades. "Moreover, the ecstasies are not spiritual but instinctive and find an outlet in the bloodlust of the deed."

Voegelin then provided an analysis of Schumann's poetry that centered on the emotion of loneliness overcome through unification within a brotherhood that would transport the individual soul into the midst of the *Volk.* The soul lost itself but became great by participating in the greater reality of the *Volk* and the *Reich.* Even so, the *Führer* must galvanize the *Volk* into the ecstasy of action. For the "oath-bound ascetics" in the SS, such as the author, the goal was endless battle as "fate" prepared to perfect itself in action. A prayer to "fate" asked for endless restlessness, because the point of the deed was not to win but only to act, and the pain inflicted on the enemy was to be experienced again in the soul of the actor. That is, friend and foe were equally to be destroyed until, eventually, the desire and the will of the actor (who somehow also is a sufferer) was extinguished. "The naked, purposeless deed as well as the self-inflicted wound and laceration are acts of mystical self-extinction and communion with the world up to the point of release in the intoxication of bloodlust: 'The deed is good if it is reddened with blood'" (*CW* 5:69). In this case it did not seem to matter whether the blood was of the agent or the patient; either way it was a splendid expression of what Arendt called superfluousness.[25]

Life after action reddened with blood inevitably ended in an enhanced version of the normal letdown soldiers typically experience after battle. Everyday life becomes alien to them, and they are left only as a standing reserve to be galvanized again by the word of the *Führer.* They are, said Schumann, "the soul of the *Reich.*"

> Devoted only to the *Führer.*
> In their steps echoes the judgment of blood.
> In their soul they bear the Grail.
> Slaves of the *Führer,* at once protectors and avengers.
> In them burns, with them grows, the *Reich!*

Voegelin introduced his conclusion by recalling that his purpose in writing the study of political religions was first of all to understand the phenomenon. The first conclusion, thus, was that the life of human beings in a political community involved more than the profane matters of law and the organization of power. "The community is also a realm of religious order" so that a thorough understanding of the political situation would necessarily be incomplete if it ignored the religious forces that were part of the political community, and the symbolic expression of them. The reason for the importance of religious symbols in political life was that human beings participated in political communities with all dimensions of their being, from physical bodies to spiritual aspirations. "The political community is always integrated into the wider context of the experience of the world and of God whether the political sphere assumes in the hierarchy of being a subordinate level in the divine order or whether it is itself deified" (*CW* 5:70). Likewise, the language of politics was always infused with religious fervor, and in this way it became, in the precise sense, a religious symbol insofar as it expressed the experience of the contents of the world having become infused with world-transcendent and divine meanings.

The structure Voegelin described was based on Mediterranean and European examples. But the elements of hierarchy whereby the sacred substance flowed from God to the community of creatures—the ecclesia as the substance of the sacred community, the apocalyptic revelation of the empire, and the sacred king, as the mediator of the divine, whose personality carried the substance of the community—were common to all advanced civilizations. In his later work, including his lectures collected in *Hitler and the Germans* (*CW* 31), Voegelin developed several analytical distinctions to separate commonsense or "first" reality from the second reality of the imagination. In *The Political Religions* he addressed this problem by relating what he would later term an ersatz religion (*CW* 5:295–313) to the specific and concrete religious sphere as understood by Christianity.

Here he quoted the anonymous fourteenth-century mystic, known only as "the Frankfurter," on the satanic practice of attributing to human beings the good things that come from God. "It is not," Voegelin wrote, "a matter of indifference how the sphere of human-political organization is integrated into the order of being" (*CW* 5:71). In good Augustinian fashion, Voegelin spelled out the alternatives. If the world-immanent religious experience was taken to be, and finds expression as, the *realissimum* by any collectivity, whether it was humanity as a whole or subordinate elements of class, *Volk*, state, race, or anything else, this act entailed "the renunciation of God." This explained why some Christian thinkers categorized political religions as demon-worship or mystical humanism, as distinct from the true faith. More specifically, Voegelin said, the Enlightenment notion of progress no less than the belief that a collective body was a mystical and divine substance, as has widely been announced since the nineteenth century, were both examples of anti-Christian renunciations of God. So far as the apprehension of the hierarchy of being, from nature to the divine, was concerned, the postulate of a world-immanent religious substance and its symbolization had the effect of concealing the essential aspects of reality. In Christian language, "it blocks the way to the reality of God and distorts the relationship of the levels of being that are subordinate to God" (*CW* 5:71).

Voegelin's final word returned to the question of the mystery of theodicy, introduced earlier with the quotation from Schelling. Neither philosophy nor Christian revelation, he said, could dissolve the mystery of God and his beings. The divine creation contained evil, the majesty of being was clouded by the misery of God's creatures, the order of the political community was founded upon hate and blood, lamentations and apostasy. Schelling's question, as that of Leibniz before him, expressed a mystery because it did not anticipate an answer: This is the way things are.

In the *Herrschaftslehre* Voegelin noted the existence of "the seed of evil that clings to all power" (*CW* 32:268). *The Political Religions* provided an analysis of the motivations that sustained a regime whose chief characteristic, as Hannah Arendt once observed, was that it was the occasion for the appearance of *radical evil,* a phrase first coined by Kant to refer to acts that could neither be punished nor forgiven.[26] If nothing else signaled a break from the traditional preoccupations of *Staatslehre,* the focus on the sheer evil of the National Socialist revolution certainly did.

As Sandro Chignola observed, with the publication of *The Political Religions,* Voegelin ended one major phase of his work and began another: "Having gone as far as he could by taking the discipline of law to be methodologically central, he was disposed to investigate political reality from a radically different point of view."[27] With the publication of the race books, academic life in Germany was closed to him; with the Anschluss happening almost at the same time as the publication of *The Political Religions,* he was compelled to leave Austria as well.

Voegelin's physical removal to the United States, his exodus, as it were, did not simply entail discontinuity. The approach to political reality first developed in *The Political Religions* was refined and expanded through the enormous wartime and postwar work that went into *The History of Political Ideas.* His focus on basic and crucial existential experiences was the theoretical foundation for *Order and History* and for his philosophy of consciousness. "These experiences," said Peter Opitz, "are interpreted and arranged, moulded into symbols, forged into terms and finally fashioned into all-inclusive worldviews. These in their turn form both the structure of political systems and institutions as well as the forms and strategies of personal and political action."[28]

Indeed, the insight Voegelin gained with respect to the importance of a public cult in the self-understanding of political communities continued in his best-known postwar book, *The New Science of Politics.* According to Dietmar Herz, the phrase *political religion* was a precursor to his use of the term *gnosticism* in his postwar writings.[29]

Herz's point, even if perhaps somewhat overstated, emphasized the continuity of what we have called Voegelin's quest. Granted that, in retrospect, as we quoted Voegelin above, he found the phrase *political religion* insufficiently precise (*CW* 34:78–79), the same could be said of *political idea* or even *gnosticism.* The process of critical clarification, as he called it, was continuous. In 1949, for example, he gave a paper at the annual meeting of the American Political Science Association. The title, "The Political Religions and Their Implications for the Traditional American Doctrine," echoed his work a decade earlier; the substantive content, particularly his analysis of Marx's early writings, anticipated his inaugural lecture at the University of Munich a decade later.[30]

This paper is interesting in another respect as well. In it Voegelin introduced the phrase *theologia ideologica* to supplement the classification of theologies by Cicero, Varro, and especially Augustine. For Augustine, *theologia civilis* referred to the politico-religious self-understanding of the Roman Empire, *theologia naturalis* to the politico-religious interpretation of Plato and Aristotle, and *theologia supernaturalis* to his own politico-religious interpretation of history. "Our modern political religions," Voegelin said, "while intimately related with the types classified by St. Augustine, cannot be subsumed under any one of them. We must coin a term for this fourth type; and continuing the tradition established by the great thinkers, I suggest the term *theologia ideologica.*" So far as I know, Voegelin never used the term again. It was replaced by other labels. Even as *The Political Religions* concluded one phase of Voegelin's quest for truth, it continued "the tradition established by the great thinkers."

Conclusion

In 1947 Voegelin published an essay, "On Sander's General *Staatslehre*," which was written just prior to his escape from Austria (*CW* 9:126–60). It illustrated well Voegelin's perspective on his own intellectual formation as a scholar who would no longer be described as a brilliant young man but who had not yet found his voice as a philosopher. Consideration of its arguments draws together several points made in the preceding chapters. The book, Fritz Sander's *Allgemeine Staatslehre*, was "the most significant" contribution "to a systematic groundwork of a science of the state." The purpose was to provide a discussion of the basic issues, the principles or the "groundwork," *Grundlegung*, of the state. Clarity about principles, Sander said, was more important than grasping details. The reason for this emphasis was a result of the lack of interest on the part of practitioners of *Staatslehre* about the principles of governance. The chief reason for this lack of interest was because the purpose of the scientific training has been to produce competent state employees, "for whom knowledge of and loyalty to the law is desirable, whereas too much speculation about foundations is not."

Voegelin then summarized Sander's argument and noted "certain difficulties" that arose in the course of attempting to evaluate it. The book was well argued and well structured; it proceeded from a series of axioms in a logical and consistent way. Moreover, his criticism of other approaches was also consistent with the "system" he developed so that "from his viewpoint, [he is] always right." Thus, "an immanent critique will only be able to confirm Sander's conclusions; but since it cannot come to different conclusions, because it is unable to move beyond the acknowledgment of a conscientiously completed work resulting in inner noncontradiction, it will also be completely uninteresting."

But a critique posed on the basis of other assumptions, a "transcendent evaluation," would lead to other problems because the reader then would ask questions that the author did not address or answer. "Since the questions go unanswered, an exchange of views is impossible." All one can do, therefore, was "formulate" and perhaps "explicate" the questions. Voegelin then elaborated five sets of questions, which he then addressed to Sander's text. These questions dealt with the problematic status of Sander's axioms and they concluded, naturally enough, with "a question mark," which is to say, inconclusively.

Even so, Voegelin addressed a number of critical remarks to Sander that recapitulated his earlier criticism of *Staatslehre.* For example, Sander adopted the system of "fundamental science," *Grundwissenschaft,* developed by Johannes Rehmke, without consideration of its applicability.

> Consequently, when one juxtaposes everything that is contained on the 113 pages of Scheler's small-format booklet on *Die Stellung des Menschen im Kosmos* [*The Place of Man in the Cosmos*] with what is missing from the 625 large-format pages of Rehmke's *Grundwissenschaft* [*Fundamental Science*], it would seem to me that a justification is in order for why Rehmke's doctrine of man has been adopted as a scientific prerequisite, rather than, for instance, Scheler's doctrine—this is not meant to indicate that I consider Scheler's anthropology an adequate scientific prerequisite for *Staatslehre.* Inasmuch as Sander does not offer any justification for this choice, I can again do no more than conclude with a question mark.

In other words, one could object to Sander's system only on the basis of a point of view that no theory of social reality that excluded the phenomenon of norms was useful. But for Sander the question did not arise because he began with Rehmke's *Fundamental Science* on the assumption that it was both fundamental and was science. "This beginning, however, would require a foundation based on ontology," and Sander neither provided one nor did he discuss the reasons why he began with Rehmke. Any argument dealing with political or even legal phenomena, in other words, eventually had to be based on a properly argued philosophical anthropology such as Scheler provided.

A second example indicated that Sander seemed to be indifferent to the historicity of the concepts he used or, more broadly, he ignored the fact that "the interpretation people gave of the social circumstances in which they live constitutes in itself a component of this set of circumstances." This had been Voegelin's starting point from the time of his writing the book on America. So far as the subject matter of a general *Staatslehre* was concerned, therefore:

> The term *state* is a *Staatslehre* expression of only secondary significance; it belongs primarily to the self-interpretation of European political thinking during the last four hundred years. The question of where the "essence" of the state is to be sought cannot be answered by an arbitrary name assignment to a random set of circumstances; instead it must find its bearings in a socially *previously given* fact "state," if *Staatslehre* as a branch of social sciences is to possess any degree of truthfulness in respect to its subject matter.

In order to justify the use of the term "state" in a scientific way, it was necessary to be aware not only of its historicity but also of its ontological basis, which is to say, its foundation in a philosophical anthropology "that encompasses the integral being of man, ranging from his corporeal and geographical ties all the way to his self-interpreting and mythopoetic spirit." Sander's refusal to consider such matters had the inevitable consequence that "whole groups of topics that would otherwise belong to *Staatslehre* are excluded. Thus the problems of social and political self-interpretation and the problem of political symbols are among those excluded."

By starting with so inadequate a basis as was provided by Rehmke, as distinct from, for instance, Scheler, "the entire historical layer of the political phenomenon, the question of sacral communities and sacral persons, of political myths, and finally the problem of norms" was overlooked. Had Sander used a "more fitting" ontology, these exclusions may not have taken place. In short, "when one lacks relevant grounds derived from an ontology of community [and thus from a philosophical anthropology] that facilitate the classification of the types of rule, every classification becomes materially pointless." Thus as was noted above, in distinguishing monarchy and dictatorship, the number of rulers is irrelevant. "One could classify states according to those in which rule is by 1 through 26 persons and those in which it is by 27 through an infinite number of persons, or according to states in which rule is vested in blond as opposed to brunette persons, etc." What counts, in other words, is meaning, which was as absent from Rehmke as it was central to Scheler.

Finally, Sander excluded the question of obligation and its origin. Voegelin argued, in contrast, that every legal order contained numerous rules or norms that those subject to it need not regard as morally binding. They may be rules that were morally indifferent, such as traffic regulations, or even morally objectionable. But even the latter had a specific quality of obligation about them. One source of that quality of obligation was the value of order as such. "Social *order* is, in the opinion of those subject to the order, better than social *disorder.*" And order, as such, had a sacral basis: "in the sacral structure of the communities," whether totemic and primitive, or the *sacrum imperium,* or secret political societies, "we will detect the social basis of the phenomenon of order and of the experiences of the quality of obligation with respect to general order and its components, which regulates the activities of the members of the community." In these remarks of 1938 we can find the origin of Voegelin's concept of order, with the famous description of the "quarternarian structure" of being, with which *Order and History* opened (*CW* 14:39).

In understanding Voegelin's early work, it is important to recall that he was legally trained rather than trained in a classical gymnasium or philosophical seminar as were, for example, his contemporaries Leo Strauss and Hannah Arendt. For a young man with legal training, the great crisis of his youth, the Great War, appeared as a practical issue of social and historical reality, not as one of the "wars of the spirit" predicted by Nietzsche. He was fascinated by the conceptual and argumentative complexity of Kelsen's pure theory of law where other Germans of comparable intellectual rank were similarly fascinated with Heidegger or Hegel. The accident of his legal and practical training helps account for why his early sociological analyses were motivated in part by a desire to understand the former enemies of Germany on their own terms.

The pivotal change arrived with his direct encounter of America insofar as the pluralism, which had been intimated or perhaps adumbrated by Voegelin's methodological reflections, was confirmed directly, empirically, and experientially. William James, to take a specific example, was every inch as much a philosopher as Husserl or Heidegger, but his concerns, his language, and his arguments were unquestionably American.

Voegelin's first attempt to deal with the self-interpretation of philosophy and of similar accounts of sociohistorical reality, *On the Form of the American Mind,* developed its own detailed and, truth to tell, rather idiosyncratic and abstract conceptual apparatus—of intellectual formations, meaningful unities, and so on. The necessity of finding his own way also enabled him to find in John C. Commons an exemplary personality unfiltered by perceptions conditioned by a philosophical education—in the European or any other sense. In Commons he was able to discern achievements in gross and in detail comparable to the achievements of European thinkers, but recorded in an entirely different register.

Starting with the race books in 1933 and continuing in his book on Austria in 1937, Voegelin reversed the precedence of the chief teaching of the entire *Staatslehre* tradition. By starting with the political reality of "ideas" such as race, he discovered there was no means of analytical access to the norm-logic of *Staatslehre.* That meant, first, that *Staatslehre* was increasingly cut off from reality. It also reinforced Voegelin's conclusion, arrived at after extensive critical analysis, that it was necessary to begin with the insights of philosophical anthropology. In turn, that meant paying greater attention to the fundamental experiences of reality that gave rise to the state. Moreover, these fundamental experiences—love and hate, for example—gave weight to the political ideas by burdening them with the emotional commitments of those who supported them, just as political ideas rendered those fundamental experiences articulate.

The race books are also significant because Voegelin criticized the so-called race theorists not simply on the grounds of philosophical anthropology but on the straightforward scientific grounds that they did not know anything about biology. To use a concept he employed when he revisited the Nationalist Socialist regime in *Hitler and the Germans,* Voegelin showed the race theorists had been constructing and acting upon a second reality.

In his book on Austria, Voegelin's concern with the inadequacies of methodological orthodoxies combined with his continuous awareness of the political situation. The chief attribute of Austria during the 1930s, Voegelin discovered, was precisely the absence of a governing "idea" into which it might have made sense for citizens to place their emotional investment. Austria was, very simply, a Kelsenian legal structure, the finest in the world.

Finally, it is clear that, at the same time as Voegelin was paying attention to the political events and realities of central Europe, he was also deepening his understanding of philosophy. Hence his introduction of Augustine in the *Herrschaftslehre* or of Averroism and positivism in *The Authoritarian State,* neither of which, at least on the surface, would appear to be natural places for such discussion. His most lasting discovery from the miserable and unpleasant experiences of the 1930s was that the conventional notion of the history of political ideas, which saw in the modern world nothing but secularism, was almost entirely wrong. One could understand neither the truth of political reality nor of human being without also understanding the centrality of spiritual experience. The discussion of Akhenaton or of the poetry of a member of the SS may appear to be a long way removed from the concerns with problems of *Staatslehre.* In the interpretation presented here, however, his discoveries and analyses of the late 1930s were part of a quest for understanding that began nearly two decades earlier and continued until the very moment of his death.

Appendix

Voegelin, Kelsen, and *The New Science of Politics*

As noted, Hans Kelsen was, along with Othmar Spann, Voegelin's *Doktorvater.* In the German universities even in the late twentieth century, a *Doktorvater* was more than the professional supervisor of a student's dissertation. The relationship also implied a sense of responsibility, mentorship, and even protectiveness on the one side and considerable deference on the other. We have seen on the basis of an analysis of Voegelin's essays from the 1920s, and especially after his return to Europe from America, that he began to question the theoretical presuppositions of Kelsen's pure theory of law. At the same time, however, he continued to profess his considerable admiration for Kelsen's achievement. In Voegelin's mind, at least initially, these were separate issues.

By 1954, when Kelsen and Voegelin exchanged letters and other documents, the relationship between the two men had changed from what it had been thirty years before. Of course, Voegelin was still formally Kelsen's pupil, and formalities continued to remain important for both men. But by the 1950s whatever deference Voegelin expressed toward Kelsen was almost entirely formal. Certainly there was no intellectual deference—indeed, we have argued that, even in the 1920s, he was ceasing to be a member of what Josef Kunz called the "Vienna School."[1] The exchange of 1954 provides a fascinating example of an exchange between a brilliant *Doktorvater* and his brilliant pupil. It is made even more compelling because, from

Kelsen's standpoint, Voegelin had, in the words of the *Book of Common Prayer*, "erred, and strayed . . . like lost sheep." From Voegelin's point of view, Kelsen's philosophical assumptions were now questionable on their own terms, because Voegelin had moved far beyond them and had come to understand neo-Kantianism, as other uncritical intellectual doctrines, as symptoms of a more fundamental problem to which he had, as yet, not attached an unequivocal name. The discussion between Kelsen and Voegelin can be seen, as it were, as the voice of a younger Voegelin interrogating what the mature Voegelin had become.

It seems that Voegelin initiated the correspondence during the winter of 1953–1954 by sending Kelsen, who was then teaching at the U.S. Naval War College, a copy of his essay "The Oxford Political Philosophers," which had just appeared in German in the *Philosophischer Rundschau* (*CW* 11:29–46). Kelsen provided Voegelin with a copy of one of his recent articles and mentioned that he had just finished reading *The New Science of Politics* and concluded that, on the grounds of his new science of politics *(neue Staatswissenschaft)*, Voegelin must consider him a "agent of destructive positivism" and, even more amazing, an out-and-out gnostic. As Martin Sattler pointed out, Kelsen was not being ironic: "there is an emphatic polemic in these words."[2]

Voegelin's reply of February 10, 1954 (*CW* 30:206–9), was conciliatory and deferential. He thanked Kelsen for sending him an offprint of "Metamorphoses of the Idea of Justice," praised it as "a brilliant summary of the fundamentals," recalled with nostalgia the first lecture of Kelsen that Voegelin had heard many years before, and noted that Kelsen's pure theory of law "has become a classic and will, I think, always be part of the canon of legal science." Because of his great respect for Kelsen's work, he was all the more saddened by Kelsen's remarks. "I believe I understand the motives for your disapproval, even if I cannot agree with your reasons. We have both grown older, and I have found my own theoretical position." Voegelin would therefore like to clarify "a misunderstanding that necessarily and improperly clouds relations with a man to whom I owe as much as I do to you."

Voegelin then characterized Kelsen's position as being a critical neo-Kantian in his theory of law and an agnostic regarding metaphysical and religious questions. As a result, Kelsen divided social reality into the subject matter discussed by causal and by normative science—Kelsen's *Normlogik.* For Voegelin there was, in addition, the problem of "the order of the soul and the corresponding science of philosophical anthropology, which is neither a normative nor a causal science." For Kelsen, however, the problems of philosophical anthropology were pseudo-problems *(Scheinproblemen),* which was fine, "for I do not intend to convince you of the critical rationality of this enterprise." But on the other hand, Voegelin's concern with metaphysics did not prevent him from understanding Kelsen's jurisprudential achievements. Voegelin was too polite to say so explicitly, but the reason was obvious: His "standpoint" was more comprehensive than Kelsen's.

Accordingly, Voegelin sketched the differences between Kelsen's "dogmatic assertion" that there were no legal problems outside the pure theory of law that admit of scientific treatment and Voegelin's view that the pseudo-problems were in fact "substantial and real." For Kelsen, pseudo-problems were quite properly to be dismissed; for Voegelin, "because I am of the opinion that these problems are real and very important, you will certainly understand that we are of divergent opinions in the evaluation of your destructive intention." Moreover, if Kelsen did not care to deal with metaphysical questions, his "subjective" attitude did not, in fact, touch upon those "substantive and real" problems at all. The most that could happen was that Kelsen's rhetorical brilliance would deter others from concerning themselves with metaphysical questions that might in fact be, for them, existentially real or important. The consequence, which Voegelin did not spell out, would be that such genuinely searching individuals would be prevented from asking what to them were meaningful questions, which, Voegelin said, was a serious matter. Finally, on the question of gnosticism, Voegelin assured Kelsen that the purity of his metaphysical agnosticism ensured that he never attempted to "fill the vacuum of transcendence" created by his attitude with any immanent type of gnosis—unlike both Cassirer and Husserl, who did so by creating positivistic philosophies of history.

Voegelin concluded by remarking that "the best thing a teacher can give his students is not a 'teaching,' but the discipline of work." Voegelin added that he learned to read, to analyze, and to exercise his critical faculties from Kelsen, "and that is the most important thing in science." Consider, for example, "poor Plato with his Aristotle." So, Voegelin concluded, "if you reconsider your misguided student, you might consider that the best students are not necessarily those who swear in *verba magistri* and remain inside the 'school,' but perhaps rather those who studied so thoroughly at school that they free themselves from it and can go their own way."[3]

Kelsen replied on February 27 and included a short essay, "Greekness," in return for Voegelin's "The World of Homer."[4] Kelsen professed his respect for Voegelin's scholarship, as Voegelin had done of Kelsen's, despite their differences, which brought him to the matter of *The New Science of Politics.* Kelsen promised to send him his critical remarks soon. He noted that he had not yet decided whether to publish them, and offered Voegelin an opportunity to respond should that seem useful. Kelsen added that he thought it was "tragic" that he was able to speak of Voegelin's science only as an opponent and that he hoped their opposition would not break their human connection.

Voegelin replied on March 7 with a three-page, single-spaced letter. He thanked Kelsen for the high honor of being worthy of his critical attention. "It is also the first time, so far as I know, that you have made any formal comment on one of my works" (*CW* 30:214–20). Voegelin reserved comment on any response save with respect to "technical details," because any "dispute over principles would be superfluous." Voegelin then turned his attention to Kelsen's essay *What Is Justice?*[5]

Voegelin said he found it difficult to comment on Kelsen's book for reasons he had already set forth in the previous letter. "I have no objection to the internal logic of your study. The problem is to be found in the premises, which you present as self-evident without any critical justification." On the other hand, since Kelsen had devoted so much attention to *The New Science of Politics,* Voegelin felt "duty-bound" to offer a few general remarks and then a couple of concrete examples. It seems clear from the context that Voegelin had not yet received Kelsen's criticism, which was in any event undated.[6] Interestingly enough, Kelsen referred to his study *What Is Justice?* in his critical remarks on Voegelin's *The New Science of Politics,* but he did not answer Voegelin's argument.

First, let us discuss Voegelin's general observation. Kelsen stated that every attempt to define a concept of justice from which the specific norms of a concrete social order followed has failed. In Kelsen's words, "the innumerable attempts which have been made from the earliest times of antiquity until today to solve the problem of justice as an absolute value by metaphysical-religious speculation have completely failed."[7] Voegelin agreed: "this observation states the obvious," namely that no great philosopher has ever made "an insane attempt of this kind." Justice, Voegelin said, cannot be positively determined but only negatively by ascertaining injustice concretely and offering reasons why it is unjust.

> The search instrument is the soul of the seeker. We do not operate here in a realm of normative principles but in an empirically verifiable realm of being. These souls are, when they become historically manifest, the souls of the great prophets, nomothetes, philosophers, and saints. And the reason why one should follow them cannot be found in a norm whose correctness can be determined through immanent scientific criteria, but rather in the response of related souls. And whether a concrete soul responds positively or negatively to the great souls (or is even at all capable of being moved by greatness) is an empirical fact. If a concrete soul cannot be moved in an empirical-factual sense then this may be regretted but nothing can be achieved through rational arguments. (*CW* 30:216)

The lack of agreement on a "definition" of justice was not contested. But that empirical fact was "the *starting point* of the Platonic and Aristotelian philosophizing on ethics." Accordingly it would be impermissible to cite the fact that stimulated philosophical thinking as an argument against any "contemplative quest."

Voegelin then took issue with Kelsen's interpretation of a couple of biblical passages and criticized the terseness with which he dismissed the notion that justice was a virtue in a human being—which was the point of Voegelin's remark on the "great souls" quoted above. It would be "pointless," Voegelin said, to produce additional criticism "if the arguments could not, seen from your point of view, be of any interest to you." Granted, therefore, that an inquiry into justice could not lead to "the construction of a critically verifiable norm," it could not then be called a failure "if one does not achieve what, according to our knowledge of the structure of being, cannot be achieved." For Voegelin, therefore, the problem of justice was "not a problem of a normative science, nor of a causal science; rather it is a problem of ontology." This was also argued by Voegelin in *The New Science of Politics* (*CW* 5:106–7).

Turning now to Kelsen's *A New Science of Politics*, it was divided into three sections: (1) "A Crusade against Positivism," (2) "A New Theory of Representation," and (3) "Gnosticism as a New Category of Political Science." This is, in fact, an accurate description of what Voegelin accomplished in *The New Science of Politics*. Kelsen, however, saw matters rather differently.

In the first section Kelsen simply rejected Voegelin's argument regarding the destructive consequences of positivism but did not engage in an analysis of Voegelin's premises or assumptions.[8] According to Kelsen, Voegelin wanted to replace science, that is, neo-Kantian science, with a kind of thinking that would be "placed under the spiritual authority of Plato and Thomas Aquinas." However, Kelsen continued, "if only that intellectual attitude had prevailed which is manifested in the metaphysical-theological speculation of Plato, Aristotle and Thomas Aquinas, modern science could not have been developed. . . . This kind of speculation [of Plato, Aristotle, and Thomas Aquinas] is not only useless to the purpose of science but constitutes a serious obstacle to its progress, is an undeniable fact, [as is] shown by the intellectual history of mankind."[9]

Kelsen particularly took issue with Voegelin's use of Platonic philosophy. "Voegelin," he said, "seems to assume that Plato's mystic philosophy of the good and the speculations of Christian ethics and politics about divine justice have nothing to do with value judgments because they have the character of 'ontology,' that is, cognition of being. But metaphysical ontology is the typical way of presenting subjective values as objective truths." Later in the book he wrote that what for Voegelin was a succinct formulation of Plato's "anthropological principle," that the polis is man written in large letters (*Republic* 368 c–d), really was no more than an "empty formula" that Plato used "in order to justify his postulate that in the ideal state a small group of so-called philosophers shall rule—with the help of the army (the warriors) as their instrument."[10]

On occasion, Kelsen was simply sarcastic. Voegelin wrote of Max Weber's account of "the evolution of mankind toward the rationality of positive science" was a process of disenchantment and dedivinization. But, according to Kelsen, Voegelin believed

> that he can hear in Weber's theory "overtones" of a "regret that divine enchantment had seeped out of the world": that Weber's rationalism was

> a mere "resignation." I have known Max Weber personally and studied the works very carefully, and on the basis of this knowledge I may say that the "overtones" and the "resignation" exist only in the metaphysical imagination of Voegelin. His imagination was probably stimulated by the laudable wish to mitigate somehow his criticism of a great master and to be able to say finally of Weber: "He saw the promised land but he was not permitted to enter it," which, of course, is the land to which political science will be lead by a new Moses, about whose identity no reader of the *New Science of Politics* can have the slightest doubt.[11]

Or again, there is another example later in the book: "As Dr. Faustus in Goethe's famous play, after having drunk the magic potion sees Helene in every woman, Voegelin sees Joachim's trinitarian eschatology whenever he finds a partition into three periods." Finally, in a very strange ad hominem remark, Kelsen asserted it was Voegelin's "gnostic dream" to see in the Anglo-American democracies the "glimmer of hope" that their institutions were both capable of representing the truth of the soul and were well defended.[12]

One might summarize this exchange with the observation that, for Kelsen, the progress of "science," which is to say, his neo-Kantian and reductionist epistemology, was evidence for the absence of any crisis. That carried the implication that the concrete experiences of Voegelin (and of Kelsen for that matter) during the 1930s were simply pseudo-problems. Likewise, Voegelin's discussion of the spiritual dimension of representation, the representation of truth, was simply a historical datum of no current significance and, more aggressively in the example of Plato's anthropological principle, an "empty formula" introduced for ulterior purposes. With the possible exception of Karl Popper, it is difficult to conceive any first-rank mind showing a greater misunderstanding of Plato.

Voegelin provided his own somewhat melancholy postscript in a 1956 letter to his older colleague and fellow student of Kelsen, Alfred Verdross:

> The conversation with Kelsen a while back was not very pleasant. He had sent me his voluminous critique of my *New Science*, apparently with the request that I should give him my opinion on the matter. And he wanted to hear my counter-arguments in a discussion. Now, for quite

> some time I have been beyond letting myself get caught up in debate with ideologues. And I indicated that to him. I further assured him that as far as I'm concerned, he can publish anything about me that he wishes, and that I wouldn't think badly about it if he did, but he mustn't demand that I answer him. In any case: the review did not get published; and I have heard indirectly that K. has discovered in the meantime that I am not an isolated criminal case, but that there is a very extensive scientific literature of this sort. He is now, the rumors have it, occupying himself with that. I wonder what he will have to say when the Exodus volume, with its overview of the literature on various individual questions, is published. (*CW* 30:270; see also *CW* 34:81)

In fact, Kelsen said nothing further.

Notes

Introduction

1. Sandro Chignola, "The Experience of Limitation: Political Form and Science of Law in the Early Writings of Eric Voegelin," 64.

2. See, for example, Andreas Krasemann, "Eric Voegelins politiktheoretisches Denken in den Früschriften"; and Manuel Wluka, *Wert und Ordnung, Ethik und Recht bei Hans Kelsen und Eric Voegelin.* The most thorough treatment is Hans-Jörg Sigwart, *Das Politische und die Wissenschaft: Intellectuell-biographische Studien zum Früwerk Eric Voegelins.* See also Michael Ley and Gilbert Weiss, eds., *Voegelin im Wien: Frühe Schriften, 1920–1938;* Michael Henkel, "Positivismuskritik und autoritärer Staat: Die Grundlagendebatte in der Weimarer Staatsrechtslehre und Eric Voegelins Weg zu einer neuen Wissenschaft der Politik (bis 1938)"; Dietmar Herz, "Das Ideal einer objektiven Wissenschaft von Recht und Staat: Zu Eric Voegelins Kritik an Hans Kelsen"; and Regina Braach, *Eric Voegelins Politische Anthropologie.*

3. Mann to Voegelin, December 18, 1938, Eric Voegelin Papers, Hoover Institution (hereinafter abbreviated HI) 24:11. The issue arose in a somewhat different form in the discussion between Thomas Heilke and Manfred Henningsen concerning the significance of Voegelin's race books, which will be discussed in Chapter 4.

4. See, for example, John Ranieri, *Disturbing Revelation: Leo Strauss, Eric Voegelin, and the Bible.*

5. Jürgen Gebhardt, "The Vocation of the Scholar," 10–34. We will discuss the meaning of *Wissenschaft,* science, in the following chapter.

6. Barry Cooper, "Eric Voegelin, Empirical Political Scientist," 271–82.

7. Gebhardt, "Vocation of a Scholar," 31.

8. Fredrick G. Lawrence, "The Problem of Eric Voegelin, Mystic Philosopher and Scientist," 35–58. Page references to these two articles are given in parentheses in the text.

9. Many of the papers were published in Glenn Hughes, Stephen A. McKnight, and Geoffrey L. Price, eds., *Politics, Order, and History: Essays on the Work of Eric Voegelin;* others were published in Stephen A. McKnight and Geoffrey L. Price, eds. *International and Interdisciplinary Perspectives on Eric Voegelin,* where the Gebhardt and Lawrence papers are to be found.

10. The seminar was called "Introduction to Philosophical Meditation" and was described as follows: "We will examine the nature of philosophical meditation as found in selected readings drawn from the Indian Upanishads, Plato, Plotinus, Augustine, Maimonides, Descartes, etc., to show that it is the basic form of philosophizing" (HI 86:3). See also Thomas A. Hollweck and Paul Caringella, "Editor's Introduction" to *CW* 28:xxvii (note 19); and William M. Thompson, "Philosophy and Meditation: Notes on Eric Voegelin's View," 115–35.

11. See the Vico chapter in *CW* 24:100ff; and Barry Cooper, *Eric Voegelin and the Foundations of Modern Political Science,* 335–82.

12. See Barry Cooper, "Voegelin's Concept of Historiogenesis," 232–35.

13. Gebhardt, "Vocation of the Scholar," 16–17, was quoting from a letter from Voegelin to Karl Löwith, February 8, 1945, HI 24:4.

14. Gregor Sebba, *The Collected Essays of Gregor Sebba: Truth, History, and Imagination,* 92.

15. "Faith seeking understanding" is the term Anselm of Canterbury used to describe *theology.* Anselm is occasionally identified as the founder of scholasticism. See also *CW* 1:294.

16. See Barry Cooper, *New Political Religions: An Analysis of Modern Terrorism,* 185–98.

17. I Cor. 14; *CW* 17:309–10.

18. See Barry Cooper, "Reduction, Reminiscence, and the Search for Truth," 316–31.

Chapter 1

1. Hans Maier, "Eric Voegelin and German Political Science," 713; Gregor Sebba, "Prelude and Variations on the Theme of Eric Voegelin," in *Eric Voegelin's Thought,* ed. Ellis Sandoz, 8; Sebba, "Prelude and Variations on the Theme of Eric Voegelin," in Sebba, *Collected Essays,* 198.

2. Jürgen Gebhardt and Barry Cooper, "Editors' Introduction," *CW* 1:ix–xlii. Much in the following paragraphs is based on this text. See also Cooper, *Eric Voegelin and the Foundations,* ch. 3.

3. Fritz K. Ringer, *The Decline of the German Mandarins: The German Academic Community, 1890–1933,* 102–3.

4. Ibid., 121.

5. See Jeffrey T. Bergner, *The Origin of Formalism in Social Science.*

6. See, however, Barry Cooper, "Surveying the Occasional Papers," *Review of Poli-*

tics, 727–51, for an account of Benjamin Franklin Wedekind, an unusual German man of letters whose parents returned from America just before his birth.

7. The implications of this commitment to democracy, not all of which were admired by Voegelin, will be discussed in Chapter 2.

8. For detailed analysis of this problem, see Robert Eden, *Political Leadership and Nihilism: A Study of Weber and Nietzsche.*

Chapter 2

1. Robert Hutchins, "Address of Dedication."

2. For details on the memorial, see Martin Bulmer and Joan Bulmer, "Philanthropy and Social Science in the 1920s: Beardsley Ruml and the Laura Spelman Rockefeller Memorial, 1922–29," 347–407; Martin Bulmer, "Support for Sociology in the 1920s: The Laura Spelman Rockefeller Memorial and the Beginnings of Modern, Large-Scale, Sociological Research in the University," 185–92; and Christian Fleck, "Die gescheiterte Gründung eines Zentrums für sozialwissenschaftliche Forschung in den 30er-Jahren in Wien." Details of Voegelin's fellowship are available at the Rockefeller Archive Center, LS/RM/III/52/548.

3. For a discussion of these problems in light of Voegelin's later work, see Aníbal A. Bueno, "Consciousness, Time, and Transcendence in Eric Voegelin's Philosophy," 91–109.

4. Horace M. Kallen, *Culture and Democracy in the United States.* Quoted in *CW* 1:126.

5. *CW* 1:216–17. Voegelin reversed Giddings's given names.

6. John R. Commons, *Races and Immigrants in America,* xviii; quoted in *CW* 1:226.

7. 83 U.S. 36 (1872).

8. John Locke, *Second Treatise of Government,* ch. 5:49, p. 319.

Chapter 3

1. *CW* 19–26. See also Cooper, *Eric Voegelin and the Foundations,* chapter 2.

2. See Josef L. Kunz, "The 'Vienna School' and International Law," 370–421. See also Edgar Bodenheimer, "Philosophical Anthropology and the Law," 653–82.

3. See John Dickinson, "A Working Theory of Sovereignty, I," 524–48; and John Dickinson, "A Working Theory of Sovereignty, II," 32–63. See also Harold Laski, *Studies in the Problem of Sovereignty;* and Charles McIlwain, "Sovereignty Again," 253–68.

4. Stanley Rosen, *The Limits of Analysis.*

5. Sandro Chignola, "'Fetishism with the Norm' and Symbols of Politics: Eric Voegelin between Sociology and 'Rechtswissenschaft' (1924–1938)," 27.

6. In "The Unity of the Law and the Social Structure of Meaning Called State," (1930–1931) (*CW* 8:89ff, note 1), Voegelin noted that the article was a chapter of a

work on "the theory of the state," that is, *Staatslehre.* In 1931 he received a grant-in-aid from the Rockefeller Foundation to support him while he completed his research and published "a book upon Principles of Government." Rockefeller Foundation Archives, LS/RM/III/52/548. The grant extended from July 1931 to March 1932. Voegelin received nine hundred dollars.

7. William Petropulos, "The Person as *Imago Dei:* Augustine and Max Scheler in Voegelin's *Herrschaftslehre* and *Political Religions,*" 89.

8. See also Hans-Jörg Sigwart, "Modes of Experience: On Eric Voegelin's Theory of Governance," 266.

9. See Ellis Sandoz, *Political Apocalypse: A Study of Dostoevsky's Grand Inquisitor.*

10. Carl Schmitt, *The Concept of the Political,* 19. This translation differs somewhat from Schwab's; see Schmitt, "Der Begriff des Politischen," 1.

11. See Cooper, *Eric Voegelin and the Foundations,* 39; and *CW* 19:18, 20:4n10.

12. Voegelin was quoting from a study by Lassa Oppenheim (the so-called father of international law), *The League of Nations and Its Problems: Three Lectures.*

Chapter 4

1. The term "Nationalist Socialist" does not appear in either of the race books. According to Gregor Sebba, Voegelin could not bring himself to use it. Sebba, "Prelude and Variations," in *Eric Voegelin's Thought,* 11.

2. David J. Levy, "Ethos and Ethnos: An Introduction to Eric Voegelin's Critique of European Racism," 99.

3. Thomas Heilke, *Voegelin on the Idea of Race: An Analysis of Modern European Racism,* 83.

4. There are other reasons as well, of course. Immigration, population movements, globalization, and so on have transformed the idea of race into something like the idea of ethnic identity. It is still academically acceptable to discuss ethnic politics, for instance. Moreover, in the immigrant societies of North America at least, cultural assimilation, which may take a generation or two, has effectively eclipsed any "racial" element, however that term may once have been understood. A Chinese American whose parents, say, were born in San Francisco is culturally an American who happens to be ethnic Chinese. Likewise a third-generation Ukrainian Canadian from Edmonton is culturally Canadian (or perhaps Albertan) whose heritage is Ukrainian. In neither case would the application of the language of race make much political sense. And if the Chinese Californian married the Ukrainian Albertan, the language of ethnic identity would also be strained, especially as regards their children.

5. Voegelin was not alone in rendering such a severe appraisal of recent biological theory, though other thinkers used rather different language. See, for instance, Hans Jonas, *The Phenomenon of Life: Toward a Philosophical Biology;* Adolf Portmann, *New Paths in Biology;* Frederich Olafson, *Naturalism and the Human Condition: Against Scientism;* Marjorie Grene, *Approaches to a Philosophical Biology;* and Marjorie Grene,

The Understanding of Nature: Essays in the Philosophy of Biology. A more contemporary analysis to Voegelin's of one aspect of the "fiasco" is Kurt Goldstein, *The Organism: A Holistic Approach to Biology Derived from Pathological Data in Man* (the German edition came out in 1934). For a discussion of several other philosophers of biology, see Heilke, *Voegelin on the Idea of Race.*

6. It also became the basis for legitimizing or at least permitting transgenetic experimentation or "genetic therapy" in the twentieth century. Some of the implications are discussed in Barry Cooper, *Action into Nature: An Essay on the Meaning of Technology.*

7. Kant, "Idea for a Universal History with a Cosmopolitan Purpose," 44. See also *CW* 3:152, 6:52–53, and 33:407–8.

8. Barry Cooper, *The End of History: An Essay on Modern Hegelianism* (Toronto: University of Toronto Press, 1984), 202ff.

9. See Cooper, *Eric Voegelin and the Foundations,* chapter 8.

10. These reviews are collected at HI 54:2 and HI 54:5. Copies are also available at the Eric-Voegelin-Archiv, Munich.

Chapter 5

1. Voegelin mentioned, as one of the glaring "deficiencies" of the U.S. Constitution, Article 5, which "requires two-thirds of the votes of both houses for a proposal to amend the constitution and omits to state whether a quorum is sufficient or not" (*CW* 7:189–90; see also *CW* 7:153–55).

2. The "juridically unique structure of the monarchy under the category of 'empire' [*Reich*] as distinguished from that of 'state' [*Staat*]" was most thoroughly developed by Josef Redlich. It was used extensively by Voegelin. See his "Josef Redlich," *CW* 9:91–95.

3. For an analysis of Voegelin's account of positivism, see Cooper, *Eric Voegelin and the Foundations,* chapter 3.

4. Leo Strauss made the same point regarding the equally positivist American voting studies. See Strauss, "An Epilogue," 305–27; and Strauss, "What Is Political Philosophy?" 9–27.

Chapter 6

1. See also Emilio Gentile, "Political Religion: A Concept and Its Critics—A Critical Survey," *Totalitarian Movements and Political Religions,* 19–32.

2. Philippe Brunn, "Political Religion: The Relevance of a Concept," 321–47.

3. Klaus Vondung, "National Socialism as a Political Religion: Potentials and Limits of an Analytical Concept," 88.

4. This is self-evident to anyone who has studied Plato's *Apology of Socrates.* Looked at from the other side, Cicero explained at great length why *re-ligio* literally "bound together" the sacred community of the *res publica.*

5. *CW* 34:78, 5:72. See also *CW* 30:144; Louis Rougier, *Les mystiques politiques*

contemporaines et leurs incidences internationales; and Etienne de Greeff, "Le drame humain et la psychologie des 'mystiques' humaines," 105–55. See also *CW* 24:47n9.

6. See Cooper, *Eric Voegelin and the Foundations,* chapter 1; and Barry Cooper and Jodi Bruhn, eds. *Voegelin Recollected: Conversations on a Life,* 161–66, 220–23, 232–33, 252–53.

7. There are, moreover, two versions of this preface, the one published in *CW* 5:23–25, and a second, longer version transcribed directly from the manuscript in the Voegelin Archives at the Hoover Institution (HI 55:33). I am using the longer version available in *CW* 33:19–23.

8. The epigraph was: "Through me is the road to the city of sorrow" (*Inferno* 3:1).

9. See, however, Gerald Schwab, *The Day the Holocaust Began,* which analyzed the response to Grynszpan's action in detail. See also Ron Roizen, "Herschel Grynszpan: The Fate of a Forgotten Assassin," 217–28.

10. Voegelin made the same observation in his "Hitler and the Germans" lectures in 1964; see *CW* 31:155ff.

11. Voegelin had a high opinion of Hermann Rauschning's *Revolution of Nihilism: Warning to the West,* for example, despite the author's questionable past. Hans-Jörg Sigwart has provided an analysis of Voegelin's correspondence in 1939 with Ruthild and Karsten Lemche on this question; see Sigwart, "Modes of Experience," 283ff. See also Sigwart, *Das Politische und die Wissenschaft,* 263.

12. This issue arose in Chapter 4 in the discussion between Heilke and Henningsen. It also was central to Hannah Arendt's treatment of totalitarianism. Indeed, as we shall argue, many of Arendt's arguments in *The Origins of Totalitarianism* (new edition) were close to those made by Voegelin in *The Political Religions.* In the preface to the first edition of *Origins,* for example, Arendt wrote that her goal was to comprehend the significance of totalitarianism and added that "comprehension does not mean denying the outrageous, deducing the unprecedented from precedents, or explaining phenomena by such analogies and generalities that the impact of reality and the shock of experience are no longer felt. It means, rather, examining and bearing consciously the burden which our century has placed on us—neither denying its existence nor submitting meekly to its weight. Comprehension, in short, means the unpremeditated, attentive facing up to, and resisting of, reality—whatever it may be" (*Origins,* xxx).

13. We have used the comparative; the *realissimum* is literally the most, or superlatively, real.

14. Voegelin here paraphrased a remark of Hegel from section 340 of the *Philosophy of Right,* that world history is the world's court of judgment. For an analysis, see Barry Cooper, *The End of History: An Essay on Modern Hegelianism,* 256ff.

15. See *CW* 5:286ff, 12:213ff; and Cooper, *End of History,* 340ff.

16. Despite the somewhat Heideggerian language Voegelin used—*Geworfensein, Verlassenheit,* the *Erregungen der Existenz,* and so on—his reference to the *analogia entis* indicated that he was probably thinking of St. Thomas Aquinas.

17. Voegelin spelled the god's name Ra; we followed the later spelling, also used in *Order and History,* of Re.

18. In antiquity the problem was nicely illustrated by the touching story of Scipio Aemilianus in his hour of triumph over Carthage being filled with anxiety that "some day the same doom will be pronounced" upon Rome (see Polybius, *Histories* 37:20).

19. *CW* 5:43. See also *CW* 23:180ff; and Cooper, *Eric Voegelin and the Foundations,* chapter 6.

20. See Arendt, *Origins,* part 1.

21. See ibid., 333ff, 363ff.

22. In his later work, Voegelin dismissed the notion of a naive or good-faith belief in "science" because the "scientist" was perfectly well aware that his "science" was based on the prohibition of questions that might expose the entire enterprise as an "intellectual swindle." See, for example, *CW* 5:264–65, 274–75.

23. Arendt, *Origins,* 243–50, 394, 400, 464–67.

24. Schumann (1911–1995) was a Nazi student leader and prizewinning poet. *Lieder vom Reich* was published in 1935; a year later he was awarded the National Book Prize by Goebbels. He spent most of the war in the cultural services at SS headquarters, but in 1944 he joined the Waffen SS. He was sentenced to three years of imprisonment after the war. See Karl-Heinz Schoeps, "Zur Kontnuitat der volkisch-nationalkonservatives Literatur vor, wahrend und nach 1945: Der Fall Gerhard Schumann," 45–63.

25. Arendt, *Origins,* 457ff, 475.

26. Ibid., 459.

27. Chignola, "Experience of Limitation," 65.

28. Peter J. Opitz, "Voegelin's *Political Religions* in the Contemporary Political Order," 53–54.

29. Dietmar Herz, "Der Begriff der 'politishen Religionen' in Denken Eric Voegelins," 209.

30. The paper is in HI 62:34.

Appendix

1. See Kunz, "Vienna School," 370–421.

2. Martin Sattler, "The Controversy between Hans Kelsen and Eric Voegelin on the New Science of Politics." Voegelin's original letter is not in the Voegelin Archives. The rest of the correspondence is in HI 20:37.

3. This translation varies slightly from *CW* 30. I have used the text in HI 20:37, which contains both sides of the correspondence, as a source; Voegelin made a couple of handwritten changes and, I believe, wrote *Schule* (school), not *Schale* (shell), though the word was retyped.

4. *Review of Politics* 15 (1953): 491–523; incorporated into *CW* 15:135ff.

5. Hans Kelsen, *Was ist Gerechtigkeit?* An expanded English edition, Hans Kelsen,

What Is Justice? Justice, Law, and Politics in the Mirror of Science: Collected Essays, was published in 1957 by the University of California Press.

6. The original 125-page manuscript, with several insertions attached to the pages by Scotch tape, is found in HI 63:13. A printed version is Hans Kelsen, *A New Science of Politics: Hans Kelsen's Reply to Eric Voegelin's "New Science of Politics: A Contribution to the Critique of Ideology"*; references are to the printed version. This edition is technically well done; it is marred only by the editor's opinion that the "critique of ideology" mentioned in the title was directed by Kelsen at Voegelin, who was taken to be a "conservative" (109ff). The titles of the two books are distinguished only by the differing use of the article. References to Voegelin's *The New Science of Politics,* however, are to *CW* 5. As a final philological curiosity, Martin Sattler said that the Kelsen Archive in Vienna claimed that "such a letter," which is to say, Kelsen's lengthy review, had "never been written" and was "not in their archives." On the other hand, Eckhart Arnold, the editor of the Kelsen volume, claims the original is in the Kelsen Archives and that a copy is in the Eric-Voegelin-Archiv in Munich (see Kelsen, *New Science,* 9). In fact, as indicated, the original is at the Hoover Institution. Voegelin sent a copy of the review, which can hardly be termed a "letter," as Sattler called it, to the Kelsen Archive in May 1973 (see the correspondence with Robert Walter of the Kelsen Archive, HI 40:3).

7. Kelsen, *New Science,* 15.

8. See Cooper, *Eric Voegelin and the Foundations,* chapter 3, for details of Voegelin's argument.

9. Kelsen, *New Science,* 12, 15.

10. Ibid., 21, 59.

11. Ibid., 28–29.

12. Ibid., 79, 107–8.

Bibliography

Eric Voegelin's Collected Works

Anamnesis: On the Theory of History and Politics. Translated by M. J. Hanak. Edited by David Walsh. Vol. 6 of *The Collected Works of Eric Voegelin.* Columbia: University of Missouri Press, 2002.

The Authoritarian State: An Essay on the Problem of the Austrian State. Translated by Ruth Hein. Edited by Gilbert Weiss. Vol. 4 of *The Collected Works of Eric Voegelin.* Columbia: University of Missouri Press, 1999.

Autobiographical Reflections. Rev. ed. Edited by Ellis Sandoz. Vol. 34 of *The Collected Works of Eric Voegelin.* Columbia: University of Missouri Press, 2006.

Crisis and the Apocalypse of Man. Edited by David Walsh. Vol. VIII, *History of Political Ideas.* Vol. 26 of *The Collected Works of Eric Voegelin.* Columbia: University of Missouri Press, 1999.

The Drama of Humanity and Other Miscellaneous Papers, 1939–1985. Edited by William Petropulos and Gilbert Weiss. Vol. 33 of *The Collected Works of Eric Voegelin.* Columbia: University of Missouri Press, 2004.

The Ecumenic Age. Edited by Michael Franz. Vol. IV, *Order and History.* Vol. 17 of *The Collected Works of Eric Voegelin.* Columbia: University of Missouri Press, 2000.

Hellenism, Rome, and Early Christianity. Edited by Athanasios Moulakis. Vol. I, *History of Political Ideas.* Vol. 19 of *The Collected Works of Eric Voegelin.* Columbia: University of Missouri Press, 1997.

The History of the Race Idea: From Ray to Carus. Translated by Ruth Hein. Edited by Klaus Vondung. Vol. 3 of *The Collected Works of Eric Voegelin.* Baton Rouge: Louisiana State University Press, 1998.

Hitler and the Germans. Translated and edited by Detlev Clemens and Brendan Purcell. Vol. 31 of *The Collected Works of Eric Voegelin.* Columbia: University of Missouri Press, 1999.

In Search of Order. Edited by Ellis Sandoz. Vol. V, *Order and History.* Vol. 18 of *The Collected Works of Eric Voegelin.* Columbia: University of Missouri Press, 2000.

Israel and Revelation. Edited by Maurice P. Hogan. Vol. I, *Order and History.* Vol. 14 of *The Collected Works of Eric Voegelin.* Columbia: University of Missouri Press, 2001.

The Later Middle Ages. Edited by David Walsh. Vol. III, *History of Political Ideas.* Vol. 21 of *The Collected Works of Eric Voegelin.* Columbia: University of Missouri Press, 1998.

The Middle Ages to Aquinas. Edited by Peter Von Sivers. Vol. II, *History of Political Ideas.* Vol. 20 of *The Collected Works of Eric Voegelin.* Columbia: University of Missouri Press, 1997.

Modernity without Restraint: The Political Religions; The New Science of Politics; and Science, Politics, and Gnosticism. Edited by Manfred Henningsen. Vol. 5 of *The Collected Works of Eric Voegelin.* Columbia: University of Missouri Press, 2000.

The Nature of the Law and Related Legal Writings. Edited by Robert Anthony Pascal, James Lee Babin, and John William Corrington. Vol. 27 of *The Collected Works of Eric Voegelin.* Baton Rouge: Louisiana State University Press, 1991.

The New Order and Last Orientation. Edited by Jürgen Gebhardt and Thomas A. Hollweck. Vol. VII, *History of Political Ideas.* Vol. 25 of *The Collected Works of Eric Voegelin.* Columbia: University of Missouri Press, 1999.

On the Form of the American Mind. Translated by Ruth Hein. Edited by Jürgen Gebhardt and Barry Cooper. Vol. 1 of *The Collected Works of Eric Voegelin.* Baton Rouge: Louisiana State University Press, 1995.

Plato and Aristotle. Edited by Dante Germino. Vol. III, *Order and History.* Vol. 16 of *The Collected Works of Eric Voegelin.* Columbia: University of Missouri Press, 2000.

Published Essays: 1922–1928. Translated by M. J. Hanak. Edited by Thomas W. Heilke and John Von Heyking. Vol. 7 of *The Collected Works of Eric Voegelin.* Columbia: University of Missouri Press, 2003.

Published Essays: 1929–1933. Translated by M. J. Hanak and Jodi Cockerill. Edited by Thomas W. Heilke and John Von Heyking. Vol. 8 of *The Collected Works of Eric Voegelin.* Columbia: University of Missouri Press, 2003.

Published Essays: 1934–1939. Translated by M. J. Hanak. Edited by Thomas W. Heilke. Vol. 9 of *The Collected Works of Eric Voegelin.* Columbia: University of Missouri Press, 2001.

Published Essays: 1940–1952. Edited by Ellis Sandoz. Vol. 10 of *The Collected Works of Eric Voegelin.* Columbia: University of Missouri Press, 2000.

Published Essays: 1953–1965. Edited by Ellis Sandoz. Vol. 11 of *The Collected Works of Eric Voegelin.* Columbia: University of Missouri Press, 2000.

Published Essays: 1966–1985. Edited by Ellis Sandoz. Vol. 12 of *The Collected Works of Eric Voegelin.* Baton Rouge: Louisiana State University Press, 1990.

Race and State. Translated by Ruth Hein. Edited by Klaus Vondung. Vol. 2 of *The Collected Works of Eric Voegelin.* Baton Rouge: Louisiana State University Press, 1997.

Religion and the Rise of Modernity. Edited by James L. Wiser. Vol. V, *History of Political Ideas.* Vol. 23 of *The Collected Works of Eric Voegelin.* Columbia: University of Missouri Press, 1998.

Renaissance and Reformation. Edited by David L. Morse and William M. Thompson. Vol. IV, *History of Political Ideas.* Vol. 22 of *The Collected Works of Eric Voegelin.* Columbia: University of Missouri Press, 1998.

Revolution and the New Science. Edited by Barry Cooper. Vol. VI, *History of Political Ideas.* Vol. 24 of *The Collected Works of Eric Voegelin.* Columbia: University of Missouri Press, 1998.

Selected Book Reviews. Edited and translated by Jodi Cockerill and Barry Cooper. Vol. 13 of *The Collected Works of Eric Voegelin.* Columbia: University of Missouri Press, 2001.

Selected Correspondence, 1950–1984. Translated by Sandy Adler, Thomas A. Hollweck, and William Petropulos. Edited by Thomas A. Hollweck. Vol. 30 of *The Collected Works of Eric Voegelin.* Columbia: University of Missouri Press, 2007.

The Theory of Governance and Other Miscellaneous Papers, 1921–1938. Translated by Sue Bollans, Jodi Cockerill, M. J. Hanak, Ingrid Heldt, Elisabeth Von Lochner, and William Petropulos. Edited by William Petropulos and Gilbert Weiss. Vol. 32 of *The Collected Works of Eric Voegelin.* Columbia: University of Missouri Press, 2003.

What Is History? And Other Late Unpublished Writings. Edited by Thomas A. Hollweck and Paul Caringella. Vol. 28 of *The Collected Works of Eric Voegelin.* Baton Rouge: Louisiana State University Press, 1990.

The World of the Polis. Edited by Athanasios Moulakis. Vol. II, *Order and History.* Vol. 15 of *The Collected Works of Eric Voegelin.* Columbia: University of Missouri Press, 2000.

Other Works Consulted

Arendt, Hannah. *The Origins of Totalitarianism.* New ed. New York: Harcourt, Brace and World, 1966.

Bergner, Jeffrey T. *The Origin of Formalism in Social Science.* Chicago: University of Chicago Press, 1981.

Bodenheimer, Edgar. "Philosophical Anthropology and the Law." *California Law Review* 59 (1971).

Braach, Regina. *Eric Voegelins Politische Anthropologie.* Würzburg: Königshausen und Neumann, 2003.

Brunn, Philippe. "Political Religion: The Relevance of a Concept." *History and Memory* 9 (1997).

Bueno, Aníbal A. "Consciousness, Time, and Transcendence in Eric Voegelin's Philosophy." In *The Philosophy of Order: Essays on History, Consciousness, and Politics for Eric Voegelin on His Eightieth Birthday,* edited by Peter J. Opitz and Gregor Sebba. Stuttgart: Klett-Cotta, 1981.

Bulmer, Martin. "Support for Sociology in the 1920s: The Laura Spelman Rockefeller Memorial and the Beginnings of Modern, Large-Scale, Sociological Research in the University." *American Sociologist* 17 (1982).

Bulmer, Martin, and Joan Bulmer. "Philanthropy and Social Science in the 1920s: Beardsley Ruml and the Laura Spelman Rockefeller Memorial, 1922–29." *Minerva* 19, no. 3 (1981).

Chignola, Sandro. "The Experience of Limitation: Political Form and Science of Law in the Early Writings of Eric Voegelin." In *Politics, Order, and History: Essays on the Work of Eric Voegelin,* edited by Glen Hughes, Stephen A. McKnight, and Geoffrey L. Price. Sheffield: Sheffield Academic Press, 2001.

———. "'Fetishism with the Norm' and Symbols of Politics: Eric Voegelin between Sociology and 'Rechtswissenschaft' (1924–1938)." *Occasional Papers* X. Munich: Eric-Voegelin-Archiv, 1999.

Commons, John R. *Races and Immigrants in America.* 2nd ed., with a new introduction. New York: Macmillan, 1920.

Cooper, Barry. *Action into Nature: An Essay on the Meaning of Technology.* Notre Dame, Ind.: Notre Dame University Press, 1991.

———. *The End of History: An Essay on Modern Hegelianism.* Toronto: University of Toronto Press, 1984.

———. "Eric Voegelin, Empirical Political Scientist." In Cooper, *The Restoration of Political Science and the Crisis of Modernity.* Lewiston, N.Y.: Edwin Mellen, 1989.

———. *Eric Voegelin and the Foundations of Modern Political Science.* Columbia: University of Missouri Press, 1999.

———. *New Political Religions: An Analysis of Modern Terrorism.* Columbia: University of Missouri Press, 2004.

———. "Reduction, Reminiscence, and the Search for Truth." In *The Philosophy of Order: Essays on History, Consciousness, and Politics for Eric Voegelin on his Eightieth Birthday,* edited by Peter J. Opitz and Gregor Sebba. Stuttgart: Klett-Cotta, 1981.

———. "Surveying the Occasional Papers." *Review of Politics* 62, no. 4 (2000).

———. "Voegelin's Concept of Historiogenesis." *Historical Reflections/Reflexions Historiques* 4, no. 2 (1978).

Cooper, Barry, and Jodi Bruhn, eds. *Voegelin Recollected: Conversations on a Life.* Columbia: University of Missouri Press, 2008.

de Greeff, Etienne. "Le drame humain et la psychologie des 'mystiques' humaines." *Etudes Carmélitianes* 22 (1937).

Dickinson, John. "A Working Theory of Sovereignty, I." *Political Science Quarterly* 42, no. 4 (1927).

———. "A Working Theory of Sovereignty, II." *Political Science Quarterly* 43, no. 1 (1928).

Du Bois, W. E. B. *The Souls of Black Folk.* Chicago: A. C. McClurg, 1903.

Eden, Robert. *Political Leadership and Nihilism: A Study of Weber and Nietzsche.* Tampa: University of South Florida Press, 1983.

Fleck, Christian. "Die gescheiterte Gründung eines Zentrums für sozialwissenschaftliche Forschung in den 30er-Jahren in Wien." *Archiv für die Geschichte der Soziologie in Österreich* (newsletter), no. 20 (June 2000).

Gebhardt, Jürgen. "The Vocation of a Scholar." In *International and Interdisciplinary Perspectives on Eric Voegelin,* edited by Stephen A. McKnight and Geoffrey L. Price. Columbia: University of Missouri Press, 1997.

Gentile, Emilio. "Political Religion: A Concept and Its Critics—A Critical Survey." *Totalitarian Movements and Political Religions* 6 (2005).

Goldstein, Kurt. *The Organism: A Holistic Approach to Biology Derived from Pathological Data in Man.* Cincinnati, Ohio: American Book, 1939.

Grene, Marjorie. *Approaches to a Philosophical Biology.* New York: Basic Books, 1968.

———. *The Understanding of Nature: Essays in the Philosophy of Biology.* Boston: Reidel, 1974.

Heilke, Thomas. *Voegelin on the Idea of Race: An Analysis of Modern European Racism.* Baton Rouge: Louisiana State University Press, 1990.

Henkel, Michael. "Positivismuskritik und autoritärer Staat: Die Grundlagendebatte in der Weimarer Staatsrechtslehre und Eric Voegelins Weg zu einer neuen Wissenschaft der Politik (bis 1938)." *Occasional Papers* XXXVI. Munich: Eric-Voegelin-Archiv, 2005.

Herz, Dietmar. "Das Ideal einer objektiven Wissenschaft von Recht und Staat: Zu Eric Voegelins Kritik an Hans Kelsen." *Occasional Papers* III. Munich: Eric-Voegelin-Archiv, 2002.

———. "Der Begriff der 'politishen Religionen' in Denken Eric Voegelins." In *"Totalitarismus" und "Politische Religionen": Konzepte des Diktaturvergleichs,* edited by Hans Maier. Paderborn, Germany: Ferdinand Schöningh, 1996.

Hughes, Glenn, Stephen A. McKnight, and Geoffrey L. Price, eds. *Politics, Order, and History: Essays on the Work of Eric Voegelin.* Sheffield: Sheffield Academic Press, 2001.

Hutchins, Robert. "Address of Dedication." In *The New Social Sciences,* edited by Leonard D. White. Chicago: University of Chicago Press, 1930.

James, William. *Pluralistic Universe.* New York: Longmans, Green, 1909.

Jonas, Hans. *The Phenomenon of Life: Toward a Philosophical Biology.* New York: Delta, 1966.

Kallen, Horace M. *Culture and Democracy in the United States.* New York: Boni and Liveright, 1924.

Kant, Immanuel. *Critique of Judgement.* Trans. James Creed Meredith. Ed. Nicholas Walker. Oxford: Oxford University Press, 2007.

———. "Idea for a Universal History with a Cosmopolitan Purpose." In *Kant's Political Writings,* edited by Hans Reiss and translated by. H. B. Nisbet. Cambridge: Cambridge University Press, 1970.

Kelsen, Hans. *A New Science of Politics: Hans Kelsen's Reply to Eric Voegelin's "New Science of Politics: A Contribution to the Critique of Ideology."* Edited by Eckhart Arnold. Frankfurt: Ontos Verlag, 2004.

———. *Was ist Gerechtigkeit?* Vienna: Verlag Franz Deuticke, 1953.

———. *What Is Justice? Justice, Law, and Politics in the Mirror of Science: Collected Essays.* Berkeley: University of California Press, 1957.

Krasemann, Andreas. "Eric Voegelins politiktheoretisches Denken in den Früschriften." PhD diss., University of Erfurt, Germany, 2002.

Kunz, Josef L. "The 'Vienna School' and International Law." *New York University Law Quarterly Review* 11 (1933–1934).

Laski, Harold. *Studies in the Problem of Sovereignty.* New Haven: Yale University Press, 1917.

Lawrence, Frederick G. "The Problem of Eric Voegelin, Mystic Philosopher and Scientist." In *International and Interdisciplinary Perspectives on Eric Voegelin,* edited by Stephen A. McKnight and Geoffrey L. Price. Columbia: University of Missouri Press, 1997.

Lessing, Gotthold. *Education of the Human Race.* In *Literary and Philosophical Essays,* ed. Charles W. Eliot. New York: Collier 1909.

Levy, David J. "Ethos and Ethnos: An Introduction to Eric Voegelin's Critique of European Racism." In *Race and Racism in Continental Philosophy,* edited by Robert Bernasconi and Sybol Cook. Bloomington: Indiana University Press, 2003.

Ley, Michael, and Gilbert Weiss, eds. *Voegelin im Wien: Frühe Schriften, 1920–1938.* Vienna: Passagen, 2007.

Locke, John. *Second Treatise of Government.* In *John Locke: Two Treatises of Government,* edited by Peter Laslett. Cambridge: Cambridge University Press, 1988.

Maier, Hans. "Eric Voegelin and German Political Science." Translated and edited by Jodi Cockerill. *Review of Politics* 62, no. 4 (2000).

McIlwain, Charles. "Sovereignty Again." *Economica* 6 (1926).

McKnight, Stephen A., and Geoffrey L. Price, eds. *International and Interdisciplinary Perspectives on Eric Voegelin.* Columbia: University of Missouri Press, 1997.

Olafson, Frederich. *Naturalism and the Human Condition: Against Scientism.* New York: Routledge, 2001.

Opitz, Peter J. "Voegelin's *Political Religions* in the Contemporary Political Order." In *Politics, Order, and History: Essays on the Work of Eric Voegelin,* edited by Glenn Hughes, Stephen A. McKnight, and Geoffrey L. Price. Sheffield: Sheffield Academic Press, 2001.

Oppenheim, Lassa. *The League of Nations and Its Problems: Three Lectures.* London: Longmans Green, 1919.

Paine, Thomas. *The Rights of Man: Being an Answer to Mr. Burke's Attack on the French Revolution.* London: Penguin, 1984.

Petropulos, William. "The Person as *Imago Dei:* Augustine and Max Scheler in Voegelin's *Herrschaftslehre* and *Political Religions.*" In *The Politics of the Soul: Eric Voegelin on Religious Experience,* edited by Glen Hughes. Lanham, Md.: Rowman and Littlefield, 1999.

Polybius. *The Histories.* Trans. W. R. Paton. Cambridge: Harvard University Press, 1922.

Portmann, Adolf. *New Paths in Biology.* Translated by A. Pomerans. New York: Harper and Row, 1964.

Ranieri, John. *Disturbing Revelation: Leo Strauss, Eric Voegelin, and the Bible.* Columbia: University of Missouri Press, 2008.

Rauschning, Hermann. *Revolution of Nihilism: Warning to the West.* New York: Longmans, Green, 1939.

Ringer, Fritz K. *The Decline of the German Mandarins: The German Academic Community, 1890–1933.* Cambridge: Harvard University Press, 1969.

Roizen, Ron. "Herschel Grynszpan: The Fate of a Forgotten Assassin." *Holocaust and Genocide Studies* 1 (1986).

Rosen, Stanley. *The Limits of Analysis.* New Haven: Yale University Press, 1980.

Rougier, Louis. *Les mystiques politiques contemporaines et leurs incidences internationales.* Paris: Librarie du Recueil Sirey, 1936.

Sandoz, Ellis. *Political Apocalypse: A Study of Dostoevsky's Grand Inquisitor.* 2nd ed. Wilmington, Del.: ISI Books, 2000.

Sattler, Martin. "The Controversy between Hans Kelsen and Eric Voegelin on the New Science of Politics." Presented at the Second International Conference on the Work of Eric Voegelin, University of Manchester, July 3–6, 1997.

Schmitt, Carl. "Der Begriff des Politischen." *Archiv für Sozialwissenschaft* 58 (1927).

———. *The Concept of the Political.* Translated by George Schwab. New Brunswick, N.J.: Rutgers University Press, 1976.

Schoeps, Karl-Heinz. "Zur Kontnuität der völkisch-nationalkonservatives Literatur vor, während und nach 1945: Der Fall Gerhard Schumann." *Monatshefte für deutschprachige Literatur* 91 (1999).

Schwab, Gerald. *The Day the Holocaust Began.* New York: Praeger, 1990.

Sebba, Gregor. *The Collected Essays of Gregor Sebba: Truth, History, and the Imagination,* edited by Helen Sebba, Anibal A. Bueno, and Hendrikus Boers. Baton Rouge: Louisiana State University Press, 1991.

———. "Prelude and Variations on the Theme of Eric Voegelin." In *Eric Voegelin's Thought: A Critical Appraisal,* edited by Ellis Sandoz. Durham, N.C.: Duke University Press, 1982.

Sigwart, Hans-Jörg. *Das Politische und die Wissenschaft: Intellektuell-biographische Studien zum Frühwerk Eric Voegelins.* Würzburg: Königshausen und Neumann 2005.

———. "Modes of Experience: On Eric Voegelin's Theory of Governance." *Review of Politics* 68 (2006).

Smith, Adam. *The Wealth of Nations.* New York: Dent, 1960.

Strauss, Leo. "An Epilogue." In *Essays on the Scientific Study of Politics,* edited by Herbert J. Storing. New York: Holt, Rinehart and Winston, 1962.

———. "What Is Political Philosophy?" In *What Is Political Philosophy? and Other Studies.* Glencoe, Ill.: Free Press, 1959.

Thompson, William M. "Philosophy and Meditation: Notes on Eric Voegelin's View." In *The Politics of the Soul: Eric Voegelin on Religious*

Experience, edited by Glen Hughes. Lanham, Md.: Rowman and Littlefield, 1999.

Vondung, Klaus. "National Socialism as a Political Religion: Potentials and Limits of an Analytical Concept." *Totalitarian Movements and Political Religions* 6 (2005).

Wluka, Manuel. *Wert und Ordnung, Ethik und Recht bei Hans Kelsen und Eric Voegelin.* Fulda, Germany: Faculty of Theology, 2008.

Index